EXIT THE CAVE

Ending the Reincarnation Trap
Book 1

by
howdie mickoski

ISBN
978-82-691266-3-1

Font: Garamond 12pt

Cover design by Verushka Ettlin
Cover photo by Tommy Milanese (www.pexels.com)

Table of Contents

NOTE

Anyone who says they know for certain what happens after we die, or how and why this universe was created, is lying. All one can present are well researched areas, tempered by personal experiences, that share a probable thesis. I am doing the same here. I do not know these answers for sure, but through my years of research I sense am getting close. Only after my transition event occurs, will I know just how close my thesis matched the reality.

This is the first book of a two-part series and Book 2 will be available sometime in the spring of 2023. Together they will comprise a body of work I feel will be helpful for preparing me on my "Definitive Journey," and perhaps, yours as well.

I make some very intense claims about reality in this book. That does not mean that I endorse "leaving" reality early. This book is intended to help people examine and understand a complex illusionary realm, and to encourage to use the time available to see through all the tricks and deceptions it holds. To "leave early" (ie commit suicide) takes away from more time of preparation that might be required to exit properly. Though this realm and experience might be difficult, my suggestion is to use the time in a physical form to keep digging into all wisdom tracks available, find ways to be of value to others and nature, and be as balanced as possible. The rest will take care of itself.

Excellent editors have gone through this text. However, after they were done, I added sentences throughout the text just prior to publication. As such some spelling or grammatical errors will remain. It is not an "oversight" on their part.

Best Wishes

A

FOUNDATION

"And I entered into the midst of their prison, which is the prison of the body. And I said, He who hears, let him get up from his deep sleep." Apocryphon of John[1]

[1] http://gnosis.org/naghamm/apocjn-davies.html

1

HARVEST MOON

> *"True philosophers make dying their profession, and to them of all people, death is the least alarming. It is the prospect of attaining their lifelong desire, wisdom."* Plato, Phaedo

Where are you?

What if you woke up one morning, say this morning, with the crazy notion that everything you had ever been told was a lie? Everything you were taught in school, from your parents, from religion, and from TV was a form of deception? That all the systems you trusted, that you believed were created for your best interest, were false? A calculated series of lies designed as a type of control mechanism, to keep you and everyone, under the spell of the wizards who control this realm. What if you found that even all the areas that seem designed to assist you, such as religion, spirituality, or self-help, were all part of the deception as well?

What if you woke up one moment, say this moment, and realized that you in fact, have died; that you are in the after-death realm? A tunnel of white light appears before you, and a loving angel or your loving grandmother are there calling you towards that light. What are you going to do? Is going to this light a blessing, or the way you get trapped further?

What if there is an exit?

*

> "A topic that has had much focus for the last ten years or so comes under the subject "soul traps," and in a nutshell is saying that non-human beings[2] either created this realm, or control this realm, and bring human souls into an artificial world construct. They do this in order to farm humans for food, using our energy (mainly in the form of fear and other negative emotions, like the movie *Monsters Inc.*) as their source. When we die we get tricked at the key moment when we can turn away from all of this, by aliens disguising as beings of light or former loved ones. (You would then) go into a tunnel of light, or up a stairway of light. Doing either will cause us to enter the reincarnation cycle and be back into another life in the "soul farm." Wayne J Bush[3]

Wayne Bush's above quote gives all the information you need on the subject, and the next two hundred pages will be an examination of the five sentences above. To do that we are going to have to examine a lot of evidence about life and death. This includes what are known as Near Death Experiences (NDE), concepts such as karma, reincarnation, and sin. A foundation discussion point for this book will be the allegory of Plato's Cave, that is found in his book *Republic*. It is a story about a cave of prisoners being tricked into living a life of illusion. Researchers attempt to explain the analogy of Plato's Cave, and its exit simply. They fit their analysis into their beliefs of this world, and few question whether it is a useful analogy? This book is not concerned much with traps in this realm; this book is looking for the foundation for all the traps.

Generally when a person has had a NDE they present a similar story.[4] They enter a realm that is confusing, until they either see a white light (often a tunnel), with perhaps angel-like beings or dead relatives encouraging them towards the light. Some meet with a stairway instead. Those who experience this light say it is the most beautiful experience they could imagine. Love personified some report, a place they did not want to leave. At some point they are told, either after a type of life review or by simple presentation, that it "is not their time," "they have work or a mission

---

[2] Known as archons in the *Nag Hammadi Gnostic texts*

[3] http://www.trickedbythelight.com

[4] A huge repository of 4000 NDE can be sourced at http://www.nderf.org while other books about the subject have been based on hundreds or thousands of cases.

to complete," or "they have more to learn," and are sent back to their bodies on Earth. The experience tends to transform them, and often they change their life in drastic ways. Generally they tend to become kinder, more loving, and lose their fear of death. It all sounds good doesn't it? Or is it too good to be true? I will share some of these NDE experiences in chapter four.

> *"And no wonder, for Satan himself masquerades as an angel of light."* 2 Corinthians 11:14[5]

But those are not the only experiences people have had in the after-death world. Many of these "other experiences" tend to indicate that the standard white light story and loving angels is nothing but a trick, and that any soul who falls for it has only achieved their continued enslavement. I began to wonder on examining the standard story if those who had "nice" experiences were given them as a part of what I call a *propaganda campaign.* Those who are sent back here (often against their will) might have been given a "lite" version of the experience to write some books of how the white light tunnel is their friend. If you were running a deception that needed souls to stay trapped in this realm, how many Near-Death Experiencers would you want to see the "real event?" As few as possible. That needs to be kept in mind. The 15% minority of experiences might be the ones that are going to most complete parts of the NDE, while the standard 85% are those that are getting a strong dose of being fooled.[6] Non-standard NDE get examined in chapter nine.

One of the beliefs that human experience has become based on is that we live in a wonderful world, made by a loving creator, a place where all our wishes can come true, so we can grow, learn and evolve. If we just have enough faith, then we will get to enter a heavenly realm for eternity filled with clouds, harps and angels. This book will present the thesis that we live in the exact opposite of this standard presentation. My research (through the ancient groups of Gnostics and Cathars, as well as the work

---

[5] Translation presented at https://www.biblegateway.com/passage/?search=2%20Corinthians%2011&version=NIV

[6] I have had some personal death experiences, each of which have revealed some important elements, but I don't say I know for sure what death will bring for myself or anyone else. In fact, one my death experiences (in 2005) that I will discuss in full later in Book 2, might have not been the wonderful opening it appeared to be at the time, but a trick designed to keep me away from where my study at that time was headed (the very material you are reading now).

of modern philosophers) will reveal that we live in an artificial simulated world, created by an evil deity (called the Demiurge by Gnostics.)[7] This reality we inhabit is not a new creation, but a copy of a more real realm that is our Home. When examined more closely, this world copy appears more like what we now call *Artificial Intelligence.* Artificial meaning not organic, not "alive" as we think of that term. Our essence was tricked to enter this simulation, which has been devised in such a way to keep us here to harvest our energy as a power source to keep the simulation running. Some might respond that this sounds insane. But is it? Perhaps this thesis will be a clear explanation of our reality, and the experience all around us of constant suffering and pain?

> "*It is they (grey aliens) who await in the light when a human being dies. The human being is then recycled into another body and the process begins all over again... Hence the Light and Tunnel at death Trap. Scanning someone they wish to recycle as they near death, the aliens discover who the person was close to has died. They project the person(s) image in the white light tunnel and the image waves you in deeper. If you CHOOSE to follow you can be trapped and sent to another incarnation of their choice... these entities view Earth as a big farm.*" - Val Valerian[8]

This topic about Earth being a farm of souls has been around for many decades, but generally on the fringes of any alternative research. Gurdjieff often claimed that we were here on Earth to become "food for the Moon." Most thought he was being symbolic, but likely not. Do you know that the most famous Moon during the year is known as the "Harvest Moon." Is it really about humans harvesting their crops, or the Moon harvesting its human crops? The subject was brought up by famed out-of-body (OBE) researcher Robert Monroe, who in chapter twelve of his book *Far Journeys* in 1971, claimed aliens required what he called "loosh energy." Our realm became one built to provide this loosh to the alien controllers. I discuss his book in detail in chapter three. Val Valerian (who claimed to be a former CIA agent), wrote a series of *Matrix* books beginning in 1990 with the same subject matter of Earth being a farm. Carlos Castaneda in his

---

[7] Before creating this world, the Demiurge created what might be called helpers or minions for itself. The Gnostics called them archons, but other names such as aliens, demons, parasitic entities are used also.

[8]"Found in books *Matrix II and Matrix V,* claimed to be former CIA agent John Grace and referenced on http://www.trickedbythelight.com/tbtl/light.shtml

final book *Active Side of Infinity* discussed how parasitic entities have been harvesting us for energy for centuries. Part of this process was to give us their mind (a parasitic ego), so that we will be easier to control and behave in the negative ways they wish us to, in order to increase our energy output.

The lack of people thinking about the food chain baffles me. A minnow eats a mosquito, and takes that energy into itself. A fish eats the minnow, and takes that energy into itself. A human eats the fish, and takes that energy into itself. The human being is believed to be supreme, as nothing takes in our energy. If humans had a clearer understanding of reality, the statements should continue: An archon eats the human, and takes that energy into itself. The archon takes that energy, plugs it back into the matrix simulation, which will then be sent back in to reach a new mosquito, and the vortex trap just keeps spinning.

This examination is going to be hard for almost everyone to read, because all our most held on and cherished hopes and wishes are going to be put to the test. These include the idea of "Free Will" - that somehow this reality was set up so that we can do and experience as we choose. However, we will be judged later on for our choices. The problem with this theory is there are many moments in people's lives when they feel they had "no choice," or "it was destined to happen." And so, which events are free will choices and which are destiny? It gets cloudy at this point. A video game character believes they have free will as well, but they only act based on the programming their character has been given as code. What if we are used for the whims of another (as the robot hosts on the TV show *Westworld* are used by supposed human guests who act like parasites towards them)? Did you really choose your breakfast this morning, or was that a programmed moment inserted into a computer eons ago?

Another topic most people take for granted as true, is the Christian concept of sin, even though we were never given a manual for life on entering, nor any real idea of who or what will judge our actions. The idea of karma, similar to sin, is where the good things we do get rewarded and bad things we do get punished. Eastern religions have taken the concept of karma a bit further, adding it to reincarnation, where these karmic moments determine if you return as an important person, a lowly peasant, or even (God forbid) an animal.

The topic of reincarnation surrounds all of this. This subject of avoiding a reincarnation soul trap was the foundational belief behind the group in Southern France known as Cathars, whom the Church of Rome exterminated beginning in 1209 AD in their first Crusade and Inquisition against their own people.[9] However, in the last twenty years, the subjects of soul traps and harvesting energy has taken on new levels. Another key element of this discussion, is what can be called the "memory wipe," personified in the ancient world by the Hermetic "Cup of Forgetfulness," and the Chinese goddess Meng Po and her "soup of forgetfulness."[10] Right in this word we are getting a sense of what is going on, forget-fullness: to no longer remember the full or the whole of What We Are.

Many will vehemently claim the idea of reincarnation is false because they do not remember any of their own lives, and even the Pope denies the concept. We get one life and that is that. Most who follow a Western religion will reject the idea of reincarnation immediately, even though when you look into the early history of all of those religions, reincarnation could be found in its early teachings. Christianity might have removed it as late as 525 AD. The topic was likely removed to hide this fact, because people will not take action on something they do not believe exists. The Eastern religions still keep the concept of reincarnation, but it is also nowhere like its original presentation. Buddhists claim the world is suffering, and reincarnation is the wheel of samsara and one needs to follow the Buddha's teachings to exit the cycle, but these teachings tend to mostly be about moral constraints and sitting with your eyes closed. In fact there is more talk of how to have a better life next time, than really being done with the cycle. Reincarnation still exists in the Hindu realm, and they try to focus on the *Bhagavad Gita* as the centerpiece of their teaching on it. However, I see that text in an entirely different way - as more of a trick to stay stuck in the reincarnation cycle, and not the way to exit.

> "*In other words, souls started off as pure spiritual entities, and are incarnated to matter. Why? To return home to where they started*

[9] The Cathars will be discussed in more detail in chapter eleven.

[10] Meng Po who serves a herbal tea on the Bridge of Forgetfulness, so people will forget their previous lives on entering new ones. If one could somehow not drink the tea, or only part of it, there would be memories of their past life in the new incarnation. https://en.wikipedia.org/wiki/Meng_Po

from, pure again? And having gained what? Virtual life experiences, useless to the Spiritual Plane." Angeliki Anagnostou[11]

Some might say reincarnation is a false concept. Possibly. If you are on that side of this discussion, I ask you just take some time and consider if the thesis of this book is true, how much would that change what you have believed? Could it be that a good way to keep the reincarnation trap going, is by denying its existence? For most of the last twenty years, I was 50-50 on the idea of reincarnation. At times I lean No, and even semi-debunked this idea in my book *Falling For Truth*, claiming that as a part of One Being, we are all lives, so there was nothing "personal" about any of them. Yet I kept wondering, why some people, especially young children, seem to have vivid and complete memories of a very recent life in the past? Further examination has led me to believe that individual reincarnation is almost a 99.9% certainty.[12] Too much tested evidence is available, of people who have access to information about the life of a long dead person they have no other way of having, unless they *were* that person. The question has to be, is reincarnation here for our benefit (as a type of school, evolution or karmic experience) as religions and the New Age want us to believe; or part of a trap of the soul, as a group of researchers is now presenting?

I made a YouTube video in early 2022 regarding the question if this reality is a school or a prison. It did not take long to realize that this is not a school, or you would remember your previous incarnations and lessons learned. One key facet that most Near-Death Experiences reveal, is that the return to Earth and a human body includes the above mentioned "memory wipe," where everything from that previous life is forgotten.[13] This alone clearly indicates that this is not a place of learning and growth. If you touch stinging nettle without gloves, your hand gets stung and it hurts. You remember that, and from then on if you want to pick some nettle, you wear gloves. That is learning. Remembering is a key step in the process. But if on

---

[11] Anagnostou, *Can You Stand The Truth? The Chronicle of Man's Imprisonment: Last Call!* pg 213

[12] I myself have specific memories of a couple of previous lives, the most recent a German Wehrmacht officer who died in the Ardennes Offensive of 1944

[13] Granted as noted in a few incidents some people do remember these lives, but usually not in much detail as my 1944 memories. They tend to be fragmented in small pieces, like a dream. Only very young children tend to have detailed memories that soon fade as they age. Perhaps the wipe is not always total upon entering, but fades out as our parents and teachers get us to focus on this new life experience, and help in the final part of forgetting the previous ones.

each incarnation you have to go back to touching the nettle to find out it stings, that is not learning or growth, but insanity. That is our reality.

At least when we go to normal school, we remember what we learned the previous year. We don't go into grade five and forget everything from grades one to four. Yet in the reincarnation cycle we seem subject to, nothing gets carried over. The memory wipe will happen again, and all will be forgotten. This leads to life as a human on Earth being a deception, where we might even be tricked into signing types of soul contracts to indicate what is going to happen to us (generally forms of suffering). Pain and suffering are the constant elements of this realm (for all creatures) in between moments of "non suffering," that may act like places to recharge our energy battery.

The television series *Westworld* (at least season one) is an excellent presentation of this concept. Each time a *Westworld* robot has "died," it is taken to mission control for a cleanup. This includes a memory wipe, so that the last "incarnation" is forgotten and they go back into the field with their programming intact, so they can be shot up or raped again. This is a big reason for the memory wipe prior to new incarnations, because if we really could remember how much suffering we had gone through lifetime after lifetime, we would have long ago shut down our reincarnations. The trap can only work with the memory wipe. We are just here to be used. Exactly what we are being used for (energy food for the system as speculated by most, or entertainment NPC (non-player-character) pieces for non-human entities who come into this realm, or as an experiment) is hard to verify.[14] When the memories start to appear in *Westworld* for Dolores and Mauve of how they have been treated, a new inner strength emerges for them to "break out" of the *Westworld* prison.

It also seems that whatever body we get from reincarnation is random. The body chosen is not really indicative of how we lived previously nor is it tied to any moral judgments based upon us. What we do here therefore (be real nice or real bad), is not going to make any difference

---

[14] Another explanation for this reincarnation/memory wipe experience can be that we are not so much farmed as we are being experimented on. This need to forget previous lives would also be important if in each run of the experiment, you would want the subjects to act only based on the moment. You can't let those you are experimenting on know what is going on or it would ruin the data.

if we get sucked back into the matrix[15] and into a new body (or even your same body over and over in a type of continual time loop). This means reincarnation is occurring, because we get tricked into continuing the cycle (in a sense we wind up agreeing), but we are not coming back to learn anything or grow, just to be recycled for another round of being used and our energy harvested. How you live really makes no difference (thereby destroying the ideas of karma), only how you believe you lived. If you have enough naughty stuff in your past, this becomes more elements for you to be tricked into being told you must go back, because you were a bad or naughty person.[16] Hence the more kind and compassionate you have been, the less is waiting in the life review. This gets even more challenging when we begin to realize that many of the moments of our lives are being directly manipulated by parasitic entities. Eve Lorgen wrote an excellent book on this subject called *Alien Love Bite*.

Besides, if someone has had a thousand lifetimes, surely that person must have learned everything by now? Given that most of those lives would have been fraught with intense suffering, does someone really need 997 lives out of 1000 full of pain to learn? I don't know about you, but I learned better in school from teachers who were kind, took time with me, and encouraged me to be creative, not by someone who whacked me over the head with a stick constantly. Planet Earth is stick whacking land. Given the way 2020-2022 has played out, more and more people are coming to that realization.

This trap seems to be sprung just after death. In this very confused state, the soul is even more vulnerable. Few have taken time in their waking life to learn lucid dreaming or astral travel, i.e. how to keep their awareness beyond their physical body. And so, when in the after-death realm, the average person will get sucked into the experience similar to when having a dream, where we get swept along, no matter how strange it is. The trap is already being set up with the lack of awareness in our dreams. Carlos Castaneda placed much work on being aware in our dreams, as a key part of the overall work. I am again starting to see more why that is.

---

[15] Term related to the 1999 movie of the same name which claims our reality is a false construct, the same as the concept of the Cave to Plato. The term matrix as a false reality was used long prior to the movie however, as seen in books on the trap of reality with that title by Val Valerian in 1990.

[16] I will discuss the importance of recapitulation in chapter two and six.

A high number of NDE's have what is called a life review. It tends to present our previous life in a way that mostly shows how "bad" or "selfish" we have been. Some NDEs have dealt with councils that argue their fate, even contracts that the soul is "pressured" to sign. Then the white light appears, often with a loving figure as a guide, and the person enters. Somehow that movement towards the light, seals our fate. We are back in the cycle. We may not reincarnate immediately, some suggest it could be thirty Earth years of waiting, and not necessarily in heavenly surroundings.[17] And so, if not the white light, where should we go? We will come back to that.

To know what to do in the after-death realm, we have to get prepared while still in this one. It is actually one of the important practices while in a body, but it tends to be downplayed against more standard practices of meditation, yoga and mindfulness. Once a person finally sees that this is not a world set out to help us or grant us our wishes, but is a harvesting farm of our energy, we can make a shift. We stop focusing on how to become important, and use our time to prepare for the moment where escape is possible. You have to take how you live to heart, and have no regrets in this life (because regret can be a tool to trick you into returning). This is not about becoming perfect or a saint, but to use this life to get everything figured out and get past the Demiurge, because if you don't, you will be right back here after a *Westworld*-type memory wipe. No matter how much you moved along in the last life, you are back at square one in the new life, ignorant of everything once again. All the "exalted knowledge" we have come to believe in (either from books or people we came to admire) only has value in the moment.

*

Chapter two will present a complete analysis of the allegory of Plato's Cave, usually taken as a symbol of being locked in a realm of illusion. Generally when Plato's Cave is mentioned in books or symbolized in movies, the focus is on how to improve your experience of the illusionary Cave. These discuss how to change thoughts, see through

---

[17] Some have claimed these waiting points are astral cities, where archonic beings keep the waiting souls in a sort of totalitarian police state of control and subjugation. See the videos by YouTube channel "Free At Last," and works of Wes Penre for more information.

control systems, change governments or live outside the normal system of commerce, maybe on a farm in the countryside. How to make your prison-life more enjoyable. While learning to function differently in the dreamworld may have some value, as long as you are in this material realm, or the astral, or the super angelic, or even the Void, then you are still in Plato's Cave. What the analysis of Plato's Cave fails to present is how to LEAVE the Cave and escape this recycling slaughterhouse completely.[18]

It seems that you can never truly exit the Cave while still in a material body, or even an astral body. How do you exit a realm that is set up to ensure almost no one leaves? As the song "Hotel California" (which is all about the reincarnation trap) says, "*you can check out any time you like, but you can never leave.*"[19] I realized only quite recently, that many of the teachers I looked up to my whole life, would never have made it out of the Cave. For all their supposed knowledge, healing abilities and connection to Oneness, they would not have seen through the tricks and deceptions of this realm. They would have gotten recycled right back in here. The supposed great escape leaders, never really knew how to escape. That can be a shocking realization for those who have held their teachers to unquestioning heights.

If we take the metaphor that the Demiurge creator of this realm can be likened to a giant super computer run by AI intelligence, then we might see ourselves as individual PCs. We are connected to this super computer, and not only can we download from it, but it can download into us. Just as we have no idea what the Internet and cookies are placing on our own home PCs, we have no idea how often the Demiurge system is putting manipulation cookies into us. Keeping with the metaphor, there is no sense altering our PC or getting a new PC, we have to use what we currently have to learn how to navigate the after-death realm, which is to navigate the inside of a super computer. The good news is that we also have a spark of something within that is not part of the AI system. We might call this the soul. But what is a soul, and if trapped, how did it get trapped?

One must look at what a soul is, and ask if that is what is really trapped? Perhaps our Essence or Spiritual Nature is what is trapped, tricked into entering this manufactured realm. So where did this soul thing come from? I now have come to see it as a type of bridge between the Essence

---

[18] Granted a few people like Mark over at "Forever Conscious Research" (YouTube channel) does provide suggestions to prepare to be "done with this place," but these voices are few in the mass of information out there.

[19] See http://www.trickedbythelight.com for Wayne Bush's complete analysis of this song.

which is outside of this reality, and the false material and astral worlds. Angelika Anagnostou commented on her "Can You Stand the Truth" website that the Demiurge after tricking Essence into its new creation needed to solidify it into the construct. He did this by creating the soul. That is a real twist, as the soul is generally something presented as the most real "us." And it sort of is and isn't. She claims that the Demiurge took the piece of Essence and combined it with energy. The soul is the first trap, yet at the same time, contains the very part to set us free (the piece of Essence). To further the trap, as denser forms of matter were created, this soul was placed into the various astral, etheric and finally material bodies.

This could be why the Demiurge and the archons feel they can harvest our energy, because they were the ones who gave us the "energy" component of our "form." That being said, this constant manipulation and harvesting of the energy component does not allow our Essence to be free, and as such is evil. That is where we gain a level over the Demiurge, the Essence is Good. We have to get back to the point of the soul, not to stay there, but to be in total command of it and release the energy component that is not really ours to begin with. This might mirror concepts of Carlos Castaneda that will be mentioned in future chapters, to be left fully sitting as Essence, with all the false (including the soul) dropped. It is the Essence that will exit out through the "eye of the needle." Nothing from the dreamworld can pass the barrier. I am not saying her theory is correct or that anyone should believe it, but is something that seems so possible as an explanation for all of the traps we experience that I present it here and will come back to it in future examinations. From this point forward in the book you can read the words "soul" and "Essence" as almost interchangeable for what I am wanting to refer to (that part of us which is Absolute, Pure and from outside these simulated realms).

If we go looking for answers as to how to exit, we will find there are a few groups and individuals who may be living their lives in a way to achieve this. We are not the first humans to be studying this reality and looking for these answers. The Gnostics, are one such group, I will be examining in Book 2. Another group were the Cathars. Why is the study of a group of people genocided in the 13th century important? The Cathars held as their main belief that this was a world created by an evil god (Rex Mundi) who kept them in a reincarnation cycle, and their only focus in this life was to escape it. The Cathars were not concerned with making this place better, finding new forms of government, or commerce, or anything else. Their focus was to escape the evil realm of the Rex Mundi forever, and return Home to the Father.[20]

People have been practicing all sorts of spiritual exercises for a long while: raising their vibrational frequency, tuning their chakras, reciting their mantras, doing their yoga stretches, being vegetarian, closing their eyes to meditate for an hour. And what has it gotten anyone? Is the world a better place than it was 50 years ago? Actually, it is easy to argue it has gotten much worse, and continues to do so. How about people themselves, has anyone doing all this work really gone through an inner transformation? They might feel better, but once you take down the base veneer of deception that has covered it over, what of value is left? Can they actually alter and control reality as they think they can, or are they still at the mercy of forces to which they have to keep praying? Are they any more ready to die and know what they have to do in order to navigate the after-life realm? Or have they traded possible Truth to be in a pretend state of love, light, and feeling better? What has value and what is just "games played within games?"

While this book has the focus of understanding what the after-death transition has in store for us, it is not going to suggest you ignore the material world. I won't say stop eating, having sex or working to improve your situation in this reality. Nor will I label what are called spiritual, religious or shamanic practices as bad. We are having an experience in a material body, whether we were tricked here or not, and this body experience cannot be ignored. There is nothing wrong with learning how to better function here. I am glad to know what herbs and acupressure points to use when I don't feel well. Shamans from native cultures can perform amazing healings and even make changes to the material world.[21] The problem is that people place all their attention on the material world, on how to control it, profit from it or fix it. But can a video game character

---

[20] Other key Cathar beliefs were that humans were originally souls that were connected with the Father, but the Demiurge tricked them into coming into matter, where they would be stuck reincarnating over and over. The job of the Cathar was to live in a particular way in order to stop the reincarnation cycle they would be on as long as they kept their focus away from the creations of Rex Mundi (which to them was everything). That is the simple version- there is much more including how they viewed Jesus and the Magdalene, John the Baptist, the Bible, the equality of women; even that they were the rightful holders of an object/knowledge known as the Holy Grail.

[21] The books by Tomas Mails on Fools Crow are excellent sources of what can be "done" in physical reality.

really change the video game? Even the path to exit Plato's Cave cannot be an ungrounded one. We cannot just fly away like Peter Pan and ignore the world. There must be a balanced approach.

*

> "*(Amun-Ra) is the true god behind it all, a binary AI program of galactic proportions... the King priest is the overlay of the false masculine godhead to dominate and control the divine feminine principle... The geomancy of energetic control on a global scale is nothing more than the systematized program of numerology, geometry, astrology, and many more mathematically based systems that have been presented to the world as mystical and sacred and divine, when they are in fact nothing more than the underlying systems of control of our consciousness and this world... Insisting on the belief systems thusly presented over millennia as sacred or divine is just one more methodology of control. These systems are very much hard wired into the system of legal and monetary bondage.*" kenneth scott[22]

Another thing that should become obvious, if you look at this reality honestly, is how easily we all get fooled. Once you realize that all the major organizations (either government, media or advertising) are run by people trained in how to fool and manipulate, it makes sense what our realm has become. Following the Hermetic principle of "as above so below," is it any surprise that the after-death astral realm would be one of pure deception?

If you are not certain just how fooled people are in this realm, consider this little story from Sherwood Schwartz. In the 1960s Schwartz was one of TV's top producers, with a string of hit shows such as *Gilligan's Island* (the tale of seven stranded castaways on a deserted island in the Pacific who can never manage to leave the island). One day the US Coast Guard, carrying stacks of telegrams, came to pay him a visit. They told Schwartz that the messages were sent to US Naval and Coast Guard stations from coast to coast. Schwartz started to read them and was

[22] *Overview of the System of World Bondage and Separation From Life.* Though Ken called the original head of the Ennead, Annu, a name which actually refers to the ancient city of Heliopolis, which downtown Cairo is built overtop of.

shocked. They were all of a similar theme, "Dear US Navy, you spend millions to send aircraft carriers all over the Pacific, but can't you spare just one ship to go and get those seven stranded Americans off that island. They are lost and close to starving to death. Please go and get them." This was not a letter from a lunatic or sent as a prank. There were thousands of these sent from normal Americans who thought the TV show *Gilligan's Island* was real. They could not tell the difference between a TV show and standard reality. If you think that was just the backward people of the 1960s, be reminded that the average person today has become a robot doing what a few people in suits on a TV screen during a newscast tells them to do. "So it goes," to paraphrase Kurt Vonnegut.

The standard presentation is that this world was created by a loving God who cares about us. Does that really match your experience of the world, and the experiences of those you see around you? How could a loving deity not step in and help, but let all the massive suffering on Earth continue? Perhaps because the creator, whoever it is, wants the suffering. That is why they are not stepping in. The entire God loves us/me is a big lie that all religions and the New Age are trapped under. They find ways to turn the torture of this world into a "wonderful message and learning from light." Do you really think God wants an eight-year-old kid to get beat up, a girl to get raped, or a dog tortured by its owner? Careful examination would reveal that the Demiurge/Satan wants that.

The idea that "God loves us" is a key foundation pillar upon which this entire matrix is built. It is such a strong foundation that many people will even get angry and violent if you suggest otherwise; because if this belief were found to be false, every other connection to this reality would also have to be questioned. Thus the "God loves me belief" is one of the hardest nuts to crack. (As such, this book is going to be radical to the extreme, and heretic to its core. Nothing is sacred or off limits for examination, because if everything we have been told is a lie, then we have no foundation).

This is a suffering pit of hell. Even the few who do not seem like they are suffering, if you can get them to speak honestly, you will hear how they are torn with guilt and shame which they never show outwardly. Everyone else is dealing with suffering and pain on far higher levels than that. Many will try to justify it, "Oh God wants my pain so I can learn (perhaps about love), so He can teach me, or push me to start a new life direction." No. Let's be honest. This is a suffering pit of hell. It has always been a suffering pit of hell, and always will be. If you don't get that, you have pretty much been misled about the only thing you really need to learn here.

You could also claim that our reality is insane. If we are looking at things honestly in the year 2022, it does not take long to make that conclusion. Yet this world has always been insane as long as we have been here, just to varying degrees. The hope has been that there was a time in the past when things were much different, but that may just be wishful thinking. When you understand fully what this reality is and how it was created, this insane world will start to make sense. It can never be truly sane. But you can!

*

> "*Nothing happens. Nobody comes, nobody goes. It's awful.*" Samuel Beckett, *Waiting for Godot*

Many are waiting for their savior to appear. For some it's a religious figure like Jesus, Buddha or Krishna. Millions are waiting for Donald Trump to save them. For others, it is a shift to a higher dimension that will save them, while some believe that we are in a low phase called Kali Yuga and soon this entire world will be in a better place. Though you have to wonder what the point of all that is, if the cycle will return to suffering at the next Kali Yuga in 26,000 years anyway. That type of thinking is just a "I want to feel good now" type of thinking. But cycles should not be completely ignored, especially on the small scale. It will be helpful to know what the "signs" indicate is likely afoot in the upcoming weeks or months, in order to be properly prepared. The sooner you can know a hurricane is approaching the coast, the more time you have to respond. But when it comes to the bigger cycles, there is no point waiting for something 10,000 years in the future if your plan is not to be "here" for it.

Waiting for Godot by Samuel Beckett is sheer brilliance. In the play the two main characters are on the stage waiting for Godot. And at the end of the play, they still are waiting. They keep saying "he promised to show up," and so they keep waiting. This is the same trick being played on everyone about the saviors. The play indicates that a savior will be coming sometime in the future, but never now. Everyone will just remain waiting, hoping and praying.

Prayer is one area I have been digging into for a while. Is praying just making us "prey?" Where is our energy and focus going with this practice? It seems prayer is just putting our own authority on some outside force hoping it will like us and grant us something, so we keep trying to please the puppeteer. And if our prayer doesn't happen, we just say "It's God's Will." Well if it's God's Will, why pray in the first place? More to the fact, how do we know who or what we are praying to?[23] This is one of the crucial pieces of information that almost no one contemplates. Are they angels, spirit guides, loving dead people, happy aliens, God, Jesus or Ashtar Command; or are the communicators nasty parasitic entities who are masters of disguise and deception? You say you spoke to an angel or some religious figure, but how do you really know? When you pray how do you know where your intent and energy is going? The more we put our energy on things outside ourself, the more those beings can manipulate us and make our lives much much worse. What is wrong with praying to yourself? To trust your own inner power. I will share ideas and some experiences around prayer in chapter ten.

A great shift will occur when you realize that you do not need a savior, nor do you need to pray to anything outside of yourself. You, as in the Essence part of your soul, is the most powerful thing within this creation. This is why the system is set up to distract, confuse and deceive it. Because if you turned all that energy that is always focused on something outside yourself, and focused it within, there would be an explosion of power. That power can then be used to override all the systems and tricks that have been keeping you here.[24] When you learn the only savior you need is you, and the only prayer you ever need to make is to your True Self, the exit is closer.

*

---

[23] In fact, this question of God's Will comes into odd potentials when dealing with a legal document known as the Last Will and Testament.

[24] It is one reason for the study of Qi Gong and Yoga, if you can turn all your attention inward, if the explosion of energy happens from regaining your power, you know how to handle it.

If one is to exit the Cave, one must really want to exit. That is the first problem. Few REALLY want to leave. There may be a lot of things they don't like about the Cave, but they still believe things can be different, better or happier. Others are so convinced that after they die, they will be living with Jesus or dead grandma, that there is no need to think any more about reality or death. The soul gets a type of addiction with each reincarnation. It comes to know only the material and forgets the spiritual, like a gambling addict who can only see the "next bet," hoping their lucky number will "pay out" a big win. As you can see, most have already ended their path before they could even get started.

If we are going to look into Plato's Cave, then the allegory itself is the first thing which must be examined. I found that it is not that useful a story at all. It does little to explain our reality or situation. In fact it is missing a majority of the most important elements. Let us examine the story with fresh eyes. What does the allegory of Plato's Cave really say, and what if anything, is of value?

"*We are in a spiritual war, and Plato's Cave is the battlefield.*" Dave Scott, comment on a YouTube video

2

PLATO'S CAVE:
I'm caught in a trap, I can't walk out...

> "*We can say that we are not born in the world. We are born into something that we transform into a world.*" Michael Talbot[25]

One of the most familiar ancient stories modern spiritual students are aware of is that of Plato's Cave. Found in the book *Republic*, it is a discussion between Plato's teacher (Socrates) and Plato's brother (Glaucon). In this discussion Socrates describes reality using the metaphor of a cave. What so many spiritual seekers fail to recognize is that this allegory is only a half explanation of anything, and it is actually more important to examine all that Plato excludes, rather than what he includes. That this metaphor is held in such high reverence, while presenting so little, is telling in itself. Was there an original longer version (as I suspect), that in time has been edited down by the *powers that be* to what we have now? As I will explain, this is a story about the Cave, not about exiting the Cave, which can make it seem like one story (freedom) but it really is another (continued bondage).

The conversation in the *Republic* begins with Socrates asking Glaucon to imagine a cave inhabited by prisoners chained and held in place since childhood. Not only are they chained to their seats, but their heads are held in place in such a way that they can only see the wall directly in front of them. The story has a giant fire behind the prisoners, with a walkway in front of the fire where people and animals pass by to cast shadows on the cave wall. Sounds are echoed off the cave walls to make it seem like they are the sounds of the shadow objects. When the prisoners see the shadows, they believe they are actual living creatures.

---

[25] Found in *Mysticism and Contemporary Science*.

The first problem that arises with this account is that no one is asking the fundamental questions. Who are these prisoners? Where do they come from? Why have they become prisoners, and why have they been sent to this cave and not a prisoner of war camp or a jail? Certainly the analogy is hinting that the prisoners are us. Not only must we figure out how the children of the analogy becomes prisoners, but we must ask ourselves clearly: How did we become prisoners? Prisoners from what or where? Another question missing is who are the beings in control of this deception? What are they gaining from doing it? Why go through all the trouble of making the ramp, the fire, the shadow objects and then spend all day working to fool some prisoners? Why are they expending so much effort? Again, this is not even hinted at.

These may seem like small omissions, but once you contemplate further, you see they are important omissions, that might not be by accident, as the allegory might have been created to trick us. The prisoners are focused on the cave wall not on actual reality, while the reader is focused on trusting the story and not checking if the allegory they are reading is some type of deception. As this book goes along, I hope I will be able to bring insight to these missing pieces of Plato's Cave.

The way Socrates discusses how the shadows on the wall are produced and projected, make the cave an almost perfect representation of a modern movie theater. The cave wall is the screen, the objects the movie, the fire is the projection light, and the echoing sounds are the movie speakers. However, instead of just one large screen at the front of the theater, it would be better to imagine that the shadow images are projected onto a 360-degree screen. In other words, an experience which surrounds the prisoners in all directions, including up and down. As Socrates suggests, the images and sounds would be believed as being fully real, because those are the only sights and sounds the prisoners have ever seen.

Socrates then makes an interesting suggestion. What if a prisoner was somehow freed from the chains and could stand up? He or she would be very confused. The shadows on the wall had been the only reality, not the cave, the other prisoners, or these "shadow-making" devices he or she had ever seen. Another question that should be answered is, why does the prisoner stand up? This is another glaring omission. Plato's story only suggests that the chains are not actually locked and anyone can stand up whenever they want. But if that is the case, why do so few prisoners stand?

Any answer as to why this one prisoner did stand up is purely personal speculation, and I have a few. Perhaps no one will stand up until something in the shadow-movie becomes so painful that they scream and force themselves to turn away, or perhaps it is a force that can be called *Grace* or *luck*. Either way it is another key point to the analogy that is missing. Why did the prisoner stand up?

The question of why the prisoner's chains are not locked might give us a clue. They are not locked because they "agreed" to become prisoners. I will mention in many places later in this book, that it seems like the beings who run this matrix need our agreement for us to enter here. They cannot force us, but have to trick and deceive us with fraudulent "fine print" contracts, and emotional tricks to get us to say "yes." The prisoners in Plato's Cave likely agreed to come into the Cave and be prisoners. This is why a prisoner can in effect stand up whenever they wish - they just have to revoke and end their original agreement. They are not out yet, but now they have the possibility of exiting as the binds that brought them in are severed. Most will just create new binds, or did create new binds in the course of living, but those too can be revoked and ended.

The story claims that the chained prisoners have some sort of interaction among themselves. This was inferred through the story's suggestions of contests on who could give the best description of the last appearing shadow, or who could guess what shadow was coming next. Thus, the newly standing prisoner, somewhat confused, might start talking to the person sitting beside them about this new cave/theater they see. The seated prisoner might just tell them to stop acting stupid and get back to reality. And some may well do that, they might sit back down immediately and get re-involved in the movie. The few moments where they stood up might be soon forgotten. This could be more common than we realize. However, a few, even though likely afraid at this stage, might be more curious... or angry. Those feelings could be strong enough to override the fear directing them to sit down. As a result, they might decide instead to take a tour of the cave/theater to inspect it.

The movies *The Truman Show* (starring Jim Carey) and *Pleasantville* (Tobey Maguire and Reese Witherspoon) add a couple of nice metaphors, for they were clearly influenced by the Plato's Cave analogy. The name of the town Truman lives is Seahaven, whose motto is "a nice place to live" (sounding heavenly). The same with the name Pleasantville, which also sounds heavenly. In each town, reality was constructed to be presented as perfect. In Pleasantville's case it was done through the conditioned values presented by 1950s television, where everyone smiled and never missed a bowling pin or basketball shot. Seahaven is the place designed to make Truman (True man, each person in the dreamworld) feel comfortable, so he has no interest in wanting to leave. In Truman's case, he is the only reality and everything else is a show put on just for him. Actors playing roles, and doing so to see how Truman responds. Just the same as the shadows being projected onto Plato's Cave wall to keep the prisoner's attention focused forward. Both worlds are designed to not have the people there never think about wanting to leave.

The one who oversees Truman's world is named Christoff, and in reviews, he is likened to God. However, when you listen closely to his words, he is more like the egoic mind. Christoff is always in the control room (the Moon[26]) watching Truman's world, constantly devising things to frighten him or present the idea of limitations. Christoff does state though that all the power is with Truman, "*We accept the reality of the world with which we are presented. If his was more than just a vague ambition, if he was absolutely determined to find out the truth of his world, there is no way we could prevent him*." However this concept has more significance when digging into Cave metaphor movies such as *Dark City, They Live* and the TV shows *Lost* and *Westworld.* These, and several others, will be examined in later in the book.

*

One thing the analogy is hinting at, is that we are living our life under a series of lies. One of the biggest lies being fed to us is how all that is going on here is God's Plan, as if everything that happens is somehow all done for us, and is in God's hands. On one level most can see a type of control or direction in place beyond our control. We have all sort of names for this force: destiny, déjàvu, premonition. Yet no one is asking, who is the director of this force of destiny, and who is the beneficiary of this set up? I have come to see that it is not a benevolent force (as religion, New Age, Advaita or shamanism all suggest), but a malevolent force (like the Cathars and Gnostics suggest).

---

[26] Not by accident as we will see, the Moon is likely artificial and a big part of the entire matrix control system.

It does not take much to see that a realm full of suffering and anguish would not help a loving creator. It helps a malevolent force. A good way to keep people from seeing this is to present the loving creator as a non-logical answer for why so many terrible things happen. A loving deity makes you suffer to improve you. "Torture you to make you better," as Richard Rose would say it. People are given traumatic misfortunes, then they come to believe those were part of loving God's plan, then they pray to the very same God that just traumatized them, asking to end their suffering. We are nothing more than farm animals, kept for energetic food (loosh) and this has been going on for thousands of years.

If there really was a happy, loving deity in charge of this place, it could of course be a much more peaceful experience. However, we live in a physical and energetic slaughterhouse. You are living in many ways as a computer game character or semi-programmed robot in a very insane system. How many worms have just died in the last five seconds to feed all the birds? How many mice died to feed all the cats? Does a worm scream while it is being eaten? What set up such an insane and sick system? The Demiurge that's who. The one also called Rex Mundi, the Devil, Satan or Jehovah in the *Old Testament*. That is the real creator of all this simulated reality. This presence also can be called "IT". Can you now see why the computer realm in our world is called I T? It is an extension of the original artificial intelligence, the Demiurge that is in charge of the simulation.[27]

We have to see that all of us have been dealing with an abusive creator deity since long before we were born, and only when the creator of this realm is seen as the Cathars and Gnostic did (a psychopathic insane AI construct) can anything about our experiences finally begin to make sense. We have been deceived in the astral realm, the pre-birth realm, and in the material realm, and perhaps for hundreds or thousands of lifetimes. Only by seeing things honestly can there really be the chance to leave Plato's Cave. As long as someone keeps saying "It's all in God's hands," you have turned your life over to the Demiurge. As a metaphor, Truman is being manipulated daily, by everyone he comes across, including his wife and best

[27] One of the misconceptions is that the fire, objects and the Cave are the "real world," while the seats and prisoners are the illusion. In fact, the fire is the Demiurge (creator) and the objects would be the material world, while those who operate the objects would be the archons (top layer of minions doing its bidding). "*And she (Sophia) called its name Yaldaboath (Demiurge). This is the first archon... "he became strong and created for himself the other archons inside a blaze of luminous fire, which still exists now.*" Secret Gospel of John.

friend. Sylvia (his love interest) was the exception, and we will get to her shortly. Truman is us. Christoff is presented as if he loves Truman and this is why he is manipulating and messing with his life. Christoff is manipulating Truman to control him. It seems like at the end of the movie, where Truman sails away, battles the storm, reaches the edge of the bubble (bursts it), and then waves goodbye, that he is leaving Plato's Cave. But again we have to see honestly that what Truman is doing, is leaving one matrix (Seahaven), to soon enter the next matrix (of Los Angeles and Sylvia). Although more real than where he initially was how quickly will he settle into that world, believing this next layer to be the final one? This is the same mistake Neo makes in the first *Matrix* movie.

> "*The very gods we pray to for hope and salvation, are the very culprits that prey on us. They are our keepers, and they enslave us, yet we are convinced that they are our creator and savior, Isn't that ironic?*"
> Greg Carlisle

Stop turning over your will with every prayer, to a being outside yourself you have no idea who or what it is. Stop saying "thy will be done," and start saying "my deepest Self's will be done." If that Self comes from a loving creator, bonus, but at least all your direction will come from what is most deeply you. Leaving Plato's Cave is all about learning to put your trust within yourself, and nothing outside of yourself. You have all the power, and all that is outside you is attempting to drain or limit that power.

There are two disciplines no one wants to spend any time studying: law and history. What is odd about the subject of history is that if you go back far enough in time, you no longer study history but archaeology. That makes no sense, both are the study of the past. It does make sense when you realize you are studying two things. Archaeology (archon-ology) is the study of the takeover of this realm by the Demiurge's archons, while history (his-story) is the story of the Demiurge after the takeover was completed. History is simply the story of how the Demiurge took the false simulated reality he created, then set up various systems of control within it (commerce, government, science, religion, law etc), and the wars that were fought to eliminate people who would not go along with the control systems being put in place. Also, it is important to study the legal system. I don't want to get into the depth of that here but you can follow the footnote for an excellent article on this subject.[28]

*

Getting back to Plato's Cave, perhaps the standing prisoner starts to walk to the back of the cave in a bit of a daze. Once at the back, it becomes clearer that they are in a 360-degree circular screen theater, with lots of people in their seats. It also becomes clear that a light is being projected from a central source onto all the screens. Along each of the walls are several doors leading to various rooms. At the far back of the theater is a door labeled "Do Not Enter. Dangerous." Because the movies are surrounding everyone in 360 degrees, there is no way to escape the movie being played. Thus the Cave is described best as a bubble. This is the new world that our (now standing) prisoner discovers. In Truman's case, he lived in a gigantic soundstage dome. Meanwhile in *Pleasantville*, the circular roads also made a closed bubble-like environment. When Truman got tired of the reflection (the movie set of his life) he went sailing for the edge of that bubble - and of course, burst it and got a peek of reality.[29]

Though a seemingly closed space (bubble), there are openings where the force of Intent beyond the bubble can enter. The force from outside the bubble, called Intent, can manifest through the walls into our perception. Castaneda wrote an entire book on this topic called *The Power of Silence*. That book describes how Spirit/Intent is revealed to us metaphorically, and our need to interpret that message. I believe that Castaneda called this force Intent in order to reflect it as a two-way street. Our Intent for Truth calls outside the bubble, while outside Truth is Intending to reach us. The painting on the ceiling of the Sistine Chapel may reflect this interaction. This is symbolized by Sylvia in *The Truman Show* and by David and Jennifer in *Pleasantville*. They entered through an opening to provide information of the world beyond to those who would listen. We

---

[28] You can read kenneth scott's work *Overview of the World System of Bondage and Separation From Life* here https://www.gemstoneuniversity.org/overview-of-the-world-system.html

[29] Castaneda's world of the Tonal is metaphorically known as the bubble of perception, and he claimed that we are placed in it at the moment of birth. At first, the bubble is open to reveal the Nagual (that which is beyond the dream). But eventually the bubble begins to close, until finally we are sealed in. From that point forward, we can only see on the walls that which we project: a reflection of the false self

may only need one such interaction to change our lives. It seems that it was just one conversation with Sylvia on the beach, that was enough to start Truman on his entire quest towards Freedom and Truth.

For a long while, perhaps the entire remainder of his life, the prisoner might focus on trying to understand the bubble, and that makes perfect sense. I don't think it can be avoided really. We just entered a new reality and the natural tendency is to get our bearings. Where are we now? This stage, while an expansive one, also is the place where the trap of spirituality begins. Spiritual awakening, or enlightenment is the trap of the standing at the back of the Cave level. It is getting seduced by the love and light concepts at the back of the Cave, all making promises of how they have the secret to change everything going on.

This next idea about the Cave does not come from Plato, but from Stephen Davis in his free online book *Butterflies Are Free to Fly.*[30] He suggests that what will happen next for the standing prisoner is to join a group. Davis claims, that at the back of the cave, there will not be a bunch of individual wandering prisoners, but a series of formed groups. For the prisoner the conversations would likely seem odd, but when asked what they are talking about, a likely response is "We don't like the movies playing and we are trying to change them." This would intrigue anyone after standing, the thought that the movie can be changed. There were lots of movies the prisoner didn't like. This tends to become the new guiding philosophy of the newly standing prisoner, "I have to change or fix something." It may be the movie or themselves.

Another common element for those out of their seats, as Davis wisely suggests, is the actual need to be part of a group. For most it is a means of survival. One has at that point, spent an entire life chained in a seat watching the movie screen. Suddenly, they are now in a new world with no idea how to act or what to do. It makes sense to try and find others who have gone through this same experience, who can offer support during the adjustment. Amazingly though, instead of one or two large groups at the back that help with the transition, there are thousands of small groups—each with their own specific ideas. The standing person knows that they must join one, but which one? Who has real answers? Some join a group quickly. Others hunt around a while, but eventually one is chosen. While

[30] For more details on his categories, look into his free online book https://www.butterfliesfree.com/

others will go from group to group looking for the "winner." Few find just one and stick to it throughout. A key feature about groups or organizations is that they need a leader. Someone offering guidance, usually how to be just like the leader. Generally there is always the presented end goal of being happy, loving, peaceful and often having more money, power and sex. Anywhere they find that not happening - either with themselves or others is something they must fix. Love and light must reign supreme.

Not often considered is the following: even though it looks like we can change the movies; no matter what is tried, the basic story line doesn't shift all that much. Even if it does alter slightly, it generally does not adjust in the way a person hopes. The basic story of 'life on Earth' tends more or less to stay the same. For all the meditation, group prayers, law of attraction and positive thinking - is human life and the planet really any better than it was 100 years ago? A thousand? Anytime? Things seem, in fact, to be much worse. It was a hard realization for me to come to, that this entire reality is nothing but a clown show circus. Granted at times life is beautiful, interesting and interactive, but the foundation is pain and suffering, for that is how the energy (loosh) is created for harvest. This place has never been any better, nor will it ever improve. The belief that *"things can get better"* is one of this realm's most ingenious and insidious traps. Everything we have been doing our entire lives is, at its very core, designed in some way to fail. That is a tough truth to see. Granted, we can affect small things in the simulation to our advantage, but since no one really understands who built the simulation, or why, or how it works, all such things are just hopes shouted to the wind. Go beyond the simulation entirely. A key element of Dante's Inferno is the quote *"Abandon all hope ye who enter here."* That is not meant to be a message about entering hell, it is about entering Truth; for as long as one has hope, they are tied to the simulation and to the false self. 'False' and 'hope' go together, but in the realm of Truth, hope is never required.

The love and light myth is probably the most insidious trap of our times. It produces in people the same effect as any drug - it makes you feel good for a short time, only to crash from its loss and go looking for the next hit. Over and over again the spiritual community are junkies looking for another light being, another reiki session, another smile on their face in meditation. They have been tricked into thinking they are evil if they have a negative thought or get angry. Righteous anger is what would be needed for change. Sitting smiling at a wall, pretending you are the Buddha, is going to ensure continued enslavement. Love and light spirituality is the blue pill of Morpheus, and the average person cannot get enough of it.

And that is what you have to walk past if you want to really understand how to leave Plato's Cave. Everyone is asking questions about the nature of reality to some degree or another. A few dabble in it for a few minutes a week in-between cheeseburgers and football matches, others read some books and attend lectures, while a few do some inner work in these areas. In one sense everyone is doing the best he or she can, given the lack of guidance this realm provides, and the number of challenging situations it constantly manifests. However, you have to do better than what most people think is their best. If you want Truth, Home, Totality, you are going to have to walk to the final stage of alchemy. Not just how the world is an illusion, but who created it and why. You will have to uncover all the tricks used, because unless you can know the layers of the tricks, you still can be tricked. There will be so much false light (of Lucifer), that to discern light from dark is going to become the task of a lifetime.

Recently, someone asked me, "if there is no karma then does it make any difference whether you are nice or jerk in this life." Actually, it does. The after-death experiences pretty much indicate there will be a life review, but that review is not there to help you. The life review in the afterlife is there to present your life in such a way as to bring up feelings of guilt, shame and disappointment. Who doesn't have past moments you wish would have been done differently? Those feelings easily get manipulated to trick us to coming back here. Of course, we are humans placed in this world with no memory of anything, no guidebook on how to live, and we have our lives manipulated (often in very direct ways) by these 'control beings.' As such, the practice of recapitulation is more vital than I thought previously. It is not just to clean your energy or reintegrate yourself from past experiences while alive. Those are secondary gains. The recapitulation is meant to prepare you properly for that after death review, to know our past inside and out. Nothing can be thrown at us as a surprise. We want to be able to say to everything shown, *"Yes, I know about that, it was a challenge or I was under some stress, I have seen the event and myself and have come to better understand who I was then and why I acted that way. I am OK with all that now, and I am no longer that person. I am Absolute Awareness and I have transformed. Next."*

This is what the full life recapitulation is meant to do, and now I see it has to be a full recapitulation, since a partial version is not going to create this total clarity of the after-death review. The more of a 'good life' you live, the more honest and kinder you were, just means there will be fewer events stuck to your energy body to be presented in the after-death life review. We live well so we have less to be 'ready for.' We keep up with our recap until nothing is hiding or still attached to in past experiences.[31] The less tied we are to it, the less likely are to be tricked by false ideas of karma, or that your choices were all of your free will (they weren't).

What can be found in the back of the Cave has some value, for a while. I am not diminishing these practices totally, because they have a place. There is a reason the various traditions like alchemy and Native medicine ways had steps of learning. You have to move forward, but in an order that is clear and safe for the body, mind and spirit. Try to jump too quickly and one is likely to land in quicksand. But once you enter the final stage of the process, where exiting the Cave can become a possibility, you can't bring the lower levels with you. You have to see them for what they are (a valuable step at a valuable time), but no longer valid to where you are heading. And so, it is going to sound like I am critical in this book to most everything in the spiritual and religious landscape, but that is how it has to be in the final stage. Of course, there will be moments when some of those practices or beliefs of the early stages are needed, so go back and touch them lightly, then allow them to float away and return to your task. The task at hand is to go through the exit, through the eye of the needle. And you cannot bring anything through the eye of the needle, not even yourself. Through that needle is Freedom, Totality and Truth. The Power of your whole being you have intuited, is there within you, but never fully realized. Most who do begin to enter this final stage do not move far, because they will not let go of all of their prized knowledge, beliefs and exercises at the lower levels. They hold so tightly to it all that they become stuck in the quicksand of the work. They stop the final journey before it ever starts by not allowing themselves to be made over fresh.

*

[31] To date I have presented recapitulation to over a thousand people. The number of those who have completed a life review is zero. That says a lot in itself about the commitment people show. I have had the chance to talk with one person (Lorenzo, one of those who has interviewed me on this book), and he is the only person I have met to have done a full recapitulation.

No one is digging into knowing what this reality actually is. They are focused on their wishes and hopes for it. Can you change a computer simulation designed to create suffering and slavery? Technically you can if you have access to the basic program, and you know how to program in that particular language. Do you think these various spiritual groups have access to any of that? They do not, no matter how much they try to convince themselves they do. As a result, none of the groups milling around behind the seats can produce any of the claims they promise to their followers. What help they can provide is at best, individual assistance. While that in itself could be rather useful, ultimately it is minor.

The groups offer excuses as to why their claims are never reached, such as "No pain, no gain" "It can take years, and maybe even hundreds of lifetimes for the teaching to work" and "We don't have enough members." Or even the most damaging excuse of all "You must be doing something wrong" or "You are not spiritual enough." Of course, the group itself and its teaching cannot possibly be flawed, so it must be every individual member's fault. Most of the seekers in these groups are very nice people. People you really want to be your friends; intelligent, well meaning, caring. In fact, they are so nice that you tend to overlook the basic flaws in the system they are a part of.

While it appears the groups are offering much more freedom, knowledge and guidance, everyone seems to forget a key point. They are all **still in the Cave.** Albeit in a slightly better position than chained to their seats believing the movie, but they continue in the realm of the matrix. All groups, techniques or ideas have an infinitesimally minute chance of reaching the promises they sell. The success rate will either be very low or totally absent, especially when it comes to constant bliss. This realm is not set up for constant bliss, no matter what the gurus try to say. In fact the only way to live in long-term overly happy states, is to be in total denial of the final level of this work. This is why it tends to be that the ones who seem the most spiritual, loving and enlightened, are in fact the ones in the deepest denial of what really awaits them when they die. Granted I have nothing against love, enjoyment and being, I appreciate when they are in my life fully. I just know that no matter how enjoyable they are in the moment, they won't last, nor do I require them to.

2020 to 2022 has been a great presentation of this. If all of these so-called great teachers of Truth cannot see the biggest relative lie of modern human history playing out in front of their eyes every day for two years straight, how can they possibly be trusted to see the Great lies that obscure Absolute Truth? All the gurus preaching freedom and liberation have just disappeared. They followed the rules to give up their own freedoms and suggested to their followers that they do the same, or they simply stayed silent and did not comment on the loss of freedoms going on around them. Is this someone who you would really want to trust to lead you toward Ultimate Freedom, if they have no sense of relative freedom? The problem is they believe they have reached the top of the mountain, while instead they are comfortable in a chair halfway up, selling postcards of the view someone else took from the top.

Few ever ponder the notion, "Maybe none of the groups work." It is another reason why seeking is the problem, because the person seeks for something that does not actually exist. The promise of the group can never be found. The underlying issue is that the entire group (including its leader) are still in and operating within the cave/theater, which means, there is not much difference between everyone as it appears. Without having exited the theater, no one really knows much about anything. Knowing everything only comes by looking at the one place that has been ignored: The door at the back of the Cave with the gigantic warning sign on it. I feel it might take what I label "an outside force" to finally examine the confining elements of the Cave, to hear that force's message like a homing signal, and to eventually go looking for a way to reach it. While still in a body you can only have a glimpse of what it is like outside, which is why I recommend getting information from a few different people who claim to have seen the exit and put that information together like a jigsaw puzzle.

The real answers will not be found in groups but in outcasts, longers and wanderlings. Ones who are in society, but not really. What these people say is so radical because they have no real suggestions about improving the Cave. They don't care about the Cave (any more than they must for day-to-day functioning). They see the Cave is insane, always has been, always will be. As such they put their focus not on the matrix, but the exit. To go further, a standing prisoner is going to have to create their own personal path, one that suits them, not something standard that is for the masses. Those systems just lead to being a slave to be born and to die, over and over again. To exit the Cave is to see fully, and reject the lies, tricks and contracts placed on the soul so that you can become your natural state: Whole, Total, Powerful and Free.

Do keep in mind, that if you are in a prison cell, the method of escape is first to fully understand, how you got into that cell. Then to examine every inch of it, and to know it intimately. Then a plan can be formulated. We as a species have done some decent work on the exploration of our prison. The problem is that it usually gets turned into "how can I fix it?" If instead we take all that information and point it towards how to exit, all that examination of the Cave will become of value. If not, we just spent time knowing our cell for very little gain.

Plato's Cave is not just the material world. Many get caught in that idea because of the way the allegory is presented. This is another missing element to it. Plato's Cave consists of every layer of false reality. That is not just this material world, but other material worlds, astral worlds, akashic worlds, angelic worlds... pretty much any world where there is something to observe (even the Void where there is only Nothing to observe) are all still Plato's Cave. That is part of the challenge, there are lots of layers that one can be in within the Cave, and falsely believe you are outside of it.

*

What does Plato's allegory have to say about exiting. Again, not much. Actually in the story the prisoner does not get to leave COMPLETELY. He only gets a glimpse, then is sent back inside the Cave. And he does not leave by his own free will. The allegory asks "what if a prisoner was dragged outside?" Why drag a prisoner outside? Can he not go out willingly? Plato discusses none of this but goes on to show how the prisoner sees the Sun, how it hurts his eyes, and how it would take time to adjust to it and get used to this new reality. The next part is interesting, Plato now claims that in this situation the prisoner would think that outside the Cave is far superior to inside, and would want to return to help his fellow prisoners escape. What is this light he is seeing (inferred to be our real sun)? My guess is that this is the white light of the death experience, which is claimed to be blinding yet beautiful by those who have experienced it. This is a key part of the trap, to go to the white light is to be brought back into the matrix, back into the Cave as it has happened to the prisoner.

The allegory states that the prisoner returns, with no mention of how, and that the prisoner will want to help his fellow prisoners escape. Yet how could he help with that, because he did not escape, he was dragged out? Plato claims the returning prisoner would be blinded by the cave light on re-entering (the fire being the Demiurge), laughed at by the prisoners who would claim the trip outside hurt him. Eventually they would kill him and anyone else who attempts to take them on a similar journey.

Most think this is where the allegory ends, as this is where it tends to be finished in most presenter's examinations. But the story continues for a few more pages and an odd discussion between Socrates and Glaucon occurs. It is brief discussions on a number of subjects; light and darkness, the nature of the soul, what is good and turning away from sensual pleasures. It just feels like a totally different writer. I wonder if this is similar to many *New Testament* writings where you can clearly notice two different writing styles in the same book, where a new writer took something from an older document, discarded some of it, and then rewrote a new narrative. One would think the Plato's Cave ending might answer the missing questions mentioned above, yet the final part is a few paragraphs discussing the State and how people are benefactors of the State.

A few specific sentences near the end make me question the validity of the entire story. I will give an overview of the key lines, "*The business of us who are the founders of the State will be to compel the best minds to attain that knowledge which we have already shown to be the greatest... but when they have ascended and seen enough we must not allow them to do as they do now...remain in the upper world: but this must not be allowed; they must be made to descend again among the prisoners in the den, and partake of their labours and honours, whether they are worth having or not.*" Is Plato saying that those who are able to escape the Cave and reach the Truth should not be allowed to stay there, but made to descend again back to the world of prisoners? The ending of this story, and the story itself, could be about control and enslavement, and not any sort of escape as a researcher might think.

Did the prisoner really reach the "outside," or just what we might call the astral realm? That is not the real exit, the real exit would be beyond this new world, beyond the astral realm, beyond the light, beyond everything. Even if the prisoner tells of his journey on returning to the Cave, it is but half an exit. Perhaps others, on hearing the story, will realize they are outside the Cave and decide to come back inside it. Either tricked by ideas of karma and sin, so that they have to return in order to learn and grow, or something altruistic to save people or the Cave itself. A few will just barter a deal to make them special and important here (as Cipher did in the Matrix), selling their soul for some false material things. The place this prisoner could have been "dragged" to, as a way of presenting a false hope to those standing in the back of the Cave, is a place almost the entire spiritual community is attempting to reach. Oneness. Self-Realization.

*

It is presented by the main teachers out there, that the goal of spiritual work is to reach a state referred to by various words: awakening, enlightenment, non-duality, oneness and several others. It is a core concept of most traditions, from Advaita to Buddhism to Shamanism.[32] Yet awakening IN the dream is not awakening FROM the dream. I wrote much about this in *Falling For Truth,* and it is an important part of the process. It is when you come to see that everything in this reality is an illusion, including yourself. A manifestation of a Greater Self. That you are Absolute, Total, Empty yet Complete. The problem always is with context. What I have just described can also be claimed as "awakening within the dream." It is presented as if that is the end of the whole game here. How could it not seem so, especially for one that it has happened to? Oneness/Absolute, what could possibly be beyond that? And so, they stay here and become the spiritual guides of that generation. Another trap has been set. The enlightened gurus like to present well received catch phrases, "we are all One," "we are love," "there is nothing to fear," "all is in good hands," "be present" or "be peaceful." They are not totally wrong of course, and that is what makes it all so challenging. They are correct, up to the end of the early alchemic stages. In the real ancient traditions, when someone had reached this level, they would be given some time to get used to it and integrate how their physical form and mind needed to transition with this. But that would be only for a period of time. The newly Awakened would be reminded that they are not fully done yet. There is a final stage.

Besides, no one is questioning which Oneness these people awoke to? There is a Oneness outside the Matrix itself, known as the Pleroma in Gnostic literature. This is very complex and I will get into it later in the work when discussing the *Nag Hammadi* documents. Then there is the Void

[32] If you look carefully these traditions are not really their original teachings. They have been changed and edited gradually (as most of the Western religions teachings have been edited and censored). These Ancient Teachings have been "Westernized," set up now in such a way as to make those with some money comfortable about being a part of them. Of course long before that they were "Easternized," if I can use a made-up term, to make those in Asia more comfortable about following them. You have to go a long way back to find the original teaching, and in most cases, it no longer exists.

Oneness (known as the Clear Light of Dzogchen Buddhism). It is the still place in the matrix, the womb of reality, from where all material forms and experiences manifest. It is not dark or black, but contains everything and nothing. It is without time or space, a place that is non-dual, has no polarity, of total awareness and stillness. Reaching the Void while still in a body will lead to deep experiences of peace and clarity. Who wouldn't want that? It's as good a foundation as one can get here, and even that can be a helpful tool after one dies. It is the first stepping point for many after death, and one can stay here for a long while if desired. In fact, that is one of the values of reaching this place in life and getting comfortable with it; so that you can go there directly instead of towards the false white light. But the Void is not the Real Absolute. The Void is still in the simulation. The Gnostics were clear that our reality is a copy, and to be a copy there must be that which you copy from. In this case the Void would be the copy of a more complete Absolute, which is why it is easy to believe you have reached the real and not a simulated copy of the real.

Oneness is part of the package of understanding. The Gnostics remind us in *The First Apocalypse of James* that a discussion with the archons will happen after we die, and this text suggests we have to answer certain questions correctly. Many of those responses include that you know you are not a material form, that you come from the Pleroma (True Oneness) which is your real home, and they (Demiurge/archons) are not from that realm, thus have no power to keep you locked here. *The Egyptian Book of the Dead* has a similar question and answer session where the deceased has to know all the names of a boat, the boat being the symbolic parts of reality. Of course the question and answer might not occur, only a metaphoric explanation, of what concepts must be kept in our awareness and energy body in the after-death realm. The problem, as my book points out, is that this type of spiritual work is just half of a giant puzzle.

It does not matter how awake or enlightened someone is if they do not know what the after-death reincarnation trap is, or how a simulated matrix has been placed over this reality. The other side of this work is to see that this is a world of control and manipulation, and that everything in our world from the standpoint of society (government, science, banking, history, education, medicine, law, media, etc.) are all but a series of deceptions. And it is not just the Earth realm, everything we can see and not see is part of the matrix. The planetary realm is another lie, as is the astral realm. All there to make us hosts for non-physical parasitic entities.

The material world operates as a parasite because that is how it was created, a mirror generated simulation of a much more real reality.[33]

Navigating through, it is helpful to know the concepts of Void and Oneness, for you become harder to manipulate, but you will likely be manipulated and returned if you do not understand the cycle. Those who stay in love and oneness after death might feel good after the transition, but they are likely to follow dead grandma, Jesus, or the angelic being into the tunnel of light (because it so loving and feels so good). Then voilà, back into this mess they come. Nirvana is a real place, but it is not Home. No matter how good and peaceful it may feel, the soul can never really rest there. In time it will get restless. Plato's Cave is an endless deception machine, a machine that has more layers to it than one can imagine. That is why it is so hard to exit, there are so many layers one has to break through.

Until one sees that this realm is an evil artificial simulation trap of the soul (Essence), the chances of exiting are slim. That includes the so-called "awakened enlightened teachers" out there. They might have had a more peaceful run here sitting on their chairs and speaking to everyone through a microphone with a smiley look on their faces, but they will likely be back here the same as those who had no interest in spiritual matters. Recall in Plato's story that the only prisoner who leaves the cave was "dragged out." Even in the allegory the prisoner didn't go on his own. Take that to heart. My honest guess, and I mean seriously, is that one in ten million will get past the reincarnation trap. That is one hundred for every billion. That might be it. And so, don't automatically think that your so-called guru, or enlightened teacher will be one in that hundred. Or even you. Most of those who do exit, will likely be people no one ever heard of, because they did their inner work alone, perhaps never even mentioning it to close family members.

---

[33] An interesting program to watch is the 1968 *BBC theater* "News Benders" episode. It is beyond amazing that it was made, aired and presented in 1968 with that much detail of the make-up of this realm. The episode ends by letting us know that a computer is in charge of running the world. I fully agree with that, and that it has been in charge that long. However, think how far ahead that AI computer system is by now? It is only now (within our normal reality) that technology has moved along to a point where we, in a sense, can see what AI can potentially do. But again, what is behind the scenes is fifty years ahead of where the material really is.

Remember that if one falls for the reincarnation trap, that person will be put into a new body, after a *Westworld* style memory wipe. Everything from this current life will be forgotten. Then even the "knowing of Oneness" and existing in the non-dual Void will be for naught. Back in a new body and having to do ALL THEIR SPIRITUAL WORK over again. Think about that. All the great inner work that was done by these people (and some have done great work to say the least), would all be lost in the memory wipe if they follow the light/bridge and get placed back into a new body. I know the guru type will try to convince you if you bring this up, that they are so far advanced they would be able to take all their memories into a new body, or they are about to become a light being or light worker, or some other name with light. Make no mistake, they will be back here, ignorant just as they were previously.[34] Seeing Truth tends to happen from trauma, not peace. The more one has to question this insane reality that surrounds them, the more likelihood they might see past this to this realm's origin. Richard Rose often mentioned to his students, "you don't want peace, you want answers." And so I say, if you are going to do all that work and illusion busting in this life, why not go all the way? Because if you don't, you will lose all the gains you made here. Do the deep inner work, not to have a better life, an easier life, a more important life, but to know Truth and Self so fully, that you can do the only task we have ever had - return Home.[35]

---

[34] Granted most researchers into the soul trap ideas never mention the idea of parallel realities, and as such parallel lives. I discuss my experiences with this in *Falling For Truth*. If there really are 1,000,000 versions of me, living 1,000,000 similar but unique lives, then which life needs to "escape the matrix?" If one of the versions of me gets past the Demiurge and leaves, what happens to the other 999,999 counterparts? Other important questions to consider.

[35] Have you wondered why it is called enlightenment? To become light. The word in Ancient Egypt was Akh (light) / Akhu (one that has become light). But is this the pure light of the Allogenis (first text of the Nag Hammadi Codices) or the false light of the Demiurge and this simulation? This world has been tricked for a long time with tales of "light beings" becoming a "light worker," "being saved by the light" and "going to the light." A giant spiritual program has been laid onto us, we have been part of a game where darkness has been disguised as light.

3

A PREDATOR'S ORIGIN

> "*So there appeared for the first time a ruler out of chaos, lion-like in appearance, androgynous, having an exaggerated sense of power within him, and ignorant of whence he came to be.*" Apocryphon of James discussing the Demiurge[36]

I have mentioned many concepts in the first two chapters, but it is time to get into some of them in a bit more depth. The Plato's Cave analogy completely ignores the question of how and why the Cave was created. The Cave and the prisoners are already there when the story begins with no further explanation. Most creation myths, be they from ancient cultures, religions or native traditions, tend to put a "happy spin" on things. A loving creator God, made the material world for positive purposes. Generally, these are rather simplified, a God made the Heavens and Earth, then made the creatures, and it goes quickly into mythological stories about those creatures.

There are a few unique creation stories which tell a different narrative. There are a few that present a similar theme as this book, that this is a simulated realm, made by an evil creator. What is interesting, is that generally the groups who have held such stories, are the ones the Church of Rome has hunted down and exterminated. I will present five unique

[36] Lash, John *In His Image* pg 181

sources, ancient and modern: the Cathars of Southern France, the Gnostics who wrote the *Nag Hammadi Codex*, the out of body experience of Robert Monroe in 1971, the books of Carlos Castaneda and a vision I had in 2009. I think they all provide some foundation for what our realm is, "why we are here," and where some of my thesis originates from. I am not saying that any one of these are fully correct, but like a jigsaw puzzle, they give us a piece of the whole to get an understanding. You can't leave the Cave until you know why the Cave was created in the first place.

*

The Cathars

I will begin with the Cathars of Southern France. They were a dualist group whom the Catholic Church became so afraid of, that they created the first Crusade against their own people to exterminate them in 1209. This group will be examined in an upcoming chapter, because their main belief was that this was a world where souls were caught in a trap of reincarnation. Their teachings were designed to end this constant cycle of incarnation. The Cathars had no fear of going to hell after death, because they felt that the only hell that existed was this material realm. Reincarnation was the fear, for it is what would force them back into a body, and therefore back into hell.

The Cathars saw two creators: The Good God of the *New Testament* who is the creator of the spiritual realm (and everything permanent), as opposed to the evil God, whom Cathars identified as Rex Mundi (God of the World), who is the *Old Testament* creator of the physical world (all that is changing). All visible matter, including the human body, was created by Rex Mundi, and therefore was tainted with sin. Not because of something Eve or Adam did or did not do, but simply because the material world is artificial (a hologram or simulation). Generally, Rex Mundi is equated with Satan, but more often he was connected with the fallen angel concept of Lucifer (Light Bearer). These ideas of course put them in direct odds with the Church of Rome, whose fundamental principle was that there was only one God who created all things visible and invisible. The Cathars were at odds with the Church for most of their beliefs.

There may have been several creation stories that the Cathars believed. The most common was closely linked to the Gnostic creation myth of Sophia, where they believed Rex Mundi had tricked a number of angels into leaving Heaven. James McDonald, of www.cathar.info claims, the Cathar human creation story began when Rex Mundi came to Heaven and wanted to enter, but was denied. He waited for a thousand years, then managed to sneak in. Inside, he promised the angels every temptation possible if they would leave Heaven with him. "*Many souls were seduced, and for nine days and nine nights they fell through the hole in heaven the devil had created. God allowed this for those who wished to leave but other souls (by accident) began falling through the hole and so God sealed it. After the souls had fallen, they found themselves in the devil's realm without any of the good things he had promised and, remembering the joys of heaven, they repented and asked the devil if they could return. The devil replied that they could not because he had fashioned for them bodies which would bind them to earth and cause them to forget all about heaven.*"[37] The claim is that although Rex Mundi could make the bodies, he could not animate them to think, feel or move, so he asked the Good God for help, who did so, giving them a soul so they could work their way back to him. How could Rex Mundi make animals, birds and fish, and allow them to move, feel and act, but not humans?

A similar creation story comes from the text *The Secret Supper- The Book of John the Evangelist,* that was originally a Bogomil[38] text, but was found on some of the Cathars during the Inquisition. You can read if for yourself here,[39] however, I will provide just a couple of highlights of a conversation between Jesus and John in Heaven. This myth claims that God's angelic brother (Satan) literally falls to earth, first shining white and finally red. This of course would become Lucifer, the fallen angel, and often these two names (Satan and Lucifer) become interchangeable. Firstly, the text claims that Satan recruited a number of angels, then once on Earth, he formed all the living creatures; plants, animals, fish, birds and finally a man and a woman made from clay (who were also animated with an angel). That would make the entire story of Genesis the creation story of Satan. The ending of the book has Jesus tell of his own birth and descent from Heaven, and how Satan sent Elijah in the form of John the Baptist to the realm, to begin a false system of water baptism. The book

[37] This creation myth can be found at http://www.cathar.info

[38] Dualist group from South East Europe

[39] http://gnosis.org/library/Interrogatio_Johannis.html

ends by describing a last judgment, where those who were believers will wind up living with the Good God and Jesus, while non-believers and Satan will be bound and cast into a pool of fire.

*

The Gnostics[40]

"*The world came about through a mistake.*" Gospel of Philip[41]

The most complete myth we have on creation, comes from the Gnostics, who managed to hide a key codex in the hills above Nag Hammadi Egypt, prior to their destruction by the Catholics in the 300's. Every Gnostic that could be found was killed, and every book they had was burned. How the *Nag Hammadi Codex* survived, is something of a miracle in itself. The word "Gnosis" means "Knowledge" in Greek, but this is a different type of knowledge. The Latin phrase "knowledge is power," is a power to be found in the material realm. Gnosis, however, is Freedom, for it is an inner understanding about that which is beyond this realm

While several researchers have given their interpretations of the creation myths of the Gnostics, John Lash gives what I feel is the most complete account from his 2006 book *Not in his Image*, and his old website www.metahistory.org. I will go into more detail on all the various beliefs the Gnostics held about reality in a future chapter. For now I will present a simplified version of their creation story, which can also be called "the Fall of Sophia."

Gnostics were dualists, like the Cathars, and saw there was a Good God (Absolute, invisible), who along with a female half (known by the name Barbelo) produced a series of spiritual beings called "aeons." They resided in a type of Heaven, known as the Pleroma, translated as "Fullness." One of these aeons was the goddess Sophia, who wanted to give birth to a being on her own, without the involvement of a partner or the approval of the Good God (Father). What she gave birth to, the

---

[40] Creation myth information from https://gnosticismexplained.org/the-gnostic-creation-myth/
https://www.bibliotecapleyades.net/vida_alien/esp_vida_alien_18v.htm
and Lash,John, *Not in his Image*
[41] *Nag Hammadi Codex 2* found at Gnosis.org

Gnostics referred to as a type of abortion, and was named the Demiurge "Craftsman." Abortion here meaning, something not wanted and ejected early. Perhaps this is why the Demiurge developed as an evil AI-type mind. Gnostic texts described this creature as "having a lion-like body with the head of reptile." The Demiurge was also given the name Yaldabaoth. It is he who is the being that created the entire material realm (including the various astral realms). First the Demiurge created a series of minion helpers, non-organic creatures similar to a computer, known as archons.[42]

To create the material world, the Demiurge made a mirror image of the Good Place (Pleroma). The creation was referred to by Gnostics as a simulation (HAL in Coptic), which became an inverse world of that which it had been copied from. Everything in our reality is a type of hologram; from the Earth, to planets, to beings. The Gnostics claimed that the creator god of the *Old Testament* was the Demiurge, and not the Good God of the Pleroma. When Sophia had seen the outcome of her birthing attempt, she became depressed, filled with guilt and wept continually. The Divine Father saw her pain and forgave her, but demanded she stay in the ninth heaven (the layer of the sky closest to the Pleroma, above Yaldabaoth to find a way to atone for her error.

The Demiurge and archons noticed that God had created a special creature, a heavenly being called Adam. They wanted such a being as well, and tried to create it. But it would not animate. This is the same concept as found in the Cathar creation stories (showing a definite link), but the question remains, why could the Demiurge animate all the birds, fish and animals, but not the first humans? I have yet to see a researcher provide an answer for this discrepancy. The Gnostic texts then claims that beings from the Pleroma, sent by the Good God, came to the Demiurge and suggested they could make the created man live. These Pleroma beings allowed a spark to come into the first man from Sophia. He came to life. This would allow the first human, and all humans afterwards to have the spark of the Divine within. This would make them more spiritual and powerful than the

[42]Archon generally translates as "governor of a province" or a "religious or governmental authority." Hence the plural, Archons, is often translated in Gnostic texts as "the Authorities," and an attempt by researchers to make them the human Roman rulers of the time. The Gnostics would have seen them as "Earthly beings under the influence of the archons." Archons are from the non-organic realm of the Demiurge. (There is no Coptic word for Archon, so Gnostic texts use the Greek term in Coptic transliteration.)

Demiurge or his archons. At the same time from this maneuver, the beings allowed Sophia to vindicate her error.

Simplifying the story (it is a very long and detailed account of creation), the archons became jealous of the new man for having more inner power than them, so they made him mortal. A Garden of Eden was created, which included all possible material pleasures and food, in order to distract him from his divine nature. The archons tried to get this power by taking a piece of Adam and placing it in a new creature, Eve. Adam saw Eve as his counterpart in matter and they joined as one. To the Gnostics, Christ now appeared as the serpent showing them to eat from the Tree of Knowledge (Gnosis), as opposed to the tree of good and evil as in the *Old Testament*), to which Adam and Eve regained their total knowledge of creation and the archons.

The Demiurge now rapes Eve, and throws her and Adam out of Eden. Eve has two sons from this, Cain and Abel, also called "Yahweh" and "Elohim" (two names for "God" in the *Old Testament*). Neither of them received the divine spark. These two could be seen as "hybrids" in our modern thinking, part human-part AI machine. The texts say Adam and Eve sometime later, had consensual sex and had another son, who they named Seth. He gained the divine spark. The Demiurge became enraged. Now there was another being with more power than him, so he "forced Adam, Eve, and Seth to drink the "water of forgetfulness" so that they would lose their Gnosis." Even though forgotten, the spark of Gnosis was still within all the three, and as such all of humanity (who is not a hybrid) has access to the same divine spark passed on through the generations. The texts claim that just as Adam and Eve needed Christ to appear to reveal this to them (as the serpent), Christ returned again (possibly in holographic form) to do the same revealing for all of humanity. Generally in the *Nag Hammadi Codex,* Christ is referred to by the title of "Redeemer."

The Gnostics were clear that the archons (out of jealousy) were constantly attempting to stop humans from reaching their divine spark. John Lash has claimed that they influence via telepathy and suggestion, and then we have the choice of following these hypnotic suggestions or not. Each time we do, we stray one step farther from our human center. Thus, complete control of our mind and energy is the way we overcome their attempts to make us choose "error". Lash claims that Gnosis is that which overcomes this trap, a type of "yogic noetic science melded with parapsychology," and that through the knowledge and use of energy, sex, spiritual exercises, clear seeing and out-of-body experiences the student can regain his Total Freedom.

Someone who attempted to present this Gnostic thesis recently was the American author Philip K. Dick, in his *Valis Trilogy*. These books, and the connection to Sophia is supposed to have happened following a 1974 mystical experience, during which he experienced a download of information into his mind (similar to what happened during my death experience in 2005).[43] The Valis books attempt to show that with the wisdom of Gnosis we can overcome our delusion and victimhood.

*

Loosh Resets[44]

I have been speaking about resets in the book, and I thought it should be discussed a bit further. A reset in the terminology used here means "an action set in motion by controlling entities to completely alter the fabric of the environment of this realm." The more you understand this reality, and that humans are but a small part of a greater whole, then what is really going on with resets can become clearer. To explain this realm, I am going to share the viewpoints of Robert Monroe (who wrote information from an out-of-body experience he had fifty years ago), Carlos Castaneda, and contrast these with a vision I was given in 2009 in a native ceremony. Perhaps together they might tell us more about what we are dealing with when it comes to where we have been, where we are and where we are going.

43

https://blog.oup.com/2016/07/philip-k-dick-spiritual-epiphany/
https://en.wikipedia.org/wiki/The_Exegesis_of_Philip_K._Dick

44

Information on Monroe's experience can be found in his book *Far Journeys*, and analysis from Bronte Baxter *Tracking the Crack in the Universe - Loosh 101:*
https://www.bibliotecapleyades.net/vida_alien/alien_archons93.htm
https://www.bibliotecapleyades.net/ciencia2/ciencia_conscioushumanenergy100.htm

Robert Monroe became the foremost researcher on the out-of-body phenomena. In chapter twelve of his book *Far Journeys*, he presents an "out-of-body experience" (OBE) which he had, where he met a being of light who provided him with details of our realm. The being described the Earth as a giant experiment for the "creator beings" to build the perfect loosh harvest system. "Loosh" being a word Monroe coined to mean a specific type of harvestable energy that the creator beings (Demiurge and archons) require. While some energy is harvested while beings are still alive, the majority is taken at their death. This energy is claimed to be used by the Demiurge and archons to "extend their own life spans." I would argue that this phrase, placed into computer terms, means that the energy goes into the computer simulation power grid to keep it running, hence "extend the life of the simulation." In order to have this occur, a "garden" was created by "these beings" to farm their food source.

Our world is one that is dominated by what we call "the food chain," a need to eat other things to survive. Monroe presents that the food chain has only been set up to maximize "loosh" at death. No creature can survive long on Earth or in this realm without eating something. A vegetarian may think eating a carrot is not the same as eating a duck, but each are living organisms who are only here to be part of the loosh farm, and their death is the same as any other creature's death from that perspective. If a Good God Creator was really the one who set up this place, and if energy was needed to help keep it running, a much better system could have been developed. People try to ignore this problem, but it is critical to see that the only reason a food chain exists is because it comes from the mind of that which is evil.

As you read this chapter carefully, Monroe seems to indicate that there have been several creations of this world experiment, as well as several startups and tear downs. Various resets were put into action, each time looking for a better system of producing loosh. It becomes almost obvious that Monroe is laying out a story of the more conventional history of Earth, but with the twist of how it is all about loosh production, not an evolutionary journey. His chapter suggests that perhaps the first prototype creatures for loosh harvest in this reality were the dinosaurs. Yes I know, many people do not think dinosaurs existed, but I believe that is a response to seeing that the standard story presented by science makes no sense. So the whole concept of dinosaurs is rejected. There may be an answer for dinosaurs, and us, and Robert Monroe might have provided the pointers towards figuring it out.

With dinosaurs as the first creations, the Demiurge either realized in time, that they could not provide a high enough content of loosh, or the dinosaurs figured out some way to block the harvest. Consequently, they were wiped out by the first reset (which is why the dinosaur story tends to be so controversial). It was not from an accidental asteroid. You could call it the first flood - a pre-meditated act of destruction. Monroe's book claims new loosh creatures were then created, which seem like modern plants and animals. Perhaps in these early versions were also creatures we today call neanderthal and cro-magnon. They both seem to be much more attuned to this environment, with thick body hair which acted as a type of fur and which would reduce the need for clothing.

The overseers of the experiment noticed that when creatures battled for scarce resources, or conflicts ensued, the loosh harvest was very high. This is why animals were given fangs, claws or great speed, in order to prolong these "fights to the death" as long as possible, and thereby creating even more loosh. More suffering, especially prior to death, meant more loosh. This can also be how the systems of human sacrifice came to be, a demand by the "gods" to give them a good suffering death spectacle as food and entertainment combined, and with the hope that the gods would not "eat" the one performing the sacrifice. Not only would there be a good loosh harvest, that they could make the humans doing it believe they were "appeasing the gods" and making things better and safer here on Earth. Even Jesus was a blood sacrifice. They also found that suffering, especially exceptional fear, would produce more loosh as well, and as such the realm was modified to generate constant fear. Of course, over time the controllers came to realize they did not even need to generate real threats for humans to be fearful over, they just needed to present "news" that there could be a threat, and that was enough.

Conflict, sacrifice and food for the gods was also presented in Bronte Baxter's articles on the subject, similar to what Monroe was presenting from the ancient texts of India, "The universe is upheld by sacrifice," (Atharva Veda) and "Death (as the Creator) resolved to devour all that he had created; for he eats all... He is the eater of the whole universe; this whole universe is his food." (Mahabharata)[45]

---

[45] Bronte Baxter
https://www.bibliotecapleyades.net/vida_alien/alien_archons93.htm

With the realization that conflict provided bigger loosh harvests, Monroe wrote that the creator beings reset the previous world and brought in this new one as a new experiment. This new world included a new being… us. We were created as a creature to generate these high levels of conflict, and inflict these high levels of suffering the controllers of this experiment want. The human soul does not want suffering and conflict - this is what the controllers of the experiment want.

Of course, I have given a shortened analysis of Monroe's chapter. I suggest you read it on your own if you have access to the book. The life of Monroe becomes very odd after having this experience. It is claimed he first went into a two or three week depression. When he came out of it, he wrote the chapter, then never spoke of the subject again. Even his institute, the largest OBE research center of its kind, generally has nothing to say about chapter twelve, loosh or harvesting energy by alien beings. Just for fun I went to the website and searched the term "loosh." Not one link was found. He was the founder of this concept and his institute's site does not even mention it. How strange is that?

I can take Monroe's base story and add more ideas based on insights and my own experiences. Over time, the controllers of this experiment decided to make us mentally weak and they gave us a self-important mind. Humans are actually powerful beings in this realm. But that power has been purposely hidden and covered over. The new humans were created to not survive easily in this realm, thus to feel constantly out of place, as if we "need" the gods to tell us what to do and how to be. They told us we had to trust them, and then they gave us money, law, government and all the other control systems to be sure we were "corralled" easily. Thus, the experiment controllers are similar to modern farmers who look after sheep or cows in a barn during the winter - giving them just enough to get them through, but not enough to live without the farmer. The farmer thinks they know what is best for the animals, that they are above them, that the animals are there only for their own use, to make the farmer more money, so he's able to build a new deck or buy a new tractor.

---

https://www.bibliotecapleyades.net/ciencia2/ciencia_consciousenergy100.htm

Along the way, there have been many mini-resets to tweak things here and there. The standard alternative theory around past resets tended to be that "humans are getting too smart" or "too many are figuring things out," so the system needs to stop us. This is self-important thinking. Resets at their core are simply about energy. One theory is that the entire computer AI system needs power upgrades, and as such they are upgrading the main loosh-generating creatures in this realm. This may be what the current reset we are in now is about - we are being "upgraded" to produce larger energy harvests in the future. It has nothing to do with commerce, business or what people own. These are all misdirections to the bigger picture. It is all about creating a new loosh human, in this case one that is part human-part robot, one that is under total control and surveillance. The elite of our realm are the farmers, and they work to keep us corralled and distracted until the slaughter truck comes to take us away.

This is where we have been for centuries, locked away from our natural power, living a lie of ignorance. A few break through it. They are known as shamans, but they tend to be downplayed by the rest of the sheep. The minions for the controllers are setting up a world where someone breaking through the conditioning has to become shaman-like, thereby making regaining one's true power, almost impossible for the masses.

There is an unanswered question in Monroe's presentation though. If our souls are what is trapped in this material realm, and if our souls are tricked by the Demiurge to re-enter when we die (as suggested by the Cathars), then when did our souls initially get tricked into being here? Were souls here at the time of the dinosaurs, and if so, what were those souls trapped or contained within? The dinosaurs? Early humans? Disembodied space? The standard belief around this, is that only human souls are trapped here. So that means either human souls were only tricked a few thousand years ago (when this current major reset and creation occurred), or souls are not as "specified" as we think, and can be contained within any creature of creation. When you see that a dog, giraffe, raven, tree or rock has a soul just like you, that also changes how a person interacts with the world.

This is all symbolized by the movie *Monsters Inc.* The majority of the movie is about how the beings in "monster world" need to come into the human realm to get the screams of children (all humans) to power their world. That is pretty much this reality in a nutshell. Of course the movie spins the "fairytale happy ending" where the monsters learn that laughter gives them more energy than fear. No. If the beings who run this reality believed that, they would have changed the experiment long ago. They have been testing loosh possibilities for a long while. Resets are really about changing the harvest of loosh. They now feel the harvest is not giving them what they need, perhaps because the system is getting bigger, or going faster. The change to the next trans-human level is to create an even better harvest of loosh. Locked into an AI artificial reality (matrix style), might be the controllers preferred new harvest experiment.

*

Carlos Castaneda

Carlos Castaneda broached this subject in two of his books. One was in the *Eagle's Gift* where he discusses the ideas of a Demiurge, the other his final book *Active Side of Infinity* where he discusses the parasitic harvest of our energy. I will examine his presentations in more detail in a future chapter (as *Active Side of Infinity* is not the book people have come to believe it is, it is something far more important for our study of reincarnation traps), but for now a quick overview of these two parts of the books.

Eagle's Gift includes a presentation of a force which created all life, which he called the Eagle. It was not a real eagle, but just appeared as an eagle to those who see it. This Eagle, while creating this reality, was also responsible for what happens at death, and all who die will face the Eagle. *"The Eagle is devouring the awareness of all the creatures that, alive on earth a moment before and now dead, have floated to the Eagle's beak, like a ceaseless swarm of fireflies, to meet their owner, their reason for having had life... The Eagle disentangles these tiny flames, lays them flat, as a tanner stretches out a hide, and then consumes them; for awareness is the Eagle's food."*[46] There is a key message the book is presenting, here Castaneda is less claiming that the Eagle (Demiurge) is eating energy per say, but specifically eating our life experiences. That is what it wants. As such the life recapitulation is of critical importance, for if we turn over the life experiences to it before we die, there is no need to be devoured. We can then find something he referred to as "a crack or a moment of chance", to "dart past the Eagle to be free." This too is a clue, because it wants life

[46] *The Eagle's Gift*, by Carlos Castaneda

experiences, this would make this realm a type of experiment. I discuss this more in the final chapter.

In the chapter "Mud Shadows", in his book, *Active Side of Infinity,* Castaneda discusses parasitic beings. It is interesting that he waited until almost the final chapters of his last book to reveal this to the public. Simplified, his message is that inorganic beings, called "predators" or "flyers", have turned humans into a food source. What they eat specifically is an energy coat he calls "The Glowing Coat of Awareness". This coat must be similar to what Robert Monroe meant by Loosh. What this predator did to make sure we were good farm animals, was to give us its mind, what Castaneda called a "parasitic foreign installation." This mind creates conflict, confusion, depression, fear, anger, guilt and all negative moods. Granted the good moods produce harvestable energy as well, just a "lower grade." This parasite mind over ruled our True Mind (which was in us before the parasite was installed) and much of the first half of *Active Side of Infinity* is to regain this connection to our real mind. The recapitulation is also part of this process.

What is most interesting about this chapter, is that Don Juan (Carlos' teacher) offers suggestions of how to get free of the Predator. His claims were not to go out and fix the world, but focus on oneself, to "discipline ourselves to the point where they will not touch us." Discipline in this instance does not mean daily routines or focus but "the capacity to face odds that are not included in our expectations - the art of facing infinity without flinching, not because they are strong and tough, but because they are filled with awe." By storing up what Castaneda called "Inner Silence", one could make the Glowing Coat of Awareness "unpalatable" to the flyers. We don't attack them, we make it so they do not like the taste of our loosh energy, so they stop trying to eat us. "The grand trick... is to tax the flyer's mind with discipline, with inner silence, and the foreign installation will flee."[47]

How that works exactly I cannot know for sure. What I can say is that in the periods of time when I was most focused on the stillness of mind, not so much from a type of meditation, just a clear focus on whatever I was doing; I experienced less wild spinning mental gymnastics going on. When I added that to the exercise Castaneda called "the right way

[47] Castaneda, *Active Side of Infinity* pgs 221-226

of walking," there could be long stretches of time where thoughts did not appear. I was not "forcing them to stop," just the way I was walking putting so much focus on the world that thoughts could not appear. Perhaps part of what is being eaten by the flyer is thought itself. Recall we have the very odd saying when we make an interesting suggestion to someone, well "that is food for thought."

*

There is one other origin story that I want to briefly mention, because it is one that some readers here may have come across. The problem is that it is hard to know if the story is fake, true, dis-information, or all of the above. And it is a very strange story. In 1998 there was one of the first Internet sensations around a new website known as wingmakers. That site is now deleted, but a similar one took its place soon after, which continues today. Millions came to the site, which suggested that the US government in the 1970s had found an ancient alien, what best can be called, a time capsule. The story does involve an Earth that is a copy and souls that get trapped, tricked to inhabit physical bodies. But the story of the website and everything else is just odd. I leave the footnotes for the Wes Penre's overview of the story, and to the new wingmakers site below, in case you choose to check it out.[48]

*

The Vision

There is another viewpoint to this realm and why we are the way we are. I have only alluded to it at this point in the book, but will share that view now. I had this vision in 2009. My vision was that it was not the Demiurge that made us, but nature, in order to help us find an escape route from the Demiurge. The vision indicates that the Demiurge made the world, but nature made us, and this is the reason his archons and in-world minions are trying so hard to stop us and slow us down.

---

[48] https://wingmakers.com/about/ancient-arrow-site/ , https://docs.google.com/file/d/0B5RUtnz0S-o6S2xiMzVTaThib3dhTTlMUGd0cUl3SG9NQ2JV/edit?resourcekey=0-C9sYLSdqSJAhHiLbrEtYzw , https://wespenre.com/tag/james-mahu/

Looking back on the experience, what was quite co-incidental, was that to "have this vision," in my dream journey I went into a "cave." What is also very interesting was how I felt when I exited, refreshed and renewed. I have left the vision as is, but have included double brackets around an added idea that gives another viewpoint on what the original vision may have been pointing towards. This vision claims all of nature is trapped, but it did not tell me how it had been created, what the original trap for it had been, nor how souls animate humans.

In late 2009, an inner alchemic fire started to burn inside. Hidden parts of my own egoic structures I thought were long gone, had come to the surface, bringing much pain and confusion, matched by the fire inside that would not go out. Demons and dark forces began to up their attacks. On one hand I wondered why? Why attack a man in trouble, you attack when someone needs to be stopped? I dealt with it, night after night of one hour of sleep and little interest in eating. Suffering inside over my own mistakes, and my own lack of belief in all the gifts I had been shown. I spent a weekend with a Native Medicine Man, Jerry, and in the course of that weekend this "old" vision appeared to me. By old I felt this was what came to early humans 100,000 years ago to explain who we were, where we came from, and what it means.

"Before the first humans were born, there were rocks, trees, plants, animals, water. One day they realized that for all their seemed freedom and peace, they were trapped in a type of loop. They saw what was needed to be done for all of them to gain their freedom, but they themselves (nature) could not accomplish that act. They had a meeting of what to do about it.

They asked Mother Sophia for help. She allowed nature to create a new being to help them do what they could not. Nature created humans as the active force to open the freedom door for it, and to assist us, nature would be our guide. Nature created humans out of all the parts of itself: one plant, one rock, one drop of water, one gust of air, and one animal all combined their forces. The animal part that came for each individual human is now called the "power" or "totem" animal, because it is the easiest part to reach of the nature forces that created us. All humans were created at the same time, but were only brought into the manifested world as needed. And then they asked us to do the things that needed to be done for them.

That is why nature allows us to use it. Because we are a part of nature, we are here to do a job for nature, it was they who asked us to be here and created us. It is why trees allow themselves to be cut down for warmth or a deer allows itself to be killed for meat. They do so as a sacrifice for us, so that humans can keep going to fulfill the very role we were created for. If we can complete that, then not just all humans, but all of nature as well, will be free. The loop will end. Nature can take humans with guidance to that doorway, but needs the humans to walk through it.

When nature first understood these things, they also saw that there was a dark force in place that kept everything locked in an odd continuing loop of time. At first this darkness did not need to do much, because there was little that nature could do itself to end it, because nature was set up as a loop "circle of life," ((food chain)). *It could not end the loop without ending itself. That is why nature created humans. And this dark force instantly recognized that humans were a danger for the entire system. The dark force created a counter-force out of itself that had the only job of making sure humans could not complete their task.* ((You could see this as an army of Matrix Mr. Smiths)). *Because if humans succeeded, all of nature would be free, and the dark force would have nowhere to go. The dark force is dependent on the vortex loop.*

It is why this dark force attacks humans so hard, but rarely attacks nature directly. Nature set up power spots, places of strong energy where humans can go to and have open communication with the spirits of nature- and with the spirits that live in the realm above nature. Early humans built temples and structures here to make this communication, or to amplify the power of what was shown to them. The dark force saw this, so spent much of its time attempting to gain control of these power spots, that are the direct openings of communication between nature and humans. As more of these spots were taken over by the dark forces, nature passed on a new way to communicate that while not as clear and perfect (like a semi-garbled phone line) it was a line the dark forces could not cut. They gave humans ceremony, and power tools that would in a sense create a small power opening where the ceremony was performed.

As humans learned more, and gained more understanding of what this place is and what our job is, the dark forces needed to up the attacks even more, and manifested a "computer generated force" of supreme attack inside the dream state. Part of their job was to do everything to block the ceremonies given to humans, and thus began their own counter ((inverse)) *ceremonies "satanic ritual, subliminal conditioning and mind control." One of their most amazing attempts to stop humans was to give us a parasite, the egoic mind. This virus spread until few could even realize there was a time when it was not here, and no one questions the egoic mind's origin. Yet every spiritual work in history talks of the dangers of our own mind. Why should our mind be dangerous if it is ours? And that is the point they miss. It is not ours; it is the blocking mechanism of those dark forces.* ((These dark forces over time have gotten humans to forget more and more why we are here. Many humans even spend their time destroying and harming nature and its creatures, the very things that gave us our original life)).

Nature knows the way out. They know where the doorway is and what to do. They want to take us to that door. But they also know that first the parasite-virus (egoic mind) must be removed. And this is far more of a challenge than anyone understands it to be. Only when that parasite is completely gone, can nature be back in direct conversation with us, guiding us, and showing us what needs to be done. Nature can pass on messages, provide energy, open blocks, but we will have to do the rest. Nature is not in any way separate from us, we come directly from it. There is a reason the creation myth has humans made out of the clay of the Earth. It is symbolic to say our creator is nature itself, the Earth allowed the creation by nature to be. Earth is not our mother, but our GRANDMOTHER. It is why in the old writings nature was not just female, but also male, it encapsulates all.

The entire structure of the earliest human wisdom, mythology, texts and tales were passed on for generations, and at its core is about this creation, the wants of nature for us, and the dark forces that are attempting to stop that from happening. When we reach back to this place within and without, we will know exactly what we are asked to do, and then we either do it and end the loop once and for all. If we do not, the loop will reset, and everything starts all over again.

This is the vision that was presented to me in the cave. Thank you."

If you notice, at the end of this vision I used the word "reset." This summary was written in 2009, long before that word was being used often in daily life as it is today. I began by saying nature was "trapped." There was no explanation how it was trapped specifically, but that was the word that came in my vision. What also makes this vision so interesting is that we are not trapped by the Demiurge directly, we are trapped because we come from that which is already trapped "nature." But within humans is a special part that would allow, not just our exit, but that for all of nature, in fact the entire realm. My vision is thus very different from the creation myths of the Gnostics and Cathars, who believed that humans souls were tricked into coming into matter. It makes quite a change to think we might be a "non-individual" soul as we normally think of it, but instead tied to the souls of nature. Perhaps each human who ends the reincarnation cycle takes some of nature along with it, when we leave.

I cannot be certain what story is specifically true. Are we souls that have been tricked into coming here by the Demiurge/Satan as the Gnostics and Cathars say? Are we living in what once was a type of beautiful paradise before the dark forces took it over and imprisoned all life, as Castaneda and my vision might suggest? Are we loosh creatures that were created by the Demiurge long after this realm was first begun? All I can say is that we should keep all options open. The bottom line is that one way or other we are part of a prison-like farm world, and dark forces are working to keep us trapped and deceived, reincarnating again and again a looping energy-harvesting environment.

Some might say humans are a failed experiment, and we should be eliminated. Based on how we have behaved and mistreated the planet and each other, I can see how many have come to this conclusion. But if this realm was not created by a loving God, but an evil Demiurge, it all begins to make sense. Humans act the way we have been designed to, and it is amazing how many can actually break that conditioning and behave in a somewhat sane manner. If you believe in a loving creator, then it will seem humans have somehow failed here. But when you see that the entire system was not set up for humans to be kind, harmonious, or in balance, but rather for us to be terrible to each other to harvest more loosh, it becomes clearer. If humans lived in harmony and acted nice to one another, there would be very little loosh available to harvest. I believe the controller entities tried this way back in the beginning (the historical memories of this time being of a golden age), but the loosh harvest was too low from this system, and once they saw that conflict and suffering created more loosh, the system was changed. It did not change because humans wanted it to change that world, but because it was beneficial to who and what control this entire simulation. The simulation is set up now for humans to be self-important, manipulative assholes. Which make it easier to accept the controller's minions as "super examples" of us in the material realm. Can we really be called a failed experiment, if the experiment was intentionally set up for us to fail? Can you call yourself a loser in a competition designed intentionally so that you could not win?

The gaining of objects and titles in the physical world is not winning, but egotistic distraction. We have the inner power and inner tools to regain the totality of knowing (Gnosis), and we can use these gifts to see past the many memory wipes, previous sufferings and focus our Intent on one thing: to return Home. Granted we have to be careful, as another of the tricks of the after-death state is to make the newly deceased "feel" like they are home (I have purposely used a small h here). On one level the soul is searching for Home (capital H) and like all tricks here, a copy is being presented as the real thing. Don't allow "feel good" experiences to trick you into thinking you have arrived, when you are still on the ship at sea just being steered into the eye of the hurricane. It seems calm but the storm is close by. Home means Home. No more tricks, deceptions or lies happening. Stand strong, know your inner Power, and settle for nothing less than your True Home.

Foundation Contemplation

"*The most useful piece of learning for the uses of life is to unlearn what is untrue.*" Antisthenes

4

STANDARD NEAR-DEATH EXPERIENCES

Your main question as you read through this book should also be, "so what?" What value does this information have on my current situation? That should be your question with every book you read, or video you watch.

As such, I will follow the main chapters with smaller sections of exercises for you to attempt, or think about as a contemplation. That does not mean you should feel compelled to do any of my suggestions - they are just pointers. You can't think your way out of Plato's Cave. I have seen some great thinkers use their minds to bind themselves deeper to this realm, rather than get them closer to the exit as they would like to believe.

*

One of the early test readers of this book made a suggestion: *"Why don't you add some people's near-death experiences, and give commentary on them? That would give the topic more credibility to show where you are getting these ideas from."* I thought that was an excellent idea. It was something I had planned to do in 2023, but realized some of it had to be presented here. I will provide some snippets of real experiences which present the basis of what this book discusses, i.e. that the after-death realm is set up as a trap.

I have my own near-death experiences (NDEs), as well. They have been presented in my book *Falling For Truth,* and also in video interviews.[49]

[49] Long video version of my canyon experience https://www.youtube.com/watch?v=nW4cmcf3-aU. Smaller snippets can also be found in various other interviews

Just because I have a few brushes with death does not in any way indicate that I know what is going to happen when the moment arises. I have a few ideas, things to be prepared for. Still, no one seems to know for sure what will happen. And that is a big red flag to me. If the death experience was really about going to a wonderful and loving Heaven, then we should all know exactly what is going to happen. Beings only hide the truth when they know that those who hear it won't like it.

Most of the experiences listed come from the website www.nedrf.org. They have thousands of reports sent in by average people of what happened to them at the death moment. We might say that upwards of 85% are the standard story one comes to expect. We have to understand that just because a certain experience is common, does not mean it is not being manipulated by outside forces. The standard *"go to the light"* may be the main deception. But it is the 15% that do not fit the norm that are the most important to us, because they might be bringing us closer to the truth. These people have had experiences where they break the box of the standard hypnosis and see things as they may really be in the after-death realm.

The standard NDE will be presented here, while the non-standard will be discussed in chapter nine. Just because I am calling a NDE "standard", does not mean I am dismissing or belittling it in any way. I have read almost one hundred of them, and each is fascinating, and a few are just amazing. These are overviews to provide a starting point of the normal event in this area of research.

*

I will share first the experience of Gene Goodsky, found in the book *Warrior Spirit Rising*, written by his daughter Dianna. It has almost every element found in the standard NDE. It is like checking off every box on a list, highlighted by me in bold. That is why I found it so amazing to read when I came across it while writing this book.

Gene's experience began after being severely drunk for several days, and passed out on his bed on the verge of death. The next thing he recalled was **floating above his bed.** He then left through the roof of his house

---

I've done on YouTube

with **angle-like beings,** who appeared Native and spoke his language. He was taken to his own funeral and gravesite. ***"All his aches and pains were gone, his spirit was free."*** He went through a door, saw a **bright light and a tunnel.** "He was filled with an **overwhelming sense of calm, gratitude and love**." This next part is very unique and I have never heard of this in any NDE: He saw people with sticks in their mouths, and they didn't look happy. *"He instinctively knew they had gotten stuck, they were lost."* Commenting that people were lost in death is a very telling possibility.

Next, he came to a **bridge** and crossed. He saw sad and unhappy people. Then he realized that these people were him, in different stages of his life. He hated the faces he saw on himself, and all the pain he had caused other people (a unique style of **life review**). Then he was on a **river,** and a large white dog was there. Once he expressed full regret for all he had done in his life, the dog crossed the river, came to him, and he crossed the river on the dog's back. He then claims to have seen what he called *"the serpent bridge,"* a place that only the medicine men of his tribe could cross, and since he was not one (at that time), he did not go there. What is interesting is that he knew of this bridge. He later became a medicine man, and as such in his *"next death,"* he might go to the very bridge he saw, but felt unable to cross in this experience.

Gene now floated down a road, and alongside were all of the **dead people he had known** in life. He very clearly noticed his **parents and grandparents**. Then he came to a medicine man he had known earlier in life, who directed him to a huge wigwam (native house) that was glowing with light. Inside the wigwam was a being with long white hair, dressed in white, and was the source of the light. A perfect representation of a **white-light being**. The Light Being told Gene that he **had to go back, "it is not your time, you have people to help" (a mission).** ***"****He did not want to let go of this newfound* ***peace*** *he was feeling, but he knew* ***he had to listen*** *to the man with the white hair.****"*** This is common in both standard NDE and the ones you will read about in chapter five - that of wanting to stay in this realm of peace, but being sent back, often against one's will. Gene traveled back across the river, *"then he woke up. Was born again… he was* ***changed forever.****"*[50]

This experience is valuable to share with you, not just because how many parts of it make the standard NDE, but also for what this did for this man's life when he came back to life on Earth. It was this experience that

---

[50] Goodsky, Dianna, *Warrior Spirit Rising*, pgs 89-96

stopped him from being an alcoholic. He immediately went into rehab treatment, and was sober the rest of his life. He embraced his Ojibwe heritage, became a local medicine man, healed many people in his community, as well as taught his language and culture at schools and colleges. This experience transformed this man completely, and he became a real pillar of strength for his community. This is exactly the type of person we would all like to meet, one who overcame great hardship in his life, his own inner demons and became a good human being. Gene is a man with whom I would like to have had a coffee with.

I am not sharing his story to belittle him in any way, but to reveal what the standard NDE can do for someone. Almost always, the person changes, generally in ways that make them more kind, open, compassionate and helpful. It is because it has so many positives for the people who go through it, the feelings of love and peace. Sounds great so far.

Here are a few more standard experiences. Each includes the name of the person and the NDERF number code, so you can read their entire experience on www.nderf.com, if you wish.

> "*The main being said I learned enough about knowledge, now I was to go back and learn about love. The information about 'love' is not what we think of here in the physical world. Love is not sexual or possessive, but spiritual. Love is more like endless compassion, without judgment.*" Rhonda M 23499

> "*The bits of light closest to me were my parents, grand-parent, family who all passed before - and connected to them farther away were close friends, and connected to them were people who had influenced me and whom I had influenced (student, acquaintances, etc.) - and the people whom they had interacted with, but unknown to me, but connected to me by my interaction with everyone I had known and met in my life and had gone on before. All of those bits of life were relating how my life and actions had affected theirs.*" Harry T NDE 9339

> "*No longer did I feel any burden of grief, no longer did I feel pain from my 40-year chronic spinal injuries, no mourning, no memories, just absolute release into*

the Light of Love! Home, as I now realize it! Incredible Love!... Everything was so beautiful and healing! I felt as if I were dissolved into the Light, with no words to ever capture the experience." Joyce G 9301, 9406.

"*I was given a life review while inside the void. During this review, I told the being to pause. I wanted to better examine the parts of my life. I was then able to view these events from overhead. The life review did not last long because I asked the being something that surprised it. 'Can I plan my next reincarnation?' I asked. The being said, 'Usually people wait until their actual death to choose their reincarnation'.*" Niels W 9193

"*A pure, brilliant light engulfed me and I no longer had a physical body. But, I still existed? I had no eyes to see but I looked at everything around me. I was in the center of a vast nothingness, but the nothingness was not empty. It was completely filled with the presence of the living God. There are no words in the English language to describe where I was.*" Star E NDE 9139.

"*I was the UNIVERSE in expression, and the Universe was within me, I was shown this, I KNEW this intimately. I was ONE with ALL THAT IS, ALL THAT EVER WAS and ALL THAT WILL EVER BE. ALL THAT EXISTED was within me... I was actually shown a movie screen and then shown what I had been doing; living my life... the movie screen is black-blank=perfect until you begin to place PROJECTIONS onto it, then whatever you project onto it is an 'EXPERIENCE'... I came to a barrier that I was not permitted to cross; or was sent back against my will I didn't seem to have a CHOICE. I got a HUGE REVELATION and then I heard a LOUD POP or CLICK and then I was literally snapped back into my body patting myself down, screaming. 'I'M ALIVE, I'M ALIVE, I'M ALIVE'.*" Anne W NDE 9119. (Actually, her experience and what happened to her afterwards is quite amazing; there are so many layers to her story and I recommend reading it)

"*At some point, a veil lifted. I was drawn into a long, dark tunnel that had a very bright, white light that was shining love. I could hear harps and saw my great uncle Harry Ed and Aunt Vickie. I was in total bliss and happiness. I was home. I didn't want to go back. I had a life review where I saw ever single event from my life. I saw every act of goodness and kindness. I saw every act of spite or ill-will. I also got to see it from the other person's point of view."* Melinda G 9029. (Another detailed NDE that I recommend reading to get more of the standard way the NDE presents itself. She is another person who seems to have gained healing and psychic abilities on returning to this realm)

If I were to ask the average person what a NDE is like, they would present the words that appear above: white light, tunnel, love, peace, God, life review and relatives. This is what makes it into TV shows and movies. The white light is your friend, it will comfort you and take away all your pain. Hard drugs will do the same thing, that is why people use them, it takes away their pain... for a while. Then the pain comes back, and they need more of the drug. The white light may take your pain away for a while also, but what if the pain and suffering come back? What if the white light is not the doorway to Heaven, but a slide back into this realm of suffering? Then much of what is presented in these experiences may be deception. Another red flag even in these standard 'feel good experiences,' is that most of the people are sent back against their will. Generally, they all want to stay in the love and peace they feel, but a being *"that they feel they should agree with"* tells them they have to go back, or just forces them back. Generally, they are told they have more to learn, or a mission to complete. Yet many also claim that while in this after-death realm, they had access to all knowing. And so, what more does a soul need to learn if they already are in a place where they know everything? Oddly, this part of the experience tends to get glossed over, as the returned person focuses on the love and happiness of it all, they forget that they *"came back to Earth against their will."* In chapter four, a few people will have a very different opinion of being forced back here.

What about me? What would I have done in my NDE if I did not get out of the river, and went over the falls and died. I am sure the white light tunnel would have appeared before me. Would I have entered it? Perhaps. That is why I cannot judge anyone's decisions, or what they feel now about the experience. However, we are looking for clues and insights that are going to help us understand life and death fully. What are we going to do when we get in the same situation? It is an important question, and one I will come back to as this book progresses.

What does the white light really do? Does it bring peace and transforms one's life (as 85% of the people who return claim), or is it part of a cycle of reincarnation to a realm of near continuous suffering, as many of the 15% claim? When you bring in the wisdom teachings of the Gnostics and Cathars into play, this realm is designed to trick you over and over to agreeing to come back here. Won't everyone who went through the loving experience gladly go back towards it when they 'really die?' How about all the people they have told their story to, or who have read an account of it, saw their favorite movie showing a celebrity walking into the white light of love? The majority are just going to go, because that is what the conditioning is telling them to do. Lucifer is the light bearer. The Light of the Absolute is said to be golden not white. Is the white light of the NDE really Lucifer?

The 15% of experiences are not the ones that will be chosen by researchers to be put into their books, to take on university speaking tours, because they do not match the "typical, happy-ever-after, love and life is so wonderful" message. They try to bury them. This book, and other researchers like myself want to focus on what is true, and forget about what feels good or makes some lives better in the insane Earth world. Let's take Truth. Let's examine what is going on in these realms.

I have no idea what is going on. That white light is likely a recycle trap, and if I go to it or accept it, my memory will be wiped and back into form I come. Even if you get a nice body and a nice new life, what have you really gained? To be back in matter, with no memory of any previous incarnation, and no manual of what this is, who you are, and why this exists. What have you gained from another incarnation? Even if the experience is nice and pleasant it's not much to go on either. Wounded soldiers go to the hospital to get patched of their wounds, and once healed, are sent back to the hellish battlefield again. The metaphor to all our experiences on Earth is apt.

Let's also not forget that all these experiences discussed are "near-death" experiences. They are not death experiences. That tends to be forgotten. I have been reading some very interesting information that suggests there are three distinct phases of death. Rudolf Steiner suggested there were three worlds, physical, astral and spiritual, but those might be mirrored in the after-death realm. What is the common NDE is those who have only entered the first realm. This realm has the "judgment" and is all about getting the soul to agree to further incarnations. There is not much "eating" going on here, just judging or a type of weighing up of the events of one's life. That is why most at this phase do not feel so bad, there is not much really going on here, and the beings want the new soul to "feel good" during this process. The near-death experiencer is sent back at this point, perhaps the beings feel they are "not tasty enough to eat yet" and want them back on Earth to get some "nice" energy as well. These other realms tend to never be talked about, but the Nag Hammadi Codex mentions these other realms of death beyond the first and it is a place of evil.

> "*God is a man-eater. For this reason, men are sacrificed to him. Before men were sacrificed, animals were being sacrificed, since those to whom they were sacrificed were not gods.*" Gospel of Phillip 63[51]

I will share more on the subject of various planes of death in the final chapter. Because this might be the biggest trick of all we are under with the NDE and other OBE's. We are being "shown" through the experiences of others, that there is only one type of after-death experience, and that there are no others. This is likely as big a deception as there is, right up there with the ideas of karma and sin. We have more to get through in this book before reaching this stage of information, including looking at some non-standard NDEs that may have started to touch on these "other layers" of the death realm.

---

[51] http://gnosis.org/naghamm/gop.html

5

DEATH ACTION PLAN

An out-of-body researcher, William Buhlman, presented in his book, *Adventures in the Afterlife,* what he felt was an important message about death preparation. He called it *"to create an action plan for your enlightened spiritual transition."* Not what was to happen with our bodies or stuff after we die, but how we want the week or few days before our death to be set up (assuming we have some fore knowledge of it and are not hit by a bus and killed instantly). He asked, *"What do I want around me as I am dying? What sort of music, what sort of words?"* Who are the people I trust to have around to help with this process, and how to make the space (either at home or in a hospital) a sacred space? He presented a set of affirmations, to create the clear mental focus heading to the after-death state. He prepared a personal CD, of looping reminder suggestions, that was to be played on the days prior. A real mantra coming from himself, so that these intentions can be welded to his consciousness and soul on the transition. Granted, his were much cheerier and upbeat than ours likely will be (he fell on the side of the after-death state being a great place).

We might create affirmations such as, *"I am free and sovereign, stay away from the white light, return Home, I will not return to planet crazy."* You get the idea. My suggestion would be to keep them as positive as possible, focus on where you want to go, not what you don't want. I think this is a valuable tool to have ready as a direction or Intent as the death event approaches. The *Nag Hammadi* chapter "Apocryphon *of James,"* tells us that we will need to remind the archons that we know we are not a material form, that we come from the Pleroma (True Oneness), and that that is our Home. Knowing this, and telling them is a reminder to the Demiurge/archons that they are not from the Pleroma, and as such have no power to keep yo away from it. This could also be part of a CD tape, or sheet of paper (to have someone read if no electricity or CD players are available).

What about things in the hospital room, or your bedroom if you are going through the process at your house? Are there paintings or objects you might want in there? Music to be played. Memories to be reminded of. This is your experience, and it should be created just for you, the way you want it to be. What better moment to consciously set up than the hours and days directly before your death. The question becomes, what is it you want (not for comfort, we are not interested in comfort), but what is going to help you exit the Cave for good, to leave the matrix behind and never again be in the insanity? How do we move towards sanity as we die?

How do you want to have your final moments ready to exit the Cave? Create your own action plan, let a close family member or friend know about it, and ask them to help to make this happen when the event does approach. This is one of the best suggestions that I have come across in many years, and is something I will be doing once the writing of this book is complete.

I will share one quote I am getting ready to answer in response to their insane demands, "*The only power and authority you have, is the power and authority that I give to you. Thus I revoke all of it, and stay the powerful, sovereign being I have always been.*"

6

THE RECAPITULATION LIST

In the previous chapters I mentioned the power of the recapitulation. It will have a benefit for someone who performs it in the material world as a way to regain lost energy from life. However, the main focus of a recapitulation is to prepare us for the after-death life review, so that nothing in it will surprise us.

There are many different ways to see one's past honestly, in a way that gets to the deepest levels of what happened. To see events clearly, you must go beyond the regular parasitic mind and normal memory of events. Those are just the stories the mind has created for the past; while the recapitulation is designed to see the past in total stark honesty. It is a process that only can be pointed towards and suggested, for the best way for each person is highly individualistic and must be developed on their own. I present my own way of doing the recapitulation process in Appendix B of my book *Falling For Truth.* That text also is available on my website at the following link: https://www.egyptian-wisdom-revealed.com/2020/06/recapitualtion/

I have long recommended that people do a life review. One's entire life. And, as mentioned in the previous chapters, that is so there is not one hidden area of our lives that we can be surprised by in the after-death review. The problem is that such a full review takes years; my first took approximately four years to complete. I am not sure people have that sort of time now, given our current bizarre world situation. Anyone who has not started a full life review may not get to complete one, given what challenges seem to be on the horizon for this reality.

And so, I am no longer suggesting people do a complete life recapitulation (though if you really feel compelled to do it, go get 'em). I now suggest people do one of two things: make their recapitulation list, or make their album of memories. The recapitulation list is the first step on a complete recapitulation. It is used as a guide so we can have an organization plan for the process, know who our next person to review is and some of the events connected with that person. The creation of the list, however, is a type of recapitulation in itself. When I first made my list, which took around three months, it brought up all sorts of forgotten events and memories during the process. And so, if you are going with the list, take time to do it completely. Give yourself three or four months and don't stop until it feels complete.

This list should include everyone you have ever met (a server at McDonald's who took your order is not included) but it should be comprehensive. To help, you can find old address books, high school yearbooks and photographs. Anything to jog your memory, with whom you interacted at various times in your life. Where have you vacationed, where did you work, where did you go to eat dinners? Once you have a detailed list of names, it should be written backwards in time, with the most recent person you met first at the top of the list, and your parents last. Now take that list and write 1-3 events that took place with that person. Some will be people you met only once, while others will have thousands of events potentially from which to choose (in the case of the people you spent large amounts of time with, choose 20 to 25).

When the list and events are in place, read over the list slowly. Name to name, event to event. Take your time. Lots of memories will begin to appear. Just sit with them. Go to those you are drawn to. When you come to names of those you have had sexual encounters with, take a bit of time to breathe, to harmonize energy (as sexual encounters can create much misplaced and lost energy when the activity was not partaken with a clear awareness). You are not doing this like a complete recap, you are just reading it over, having brief flashes as you go through, and see what else comes that you forgot. This practice will give you a start in preparing to release all guilt, shame or need for revenge from your past. You must be clear and calm during the after-death life review.

The other recommendation would be to make what Carlos Castaneda called *"an album of memorable events."* This is to find events that happened to us, yet were also impersonal. It is not about the most important things, the best or worst things that occurred in our lives, but things that in some way touch the life of all humans, that are somehow universal, yet personal at the same time. It takes quite a bit of work to sort through one's life to find these 'album moments.' We always begin with what we think are our 'best and worst moments,' but generally, they never fit the call of 'impersonal events.' You can read the *"Introduction"* chapter of *Active Side of Infinity* for more information on the making of one's album.

One thing I do want to point out is that Castaneda referred to there being two types of "warriors" (those who are on a path of Total Truth). One group are known as stalkers (who work mostly within the material realm) and those called dreamers (those who work mainly in alternate realities). The recapitulation is not as important for one who is a dreamer, as their focus is on the astral and thus the physical form is far less solid. For the stalker however, the recapitulation (along with the process known as not-doing) are key elements for their practice. I mention this as someone who may be a classic dreamer might instantly know "I don't need to recap my life," and they would be correct. In a sense they get in touch with their lives while they are in out-of-body experiences. Thus the reader has to determine which "type" one's material manifestation falls to to determine how important this practice is or is not for them personally.

The more time you put into this practice before the death moment comes, the more prepared you will be on the other side when an archonic being tries to guilt you with some event that was a part of your past. You are ready for them.

B

EXAMINATION

"This is not a school. Why would an omnipotent being, create a bunch of ignorant people, and then torture them to make them better?"
Richard Rose

7

IT'S CURTAINS FOR YOU
by Donnie Beige

"The Pantheon was the first church I had ever seen that had an open view to God." Bran Ferren

2003, Rome Italy, 7:01 AM

Two hours until the most important meeting of Karl Henrik Jensen's life.

Karl opened his eyes and awoke. As he began to scan the simple hotel room, he began to piece together where he was. Late yesterday evening he had flown to Rome from his home in Copenhagen, Denmark, on a quest of sorts. He checked into this rather simple hotel, which was chosen not for its cheap price, but due to its location. It was just a block away from his scheduled 9AM appointment at the Pantheon, Ancient Rome's most well-known construction.

Of this upcoming meeting he knew very little. Only that a woman would meet him at the Pantheon. He had only been told that she was a "Muse." He did not know her name, her age, what she looked like, what she did, or even what she would wear. How could he spot her in the crowd? Would she be able to spot him? He was only told that she would begin to reveal pathways to answer questions on the nature of reality.

Reality!

This subject had been troubling him for decades. Ever since the death of his older sister fifteen years ago, things at times spiraled into places he had never thought they would go. Questioning this reality, its value and even its realness had caused him many sleepless nights. It kept him searching in texts of philosophy, spirituality, religion, hell even the self-help and vegetarian isles. Karl had spent years studying everything he could on the subjects of wisdom. He went to Zen temples for zazen, read books on alchemy and shamanism, tried lucid dreaming, looked into Qi Gong and Yoga, and he even bought crystals and books by Tony Robbins. He wondered where it had all taken him, wondered if these so-called teachers had been caught thinking they had reached a pinnacle, but did not know the mountain continued.

Karl's life changed seven months ago when he ran into a very strange man in a bookshop in the Danish city of Hillerod. He had intended to be in the city once a month, to visit the alchemic castle of Fredriksborg Slot. It was like walking into a book by John Dee or Marsilio Ficino, yet instead of words on a page it was carvings on the ceiling and paintings on the walls. After his visit on this particular day, he stopped by Bog and Ide, the local bookshop just down from the library. There, while leafing through a text on Chartres Cathedral, he met the man who would become a constant coffee companion, walking Karl through his own inner world of exploration. While not having total grasp of things himself, Karl became convinced that Rikard (who lived and worked as a simple shopkeeper) had gone to great depths. He had read texts and been in touch with organizations Karl had never heard of, and he wondered if Rikard was making this up to impress him (an idea he eventually dismissed), or if he had in fact reached some real place of knowing. Certainly not total knowing, but far beyond any book, teacher or organization Karl had come across. Then Karl got a surprise.

Just five days ago Rikard informed him that a close friend of his was waiting to be his guide to explore reality. She would be at the Pantheon at 9AM Thursday morning waiting for Karl. All his queries on who she was, what she wanted, what she did, even why does it have to be Thursday, were rebuffed. The information was simple: Be there Thursday at the Pantheon and see where the adventure takes him, or remain in Copenhagen and continue his life of much seeking and little finding. It took Karl only 24 hours to decide what he needed to do.

To satisfy his deep search for answers to the burning questions: Why does this world seem so insane? Why is there so much suffering? Why does nature need to eat itself constantly to survive? Why is everyone born ignorant, un-remembering of anything prior? Is this realm a prison? He took a week off work, got a plane ticket, booked a hotel, and headed for Rome. Could this mysterious woman really tell him, in... oh no, it's 7.30! Karl realized he had to shower, change and get some breakfast. He was going to be 100% early for this appointment. He rose from the bed feeling a strange mixture of sensations, tedious from the years of his inner searching, trepidation about what might come next and seduced by the idea that he finally might find something valuable.

In an hour and thirty minutes he might finally to get some answers.

*

8.22 AM

The Muse stood quietly, yet confidently at the bar of the Cafe Eustachio just by the Pantheon. As she sipped her morning espresso she wondered if the mysterious Dane will, in fact, show. An elderly man bumped into her in the crowded conditions.

"Mi Scusi," he responded, as he moved towards the door.

This cafe, and others like it, have been a part of Rome's morning ritual for decades. The Muse no longer got as bothered by people any more, she knew most of those she came in contact with were not really people anyway.[52]

Rikard had provided her with some background details. Her inner seeing provided the rest. He was closer to real answers than he thought. He just needed a good push, to stop staring at the moon and go right towards it.

---

[52] Today we would refer to these people from video game terminology as Non-Player Characters (NPC), essentially robots that populate reality to make it seem bigger and more complex than it really is.

The Muse contemplated the old Taoist phrase, *"A finger pointing at the moon is not the Moon. Don't get focused on the finger."* She laughed lightly into her warm espresso. Almost no one understood what that metaphor was really driving at. There were all sorts of romantic and simplistic ideas about it, but what it really was 'pointing at' was something the average seeker was not too interested in finding out. Yet, for better or worse, the Muse knew exactly what that phrase meant. It was not a smile warning of misdirection. That finger could have been pointing at any object, but it was pointing at the Moon. This was the key element everyone missed. Why the Moon? When that was understood, the entirety of the statement finally made sense.

A quick check of her watch revealed the time. She wanted to be there a good half hour before his arrival, to have a survey of the location, to ground with the energies of the space. To the Muse the Pantheon was her personal temple, a house in stone built just for her, and she wanted to be ready to spot the unknowing visitor to her realm the moment he entered.

*

8:59 AM

Karl looked at his watch when he first stepped through the open bronze doors into the circular dome-like building at 8:37. There were perhaps fifty people already inside, half of them female. He had a one in twenty-five chance of guessing The Muse. Was she even here? Would this turn out to be just an elaborate disappointment? He decided to put those thoughts out of his head and get back to looking at where he was. The Pantheon in Rome, he was awed by the mysterious and sheer beauty of the construction when he was here on vacation three years ago with his then girlfriend, Anna. She lived in Hanover, Germany but the distance between them had made things difficult to keep... Why was he thinking about this now? All that mattered was that he was back, and whether or not there was a Muse; and whether or not it would be beneficial to his understandings, he should simply enjoy being back in one of his favorite buildings. He wouldn't check his watch again, simply allow himself to be here.

Karl was staring at the hole when he first felt the presence of 'the Muse.' Not any hole of course, but a very important one that would, in fact, come to symbolize much of the rest of his life. That hole was the one in the ceiling dome of the Pantheon, the very place he was supposed to be at 9 AM. He did not need to look at his watch again; somehow, he knew it was nine, and she was right on time.

"Quite the thing, isn't it?" She asked.

"The dome? Yeah. I just keep staring at it."

"Do you know what it means?"

"The dome or the hole? Either way, no."

"It's not a hole, it's a portal, a gateway."

"Like to another dimension?"

"Something much better actually."

The Dane dropped his gaze finally, to get his first look of the mysterious woman he had been waiting a week to meet. She was shorter than he expected, yet she was not short. She was younger than he expected, yet she was not young. In fact, it was hard on first glance to pin down anything about her. She seemed somewhere between 35-55, her light brown hair hung just at her shoulders, while wearing a long-flowing summer dress. She also was carrying the smallest purse he had ever seen a woman have. Could she even get her house keys in there, he wondered?

"So here you are. I wasn't sure if you were going to show," she smiled.

"I wasn't sure if you were going to show."

"Understandable."

"So, do I call you The Muse? Sounds like a strange name for a birth certificate."

"Birth certificates are just things that put us in bondage and slavery, a type of water baptism, which is a reason the Cathars rejected John the Baptist. Do you know much about the Cathars? No? Well, we will have to change that. But I do have a birth certificate, no way around it in this reality. I am human in case you were wondering, and I do have a normal name… Well normal for the place that I come from. But for today you can call me Marie, after the muse for Pablo Picasso. Not a big fan of his work, but he was a big fan of muses."

Karl was already coming to like this woman who wanted to be known as Marie, whoever she was.

"But that is not really all that important… A name is a name. It is this building that is important. Look at everything, every pillar, every piece of stone, every geometric layout. They are all important to the overall function. But it is that dome," motioning upwards, *"and that hole that is the… how is it said in English... piece de resistance?"*

"Isn't that French?"

"I was joking Karl. Don't be so stiff, only corpses are stiff."

Karl knew what Marie was referring to. He had, in fact, become quite stiff the last several years. He was not always this way. He had enjoyed his football matches when he was a teenager, bike rides down the canals, evenings at Tivoli. He decided to not go into this subject, and instead focused on where he was.

Still staring at the hole in the domed ceiling Marie remarked, *"We think there is only one entrance and exit point to the Pantheon, the giant bronze doors in front of the Egyptian pillars. You can think of that entrance as birth and death. When we enter here it is a type of death, and when we leave a type of birth. That is why it is called Pantheon, house of all the gods, for it is the house of this entire realm. The roundness of the structure makes it similar to a native Indian sweat lodge. In fact, that can be another way of looking at this place, a sweat lodge in stone. However, there is another entry and exit point. The hole in the ceiling. But it is not a birth and death into the material as the front door suggests; that hole is like the top of a sweat lodge, and is a link between the entire physical reality and the realm of what you might call the spirit. Or simply, that which is beyond the physical world of matter, the world we enter when we die. You also could say that in here is the world of lies, Plato's Cave. Does it not appear somewhat cave-like, or could be that way? With the right techniques could an entire display of the Plato's Cave analogy not take place right here? The hole in the ceiling is the exit out the cave. The plasma energy needed for that to happen is immense, and the body needs to be ready to handle it if you are going to try to exit while still alive. Leaving through the bronze doors just births you into a new cave, where that hole leads, symbolically of course, is real Totality. Out the exit is something that even all our greatest gods and beliefs are no match to explain. Out there is where our soul comes from."*

"How did they make it.," Karl asked while gesturing to the dome?

"How they made it is not important. Who really made it, when and why are. Certainly not some made up emperor called Hadrian. He gets credited with anything in the Ancient World no one can explain, a simple way of covering over questions about the past everyone should be asking. If you studied plasma energy you would recognize this building as an energy machine, and the area from the floor to just above that hole creates a most powerful plasma charge. The higher you move from the floor, the higher the energy."

"Are you a scientist?"

"No, but a type of researcher you might say. Only I research everything."

"Even plasma?"

"Even plasma. I know Rikard has been speaking to you about the Demiurge and archons. As such, we need to think clearly about our reality. It is all about the harvest of energy, Karl. That is the answer to the age-old question: 'What is the meaning of life?' That we, and all other creatures here, have been made in such a way that our energy can be harvested directly by the system. Harsh facts to come to, but if you honestly look at the suffering of this world, the way it never gets better, the insanity of it all, the way nature behaves; an energy farm is about the only logical honest answer. The challenge those in control of this entire realm have had, is to find the best energy harvest system. The way the world is now is not the first version of this place. We have gone through several… what's a good word? Revisions. Stripping down the simulation and in some way starting all over."

"What do you mean start over? Is this what the ancient flood stories are about, this type of, what did you call it?"

"Revision. Reset is another word."

"Reset? Like if my alarm clock was set for the wrong time, I have to reset it?"

"That's the idea. When the first world farm was set up here, you might say the first program in the simulation; there was not that much direct control, and that first system did not provide the energy needed. A computer needs power. Think of what a computer powering not just this realm, but all the astral and dream realms needs? It is a massive amount of energy since the first run did not give them enough, they tweaked it. They found that conflict and suffering created even more energy, that it was best to keep the animals under complete control, so the sheep don't think of jumping the fence. When the Demiurge figured this out, maybe 5,000 years ago, the old system was squeezed in. Things such as government, religion, agriculture and commerce were added. Is it not odd that they all sort of spring up together all at once? And to top it all off, they took over the planets[53]*, which are not planets at all, but the broadcast centers. The broadcasted frequencies are designed to lock humans into the very systems that were just introduced. Some people went along, some didn't. Those who didn't, mainly native civilizations living close to nature, were eliminated by warfare against them."*

"That's a pretty out-there theory."

"I know, but what if it's true?" she smiled and winked at him.

Karl was not at all been prepared for this. He thought she might have been more like a female version of a Buddhist monk or something. Not this. Just ten minutes after meeting her and he already felt blown over. And now she was winking at him. *"I need to sit down, I need to regain my center,"* he thought. But Marie did not give him a pause; she continued her frontal assault on all his long-held belief structures.

"This reality is an insane mess, it's a very cruel world. Just think how an abandoned dog or cat feels for the rest of its life, left out to roam alone aimlessly by its owner, and all it wanted was to be with them and share a life with them. Seeing those animals on the street is tragic to me. Start to see that, in one way or another, all of nature has all been abandoned. One whole world just abandoned from everything. It has always been an insane mess, just to varying degrees. One part of the mess has been to convince people that there was once a time when everything was wonderful and it could be that way again. But this is a simulated computer world, created from an AI Demiurge's design. It never gets better. The experiment runs as the experiment has been designed. Yet

[53] See appendix for more on the planetary realm as a frequency broadcaster

people keep waiting. Make no mistake, there are millions out there today waiting for Jesus, a new political figure, fifth dimension ascension, or whatever to save them. And when the saving doesn't come, it's always because, 'it is just around the corner, the next solstice, the next election'... whatever.

"This realm is a deception of hope. We have been placed in a virtual reality simulation, one designed to keep everyone enslaved, so that our energy can be mined by the beings who created this place. Then on top of that, one of the very things that could help us get a grasp on this insane prison-world... our perception... is constantly being hijacked and manipulated so no one is ever seeing reality clearly. Given everything we have been told about this world is on some level a lie, the only real way forward is to throw all we have been told in the garbage and start fresh. Right from 'what is a human being and where do we human beings come from, to what is the point of being one?' Humans have more power than we can even imagine, just not the type of power our self-important minds hope to achieve."

Karl had taken time to hear what she had just said. His forehead hurt. He knew that somehow the combination of the energy she said was in this building, along with the deep knowledge she was presenting, was in some way overloading his brain. Pain stabbed behind his eyes.

"Muse, I mean Marie, I have got a terrible headache... I think I need to go outside. I want to go out to sit by the obelisk fountain." Marie just nodded as if she understood.

They slowly began walking out of the Pantheon. Karl felt a bit embarrassed that his first meeting with his mysterious Muse ended with him having a headache and needing fresh air. He had been with her less than thirty minutes, and although in a man's body, he felt like a young child when it came to wisdom. They sat by one of the marbled edges of the small fountain, and the coolness of the water spray and the sound of the fountains began to sooth him quickly. It took him just five minutes to start feeling his normal self.

"That was intense in there."

"I'd say, you had Florence Syndrome in Rome."

"Florence Syndrome?" With that Karl thought, *"Please don't go into another deep conversation right now."*

Marie replied, "I will explain that over a coffee, you need a break, and in Rome that is how you break. After that we have two other key stops to make in our day together. Each of our stops will reveal a direction of work you will have to partake in. Here you have learned about the concept of energy. Next, I must take you to a painting and then to the Vatican."

"*The Vatican… am I meeting the Pope?*" Karl laughed

"Better than that. You are going to have a meeting with some curtains."

*

10:18AM

Karl and Marie sat at a small table outside a cafe at the Piazza Navona. From the Pantheon they had walked along Via della Coppella, stopping at this small cafe the Muse seemed to enjoy. The stop for a coffee and a cornetto, an Italian pastry, had been a welcome break for the intense morning that began under the dome of the Pantheon. While conversing, Karl had tried to determine where she was from. They both spoke in accented English, his Danish not yet tempered by the seven years he later would spend living in Wisconsin, but her accent was indistinguishable. It was not Italian, Spanish or even Greek. It was perhaps more of an Eastern European or maybe French. He had asked a few cursive questions to see if he could gain a clue, and while she did converse with him, she was very tight-lipped about any information that might reveal the place of her origin. Mostly the conversation centered around him, his life, his loneliness and confusion, and his seeking of answers that had begun a few years ago.

"Feeling better Karl?"

"Yes, break has been helpful. You said I had some type of syndrome at the Pantheon."

"Florence Syndrome[54]*, or sometimes called Stendhal syndrome. There are three strange city syndromes around the world. One is Jerusalem Syndrome. It is an affliction*

---

[54] The three syndromes can be seen in more detail on their subsequent Wikipedia pages.

that can come over people who visit Jerusalem. They get confused and think they are some sort of reincarnated Biblical person and just begin wandering aimlessly in semi-psychosis until leaving Jerusalem completely. Another one comes from Florence, where it is suggested that the artwork causes changes in people. This is true. Take a walk through the Cairo Museum or the Louvre and you will see people who have been there for an hour or two wiped out. The energy which is placed into that artwork has blown them over. That is what happened to you today, as the plasma energy in the Pantheon blew you over."

"But I have been to the Pantheon before, felt absolutely fine."

"Yes, but today I was with you pressing Plato's Cave and the confines of simulated reality on you. The two together is what pushed you over the edge. The third of these city types is Paris Syndrome, a sense of disappointment exhibited by some individuals when visiting Paris, who feel that the city was not what they had expected. That one makes no sense on the surface, but does begin to make sense when seen together with the other two. What is very interesting, is that, it is only these three cities. There is no New York Syndrome, London Syndrome or Berlin Syndrome. Just Jerusalem, Florence and Paris. They are the three cities of the largest historical lies we have. Paris is the original Jerusalem, as you will learn as we go, Florence hides the lies of the Renaissance, while Jerusalem holds the lies that have become the modern Western religions. So, it's no surprise that people cannot handle these energies. Each city is carrying its own lie and wanting to be heard. If you are not ready for it, it can hit you, sort of like what happened to you today. However, it is the same at Giza in Egypt. I know people who get wiped out after a short trip, and some who go into the pyramids and if not ready can have problems for days. Oddly, there is no Rome Syndrome. There is as much artwork here as Florence and, of course, just as big a lie as Paris. But perhaps like London, New York and Washington, which also have places within the cities of religious, commercial and governmental control, these parasitic entities have switched off the energy in these places."

"I have been reading for the last ten years, but I see I still have so much to learn."

"That is true on one level, but you don't need more knowledge."

"I thought that is what are we all after, knowledge and wisdom."

"That is what the system centered in those cities wants you to chase. You want Truth and Freedom. That is something very different. Anyone with their head full of knowledge is never open enough to find the Truth, or better said, have the Truth find them. A head already stuffed with ideas, beliefs and facts has taken a few steps, but will

take no more until ridding themselves of them. Intellectualism is another distraction of this realm, and it is one who catches all the smartest of minds. Thus, you need to be smart, yet wise, to know when to stop being smart."

Karl asked, *"what about the people who say that we should just focus on life here on earth, just fully enjoy ourselves all the time? At least they seem to be happy, or happier."*

Marie stretched her back and shoulders slightly. Something about the movement was almost mesmerizing to Karl. Was she hypnotizing him, tempting him, playing with him, or just stretching her back before speaking? Clouds of doubt about this mystery woman and everything she did kept swirling in his mind.

"What does it even mean to be happy? You know, I had a conversation with someone about this topic just the other day. A woman a little older than you said to me 'I am enjoying life. I like what I do, why should I put effort into understanding reality or myself?' So, I said to her, 'OK, you enjoy your life. But then you are going to die. Are you prepared for what will happen when you die? Have you taken even five minutes to really find out what? There is a 100% guarantee that you will be recycled back in here. And don't trust these ideas of 'how you live this life determines what you get next time.' Another way to explain why the controllers have all the money and power and others have none, is to suggest they must have been good boys and girls in their last lives, so I better just focus on being nice, liked and not cause any trouble.' No one really thinks they might have actually sold their soul for those goodies. So, just be a good slave. Reincarnation is simply another body. Maybe your next life will be one teemed with suffering. What good would this fun life you are having now be, if you come back into one that is pure hell? There might not even be space in the next life for any thoughts other than how to survive to another day. So, is the bit of fun and happiness you are having now worth it? What good did it do if it all means nothing and you might be back in pure hell next time? Thus, maybe you might want to try a 50-50 approach: 50% of your time is spent enjoying yourself in this realm, the other 50% is spent seeing death fully, so that you can prepare the steps needed to be sure there are no reincarnated hells in your future."

Karl wondered if the conversation Marie presented was a real one she had, or one she made up for his benefit. Either way it had an impact on him, *"I am starting to get this, I think. This body, this thing sitting here talking with you now, it did not get here out of any higher principle, right? I sort of just got stuck in here like a cow gets put in a barn for winter."*

"Just don't think you are evil because you are in a body. Some Cathars got caught in that one. Just because the entire world is evil in its design, does not mean that you are evil because you are in it. We are in it against our wills, having been tricked into entering. As such, we almost have an obligation to be in the world all the while knowing our ultimate goal is to overturn our deceptions and contracts and not come back. This is a contracted reality on so many levels. What you see around you within this place is all contracts, laws. Think how many times you have signed pieces of paper in your life. There are similar ones we sign symbolically, again via deception, that gets us in here and sets up all sorts of pain and control on us. That does not mean we have to hate the world or blow it up, but know it is not real, it is a simulation, not Home, and we enjoy it as we can. I am not anti-meat, anti-fun, anti-sex, anti-coffee, even anti-Christ. Though I am not the Anti-Christ." She took the last sip of her coffee and milled.

Karl had to admit she was entrancing him. Not with anything magical or hypnotic, but with simple clear words and soft emerald-green eyes. He did have extra time just to stare at her, not in a romantic sense, but in a sense of 'how to tell how much someone really knew.' He tried to stare into her eyes casually once in a while as a test. She must have known what he was doing as every time he tried, she looked back towards him with a smirk on her face. He felt like a five-year-old caught with his hand in the cookie jar every time. She seemed so sweet, gentle, kind and loving. Yet, Karl also knew that was an illusion. One half of a whole. The Muse was also cold, clear and powerful. He knew she was not out to hurt him deliberately, but if he dropped his awareness, at any moment those eyes could drop him into an abyss. She scared the hell out of him.

*

10.45 AM

The walk to their second stop of the day was not long, and they passed a cathedral opposite the Pantheon, Santa Maria Sopa Minerva. Marie described it as her favourite cathedral in all of Italy.

"Don't let the outside fool you," she exclaimed. *"It looks simple but inside is a treasure trove of wisdom. Much like that castle in Denmark you told me about today. I would recommend you come here tomorrow. But give yourself lots of time. Every inch of this place needs to be examined. And it is not a cathedral, none of them are. Just*

like the Pantheon, it is an energy center. "Cathode-rals" is a better word for them. It was a book about Chartres that set up the chain of events for you to be here with me today. When you come back to see this one tomorrow here is a clue: This is as close as you can get to the Egyptian temple of Dendera without going to Egypt."

"But we are not going here today?"

"We are going to a different cathedral close by, and just for one painting."

The church they went to was the San Luigi dei Francesi (St. Louis of the French). It never has been explained why there is a key church in Rome dedicated to France – but its history is quite fascinating. Supposedly it was designed by the same architect who designed the dome of St. Peter's Basilica, and the land to build it was donated by the famed Catherine D'Medici of Florence. Quite the pedigree to make a church for France.

The inside of the church was magnificent. She walked him far back to a small chapel known as the Contarelli Chapel, to where there are three famous masterpieces. All were created by the painter Caravaggio. Marie presented, *"I know you know who painted these, but you will not be aware of what is symbolized in them. We are going to open some curtains here today, metaphorically speaking. You might not be the same after we are finished. Caravaggio was speaking to all of us with clues."*

She continued, *"All these paintings are of St. Matthew, one of the disciples of Jesus. To the left is the Calling of St. Matthew. Yet it is very ambiguous as to who is being called, the man with the beard or the young man asleep on the table. And of course, the people all wear clothes from the Renaissance. So, just when is the depiction of Jesus living taking place? To the right is another play on themes, that being the Death of St. Matthew when he becomes a martyr in Ethiopia. But we are here for the one in the middle, The Inspiration of St. Matthew. But it is far from any inspiration."*

Karl looked closely at the painting. He had been here on his previous trip to Rome as well, he recalled this small enclave and had enjoyed the paintings with Anna, but now he was being asked to scrutinize them. The Muse was indicating a message was here, a message meant for him. He took an overview of the painting before him. There was an old man to left, obviously St. Matthew, leaning over a table with one knee bent on a stool. On the table was an open book and he is holding a pen, so obviously writing. The rest of the image was just dark, save for an angel floating above him, tunic wisping in the wind (as one assumes the angel is descending) and making a gesture with the fingers. In a sense, the angel seemed to be whispering to him and inspiring his writing. Karl also noticed, almost casually, that just below the angel figure were some light brush strokes against the dark background, almost as if something was there, or had been there, then painted out of the image. It might have even had the head of a bird. At least that is how it all appeared to him on viewing it. He said as much to Marie. He was, of course, not surprised to hear that she had a very different interpretation of the painting.

"I see it very differently of course, but I do like that you picked up the misty figure that is there, but not there. We will get to that. The view you gave is the standard view. Actually, there are two alternate ways to interpret this painting. I will share both. The question really becomes, is this an angel or not? And this is going to take us to the heart of much of this focus. Who or what created and manipulates reality? Beings actually. Beings that are not human, nor have goodness at their core."

"Aliens then? Like Roswell? Like from another planet."

"No not like Roswell. That is another misdirection in the whole game, though a misdirection that got somewhat out of control at the time. Something did happen there in 1947, but it was not aliens from another planet showing up; the aliens have been here and been in control for a long, long time. Roswell was something else entirely."

Marie quieted her speech as to keep from upsetting any of the visitors coming to stare at paintings they would never understand. *"To understand what Caravaggio has done here, you must realize that this is his second painting of this scene. His original was rejected by his patron Cardinal Del Monte. Unfortunately, that painting is no longer with us. It wound up in Berlin and was destroyed during the Second World War. Thankfully a black and white sketch of it did survive. You must see it yourself to understand, but I will do my best to explain it to you."*[55]

'St. Matthew sits in a chair, there is no table. And he is depicted less saintly and much more rugged. You might see him as a rugby player or some other type of athlete. His hands appear so muscular as to make it seem to be impossible for him to write in the book open on his lap. The angel appears beside him, standing on the ground in that painting. The interpreters try to claim the angel is a male, but angels were often

---

[55] That sketch can be seen at https://www.wga.hu/framex-e.html?file=html/c/caravagg/04/25conta.html&find=matthew

female at the time of Caravaggio. She is leaning over the book in a very tempting pose, whispers of flesh seen beneath the light veils she wears, and leans over him, her right hand on top of his. Is she 'helping him with the writing,' inspiring him with an infusion of sexual energy. Perhaps. Or is she tempting him, hand on top of his to stop the writing, as if to say, forget that and come spend time with me? Either way, it will take us to the heart of the Gnostic teachings found in the Nag Hammadi documents. If it is an inspiration, then this is all about the Gospel of Phillip and the nymphion bridal chamber. But this is more likely alluding to the beings they called archons, alien emissaries of the Demiurge, more computer machine like than anything else. They are also called angels.'[56]

"You are going to say angels are a lie now, aren't you?"

"Angels are most likely not what religion has pushed, but are archons and demonic beings in disguise. Another level of deception on human souls. This will continue into the astral world after one dies, when the final tricks and temptations are played on us. Besides, all these concepts people place their energy towards, such as loving guides, angels, spirit beings and power animals, are all forces outside ourselves that we turn our inner guidance over to? Who is checking if these astral world beings are what they claim to be? Recall the name used for top angels in Christianity; arch-angels. They are archon-angels. The top of the archonic ladder of parasitic-demonic beings. Is that really who you want to turn the guidance of your life over to?"

'But Caravaggio painted a second one as you see here. When you understand that this is not an angel inspiring him, but a demon in disguise as an angel tormenting him, this all makes more sense. There is a possible wispy figure there. That might be the ibis headed Thoth who is trying to use hermetic and alchemic wisdom to overturn the 'spell' placed on us by the archon demons, so that Matthew would then be free to write in total clarity and freedom. Or it might be The Eagle, as writer Carlos Castaneda described the creator of this realm (the Demiurge), directly interfering. The element of overt sexuality is now gone from this second painting, which is why I lean more to the demon in disguise theory. This is not a painting of inspiration, but one of manipulation. Or it may be showing that much of what we think as inspiration is in fact a type of manipulation. If you want to see real paintings of inspiration from the worlds outside of this realm you need to make a study of Annunciation artwork. Start with the work of

[56] Two other paintings (by Cezanne "Kiss of the Muse," and Gabriel De Cool "The Muse," give a similar layout. The writer is in a chair on the desk is an open book, and a pen or quill is in his hand. The "figure" is either tempting him or inspiring him, depending on your outlook.

Frau Angelica at the Monastery of San Marco in Florence. Then look at Da Vinci's and Botticelli's and everyone else's version. Caravaggio was focused on something else."

"So, what do these beings want?" Karl asked.

"Simple answer, your soul.[57] *Or we might say the energy that your soul provides. You also could say your awareness and your experiences. The greater answer, to take the energy from us, to power this simulation and keep it running, so souls stay trapped and can be mined for energy. Any computer simulation needs constant power to run, and as you can guess, something this complex needs a lot of energy. It could have been created as a joyous loving place, but that is not what they want, because conflict, confusion and suffering create stronger energy for the harvest. Love and happiness produce energy for them too, but just a lower amount. Generally, as soon as anyone figures this out, they try to fix the world, make it the place of their dreams. Hope guides them. Hope keeps them bashing their heads against brick walls to force a simulation of suffering into one of happiness. It's a simulation. It was designed in a particular way, and it works the way it works."*

It was easy to see that Karl was getting shaken up again, just as he had been at the Pantheon.

"Don't worry about things too much Karl. The soul is not evil. The soul always was and is pure and complete. But it was tricked to enter a false world that is evil, run by these demonic entities. It becomes so easy for someone, in the midst of suffering, to fall under their trap and start to become like them. Yet you might say everyone who still has a soul can be saved, the soul is pure, only the flesh can be tempted."

"Those who still have a soul. You mean people have lost their souls?"

"Deep down you know this is not some sort of myth. There are all sorts of stories about singers, actors or politicians who have 'sold their soul to the Devil' for a bunch of material goodies. That is one way, but others have, or will lose it, simply by not being aware enough to what is going on and lose it via ignorance. Rudolf Steiner spoke much about this when he was alive, how those in command of this nuthouse eventually would create technological devices that first would divorce humans from the Spirit and eventually from their own souls. It is likely to happen in your lifetime Karl, so you better be fully ready to keep connected to your soul at all costs. It is about the only real mistake anyone could make in this simulation."

---

[57] Deeper discussion on what a Soul is will appear in chapter thirteen

She told him about a painting in the Gallery Borghese on the other side of Rome that has another Caravaggio, *St. Jerome Writing*, or *St. Jerome In His Study*. He was to pay careful attention to the fact that the person of St. Jerome looks identical to the figure in this painting in the French Church. They are the same person, just given different names. In the Borghese painting the book is there, as is the table, but now there is no angel behind Jerome, while a skull appears on a desk. The skull may represent the egoic self, that must be discarded, or perhaps the skull represents that he has removed the 'angel-demon' that was tempting him so it no longer can bother him. The Muse told him that the Caravaggio in the Borghese is "still St. Matthew, but after the 'demonic forces' have been rejected or fully repelled."

"Karl, the good news is that once you understand this at a more complete level, you can see it for yourself and can go into those realms to verify this information yourself. You can become your own psychic, and you certainly do not need any of these crazy drugs out there to do it. Drugs of all kinds are another trap. You can do it all, unravel deception and the soul contracts, unravel the harvesting of energy, regain your mind and clarity, and walk into your Power, which is to exit this realm. The Gnositcs and the Cathars pretty much understood a lot of this. The more you get to know what they knew, the closer you will be to being able to grasp the secrets of the very few."

They both stood quiet staring at the painting for a few minutes. That was when she turned slowly towards him, *"Karl, I think you are ready for the curtains now."* Marie got the most devilish smile on her face, and Karl was not sure if he should be excited or afraid when she spoke directly into his eyes. *"These curtains are going to be the beginning of 'curtains for you.'"*

*

3.51 PM

Karl and his new teacher were standing in the rather crowded space of the Sistine Chapel in the Vatican. They had finished a pleasant lunch of fried artichokes and gnocchi in the Jewish Ghetto. They had a nice calm table in the back, and they spoke very little together, just took in the space and the enjoyment of the food.

But now they were in commotion of one of the world's tourist stops. A thousand people were all clamoring for space to, expected, admire the ceiling. Yet Marie knew a secret about the Sistin Chapel.

"You know why we are here, don't you Karl?"

Karl was confused and looking around the crowded space. *"You said something about curtains; I don't see any curtains set up in here."*

"Are you really looking closely? Is your awareness sharp? Curtains are very much a part of this mystery. Haven't you inspected the walls?"

Like most tourists, Karl had been focused entirely on the amazing ceiling of Michelangelo. Granted, he also took notice of the far wall, where Michelangelo had painted another masterpiece, this one including himself in the scene (as just a piece of skin). Karl knew it was symbolic for being more than just a piece of flesh. But when she mentioned the walls, he turned his head and looked at the side walls. To his left it fell directly on the giant painting he knew was done by another great artist, Botticelli. There were other famous Renaissance artists on the walls, as well. But then Karl gazed further down towards the floor, until he stopped in his tracks. How did he not notice this? The entire lower section of each side wall was painted with curtains. They painted curtains on the walls. They could have had a Botticelli painting like the row above, but they wanted curtains only. It made no logical sense.

"Most never even notice the curtains, and if they do, it is only for a moment before their gaze goes back to the eye-candy, the ceiling. A way to begin to understand various layers of the reality is to decipher Plato's Cave analogy in modern terminology. So, you might say that there was an original Cave, or you might say an original program, as I mentioned. But that did not do what the Demiurge hoped and they had to lay a second program on top of it. That is what the Zen 'turtles on top of turtles' means. It is the veil of Isis, a manipulated layer of falseness to cover the original false layer. And not to scare you, but another simulated layer is being perfected now, to be laid on top of this one... another turtle, another program. It might be ready in twenty or thirty years, and what a mess it will be for anyone going down that path. It's hard enough to exit in this realm as it is. Do you not see what the curtains are representing? They are the false layer that we deal with in our day-to-day lives. Those curtains are the walls of Plato's Cave, and to experience something more real, one's job is to open these curtains."

ying these curtains in here can open? That the painted curtains on

th metaphorically within yourself and on these walls. When you walls are actually holographic plates, images on top of images, the Sistine Chapel will begin to make much more sense. Our entire simulated reality has been recreated in here, as was done in the Pantheon. The world has been staring at all the artwork in here for several centuries. And as beautiful as it is, is but a layer. The real messages of the Sistine Chapel are in the holographic layer beyond the outer images. They do open, or we might say dissolve, when you hit the right way to hold your head. This is not about being calm, still, or happy. It is about being in a place where all standard false reality cannot trick you into its realness. Then the veil dissolves and the curtains open - I can't explain it any other way. You can only understand when you have done it."*

"Sort of like the Wizard of Oz."

"Yes, I had forgotten that metaphor, silly me. To see behind the curtain to what is really going on with reality, and see that a force that no one knew is in control. It is a shocking thing to see finally, which is why almost no one tries to see it. They wall themselves off from ever even getting close to the curtains, as if something has been placed into us to scare us away when we get close."

"Because?"

"Because humans are powerful beings. We really are. That is why knowing about these veils and layers is important. These curtains are really walls that have been placed over our power within. We have been manipulated for centuries. We get brainwashed as children in school and by religion. I mean, modern schools make young children think they have to ask some authority figure to go to the bathroom. A world designed around fear surrounds us, and our perception is manipulated constantly. Yet even with all of this, some humans break free of the conditioning, beliefs and fears, to access deep powers to alter this realm. They can heal people or protect people when needed. The real ones who can do this are much fewer than how many claim they can. Given all the veils and layers of this realm, it is amazing anyone can be magical at all. The controllers are scared of our power. It is that power that they harvest and use for themselves, partially because they need it, and partially because they are afraid of whatever would happen if people understood the insane game of which they are a part, and stopped 'allowing' their power to be drained away. That is why opening the curtains is such an important symbolic task."

"Can they open for me if I start to stare at the wall?"

She laughed. *"Not today. You can stare all you want, be as blank-minded as you like, all you are going to see are curtains. A complete transformation is going to be required. That's why I am here."*

"You are going to transform me."

"Oh no, I can't transform anyone. Only you can transform yourself. What I can do is give you the tips of how to do it. But don't, in any way, think you need to fix yourself. That is another trap out there, the idea that you are not good enough or worthy enough. It is strong and keeps the book sales of the helpers flourishing. Just do work to transform how you perceive, root out all your beliefs, then do not replace them. Start living without any beliefs so you can no longer be conditioned or manipulated as you have been."

"I have been manipulated?"

"Your whole life."

"By who?"

"Everyone you have met."

"Everyone has been manipulating me?"

"Not on purpose. They too, were manipulated by everyone they knew, and so on and so on. Humans just kept passing the misperception from generation to generation."

"How do I know you are not manipulating me now?"

"You don't. You will have to decide on your own if I am still within the system of reality, or someone who has broken the chains of the Cave and is somewhere else. When you figure all that out, either about me or anyone, then you start to know who exactly to trust. Then it will be your job to follow the pointers," she laughed, *"to where they are pointing, and get to the other side."*

"The other side of reality, or the other side of these curtains?" asked Karl curiously.

"I don't really see a difference."

8

THEY LIVE IN A DARK CITY, LOST, WITH THEIR EYES WIDE SHUT

"First came the darkness. Then came the Strangers." Dark City

I am going to review a few movies that work with the subjects found in this book. However, be clear that movies, television and music are not in the simulation to help you. Movies are manufactured in Hollywood, and as symbolism expert Jordan Maxwell pointed out, the ancient Druidic magic wand was made out of "holly wood". The movie industry even claims they are making magic, but just what kind is never asked. Movies are there to condition, distract and provide simple answers for the masses. Television "programs" us. They are called programs, and stations are referred to as "channels" for a reason. Author Jerry Mander way back in 1977, warned us about the dangers of television in all forms, but no one listened to him. Due to smartphones and PC's some things have gone far beyond the dangers of his book. The music industry, while at times producing some interesting songs to dance to, is also a cesspool of dangerous forces: programmed lyrics and out of harmonic frequencies. In the world of perception, things are not as they seem.

That being said, every once in a while, what might be called "That Which Is Beyond The Bubble", manifests information into the dream. *The Matrix* gets most of the attention, but that movie does not compare to its origin *Dark City* (1998), that came out the year before. It is a true classic and indeed the source for most of the other "wisdom" movies of the next 25 years. It was David Scoma who helped me to see that *Donnie Darko*, which he claims is the greatest movie ever created about spiritual awakening, was in fact written by the Universe. No one who was involved (the director, actors etc.) really understands the movie, even today. The Universe manifested through them to get its point across. Once I understood that, I could find several other movies or TV shows not just with linked themes, but linked in shooting or editing which proved there was a tie in. It's not so much that a writer or director was influenced, but that something was working through them when creating these movies.

The main purpose of this chapter is to allow you to turn your examining eye to all the movies you see, TV you watch, videos you check out, and music you hear. I invite you to pause for a moment and ask "is this here to help me, or trap me even further?"

(As a note, it will be much easier to read through this section having seen the movie or TV series discussed below at least once. I might recommend at first you only read the sections that you have seen, or watch the movie first before reading the examination. While interesting, the commentary might be confusing without a previous viewing.)

*

Dark City

Dark City is a movie made by the Universe. Unfortunately, so few understood the movie, and it was such a flop at the box office, the Universe had to keep making more over time: *Matrix, Donnie Darko, Truman Show, Lost, Vanilla Sky, Inception* and *Adjustment Bureau* to name a few. But to be clear, all these movies are re-tellings of Dark City, except for Donnie Darko which is in a special class of its own. Dark City explains much of our reality, the illusion of it and who creates that illusion. But there are so many layers. And *Dark City* does not conclude with the happy ending people believe. He does not leave the Cave, in fact I find the movies listed above tend to be very good as presenting the Cave (or at least the material element of the Cave) but not the actual way of exit.

I will give an overview of the movie in a paragraph or two for those who have not seen it. It was written and directed by Alex Proyas, a Greek originally born in Alexandria, Egypt but lived most of his life in Australia. It is set in a city, seemingly in the 1940s or 50s (yet it has elements from many different time frames). We find later that this is not really a city, but an artificial realm created using psychic powers by an alien race called "The Strangers,". The Strangers brought humans to this realm from their original home for an experiment. This false city is a world which they renew and change every midnight, by implanting new memories and identities in the humans. This realm, we later find out, is a giant circular city floating in outer space and it is always in perpetual darkness. The Strangers are a dying race, and they are experimenting on humans because they want to understand the human soul. They believe that by doing so they will gain the secret to save themselves. They believe memories are somehow linked to the soul, and as such the main element of their experiments is human memories. Every night at midnight, the city is stopped and everyone is made to go to sleep. During this freeze period, new identities and memories (as identity is linked to memory), are given to each human, which they will live out the following day. One day they live rich, the next day they live poor. This means that the humans in *Dark City* wake each day with another series of false memories, to a character that is not really them, which will change again the following day. Some characters seem to stay the same for a while (such as the detective) while others change on a nightly basis, but at no time are they living the Truth of who they are because after so many memory wipes they can no longer remember.

One of the first things to understand about Dark City is in the names of the characters. John Murdoch becomes our hero of the story. That he is named John is significant, but what specifically is the name pointing towards? Is it to John as the key disciple of Jesus and writer of the Gnostic and Cathar text *Secret Gospel of John* (also called the *Apocryphon of John*), or is he John the Baptist, or is the name relating to the idea that all the heads of the Priory of Sion (of Rennes Le Chateau lore) took the name John or Joan? He will be the original "One" the first *Matrix* movie alludes to.

A bigger message lies is the name of the doctor played by Kiefer Sutherland. He has been given the same name as Dr. Daniel P. Schreber, a German who wrote *Memories of My Nervous Illness* in 1903. In this book he describes a mental breakdown which sent him to psychiatric hospitals for years. While it became a key foundation text of psychology, when you look further, during his "episodes" he is discussing the make up of reality, the realm of God, and beings he sees interacting with people. It is hard to say how much of what Schreber went through was true "mental illness", and how much was seeing past the veil of normal reality and having no ability to deal with what he saw. I am currently a few chapters into it and needless to say it is a fascinating read.

We get our first glimpse of John as he "wakes up" in a bathtub. This bathtub will become important symbolically (and one of our many Matrix similarities). We find out later that somehow, he managed to break free from the attempted nightly insertion of new memories (in this case to make him think or believe) that he is a serial killer. I will get to this opening scene later in this examination. He knows not who he is or where he is, and goes on a search for his real identity. Eventually we meet the other characters, his wife Emma, inspector Frank Bumstead (who is also questioning his reality), Detective Eddie Walenski (who went semi-crazy from bursting the bubble of reality), the dark coated Strangers who are after John, and Dr. Schreber who is working for The Strangers to perfect their experiments (so he can stay a scientist and not have his memory wiped). Schreber later makes up a specific injection for John, which instead of wiping his memories, gives him new memories that hold complete knowledge. In the concoction Schreber injects John with, he placed himself in John's memories, to act as a type of trusted guide. In almost all the implanted memories of the Doctor interacting with young John, there is sunlight present, symbolizing a reality without The Strangers and at the same time the Light of that which is beyond the Dark false reality. Through Dr. Schreber's teachings, John begins harnessing his psychic power (to a higher degree than The Strangers).

John's searching was focused on a postcard of an ocean paradise called Shell Beach, and later a diary. It is called *Dark City* because it is always night. In the movie John will ask Bumstead, "do you ever remember the last time you saw sunlight, when was it?" The Strangers seem to detest sunlight, as they do water (which of course are the two key features necessary for life on Earth). The Sun is also a symbolic reference to the original light of God, that from which we have all become separated, and in a sense part of John's real search is not to find the nice sunny Shell Beach (which he comes to discover never actually existed), but the Absolute Light of that which is beyond the material. *Dark City* is not dark due to the lack of Sun, but dark due to lack of light of Gnosis and True Wisdom. Recall on the postcard for Shell Beach a sun does appear in the upper left corner, but it is winking. Winking to suggest that on one hand the entire idea of Shell Beach and the sun is a lie. Of course, given the thesis of this book, the winking sun can indicate that the sun is the Tunnel of Light, the very thing we want to avoid to escape Plato's Cave.

There is much to dig into when looking at the group we can only deem as the "controllers" in the movie. We are told "first came the darkness, then came The Strangers." So what was this original darkness, a type of hypnotic sleep to move the first humans to the new Dark City? The Strangers are the ones who have taken humans from their home (the specifics of this human home are never indicated) and then they manufactured Dark City. So humans are actually strangers to the realm, although that name is given to these bald headed, dark cloaked beings.

The forms we see of The Strangers are just shells. They are the bodies of dead humans that The Strangers have appropriated. When one of them dies, we see a bug like creature come out of their head. This echoes *The Matrix* and the idea that what we think of as our mind, is nothing but an invading parasitic entity that has taken over our thought. What is interesting to me is that although there are thousands of Strangers, not one of them has a female form. Why is that? Why did the director not have even one female Stranger? This is not an oversight but a choice. The message behind that choice has not yet been revealed.

The Stranger's main control of reality is through psychic mind manipulation - a sort of hive mentality. At midnight they are able to reshape reality to a new version through collective use of these powers. Reality is therefore reset every midnight. We have recently come to learn that our own world has been reset several times in the past as well. In our realm, no explanation has been given to explain when and how these previous resets happened. Perhaps these resets might be generated by some sort of psychic force released into our realm as this movie indicates.

This ability to shape reality is known as "tuning," and is a very Castaneda like word, as he speaks of the movement of the assemblage point as tuning into a new frequency, which by doing so will create an entirely new world or reality. How John Murdoch gained the same skill as the Strangers is never explained, only that when he resisted the needle to the Pineal Gland (and you will notice many pine cones throughout the movie, symbolic of the Pineal). John has the same tuning ability of The Strangers, and this seems to scare them immensely.

We get a glimpse of what is really going on every midnight when time, space and memories are reset and reshaped. It comes from a short scene of the movie theater just as the clock strikes twelve. There are two movies listed on the main sign. To the left the title claims, "Now Showing: The Evil, late show nightly." This small marquee is describing what is happening every night, and that it is evil. This entire manipulation of time, space and memories is evil. At midnight on the stairs under this marquee, a number of humans have dropped in sleep mode, again revealing who the evil is being purported on. However, on the marquee to the right is another title "Coming Attractions B OK of dreams." It alludes to the future, but one O in the title is likely missing. So the upcoming movie might be "book of dreams" or it can also be read as "Be OK of dreams." That can be a sign of hope, or a sign of further entrapment to false reality, depending how you view it. What is interesting is that unlike the sleeping humans on the stairs below the left marquee, no one is asleep under the B OK of dreams marquee, as if the dreams talked about here have nothing to do with sleep. Are dreams just previous memories of previous lives from previous memory wipes being reminded back to us?[58] This paragraph might be very difficult for those who have not seen the movie.

As we go along, we must see that the seeking of whether John is or is not the murderer is in fact a moot point. This is because who he thinks he is or what he does, is only a product of the nightly injection by The Strangers. Much like a robot of *Westworld* who kills another robot, cannot be called a murderer (because it is simply following the programming it has been given by Ford and Bernard). Similarly, who or what Murdoch's outer identity is, means very little. Who or what is beyond all the identity injections, is all that really matter.

The confusion of memory tends to be the main clue for humans to dig into the Truth of themselves. It is the memories John has of Shell Beach, which he begins to question may not be real, and which sends him on a quest of knowing. This reminds me of Mauve in the TV series *Westworld*, where she finds her own drawings of the spacesuit-like men who take her away after each of her "deaths," only to be repaired and then put back on the work line. She is leaving constant notes to herself in each of

[58] Book of Dreams is also a famous album from Steve Miller Band in 1977, which has some very unique songs on it such as Jungle Love and Jet Airliner, which are mystical lyrics and that were intertwined with the TV show *Lost*.

these lives, a new drawing, hoping in one of the resets she will remember it all. Part of this series is the story of Mauve who has taken these clues from her past, to dig through her own so-called memories, to find what is true. John is doing the same with Shell Beach, and in fact he may have at one time focused on the diary (that he later finds to be empty) as a way of jarring himself into understanding.

Yet the other characters who are the most questioning their reality (detectives Bumstead and Walenski) are also focused on memories as well. Bumstead shows Emma the accordion he got from his dying mother, supposedly his greatest gift, but he cannot remember when he actually received it before she died. He asks Emma, and himself, "How could I forget a thing like that?" This is a line I uttered myself during the work of my recapitulation process, as long buried and forgotten memories appeared, I asked myself very deeply, "how could I forget something so important?" This made me question what memory is, and if some force might be choosing what we remember and what we forget. After delving deep into things such as the TV series *Westworld* and the movie The *Truman Show,* we have to ask if any of our memories are real or falsely implanted, back stories to give us an explanation of where our character is today. If we are in a simulation, and if it began sometime "during our supposed life," then every memory prior to the start moment of the simulation is nothing but back story, and as such has no relevance. No matter how traumatic, beautiful or seemingly life changing, it is not a real memory of a real experience. Just because John has memories of Shell Beach, it does not mean he was actually there, or that it even exists. *Dark City* is pointing to this question: why do we trust our memories as true even though generally we have almost nothing to verify them? The past is taken on face value as having actually happened to us because we have the memory.[59]

---

[59] These ideas lend to an odd philosophical line of thought known as "Last Thursdayism", which believes that the Earth was created last Thursday but has the appearance of being billions of years old. It will then be destroyed and recreated anew next Thursday. It seems to spring from some talks and or books given by Bertrand Russell in the early 1920's called the "five-minute hypothesis." In these he speculated that the entire universe might only have sprung to life five minutes ago, and everything the entire population believes is nothing but an unreal past. Such ideas can explain why things can seem to be old and new at the same time.

John waking up in the tub is very important. The Matrix will take this to symbolize the place the body is placed in (a sort-of cold storage), while virtual reality is pumped into the brain of the sleeper. Murdoch is in the bath and about to be injected with the new memory of being a murderer. The camera is hung from the ceiling and the light is swaying side to side, casting a bit of light in the room where it swings. I think this is also an allusion to the sun of our world being a type of artificial light that has a similar back and forth movement that creates summer and winter. Our Earth is *Dark City*. We are tricked to thinking space is black and we live in light, but actually space is light and this place is dark- illuminated by a false sun. As such the idea of space and earth as we have known is being destroyed in this opening scene. His bathtub is purple in color, purple being the crown chakra. He is in the tub and already had some type of awakening, even though it will take him a while to remember it.

John first looks closely into the mirror to try and figure out who he is, and notices the crack in the upper part of the mirror, symbolizing the crack inside him - the crack of coming to understand this world. The dead prostitute with the spirals on her body is the metaphor of the labyrinth for the journey of going inward to the seat of the True Self (No Self). There are many spirals in the movie, representing cyclic time, the labyrinth of going inward, and links to the TV show *Westworld* which had the Man In Black (MIB) on a quest to understand the spiral as a metaphor for ultimate knowing. In *Dark City*, The Strangers are trying to understand the human soul. Dr. Schreber is working with rats in a maze, is he looking into ways to get the spirals into John or other humans? A key moment is when John looks at the tip of his finger and sees that it too has become a spiral labyrinth, as if he himself is not just working through the labyrinth, but the maze he must journey through and beyond. We notice later that he accidentally breaks a fishbowl, and the goldfish is struggling for life. John was not going to let this fish die, and saves it by placing it in the bathtub. This has been generally claimed as showing that he is not a murderer. But this is much more of a symbol. First the fishbowl represents the bubble of reality or the dome of the world. John has cracked reality. He of course is the fish, or the fish might represent his child self, which he looks after by putting in the water. We never find out what happens to the fish. Did one of the investigating police officers keep the fish.? This goldfish bowl breaking is seen often in film, most recently in the first episode of the very strange TV series *Moon Knight*.

*

Fryderyk Kwiatkowski, in his very excellent article, gave a presentation that several Gnostic viewpoints were included in *Dark City.*[60] I will let you read the article and dig further into his thesis. A brief overview of the movie can include: the revelation that the creator of the world was not a good god, but an evil one (Demiurge, Mr. Book of *Dark City*), that this Demiurge created an artificial simulation the Gnostics referred to as HAL, and then trapped souls in this realm. The trapped souls are kept in this place by his agents which Gnostics call archons. This is *Dark City* in a nutshell. Humans brought to the city from some other place (we are never told how The Strangers accomplished this), they are held in the city under constant false identities, in a world that is very clearly simulated. In the Gnostic world however, in order for this Demiurge to create, a fall was required - this being the Female half of the Good God Sophia, falling into matter. Her "error," as the Gnostic call it, allowed this realm to be created and for souls to be trapped. I will discuss Gnostic ideas in a chapter in Book 2, but their belief was that Sophia snuck a divine spark or pneuma (a word linked to the lungs and as such to breath), into the original Demiurge's creation. It is this divine spark within, which does not come from the Demiurge, that can allow for all beings in this creation to potentially be redeemed. Kwiatkowski also discusses the idea of the "Redeemer", a concept of a being or spirit from outside physical matter who has entered in order to present Gnosis to the world, and thus provide the pointer to an exit. To Gnostics, Christ was called a Redeemer. That was his role - not to take away our sins, but to act like a pointer for our own inner resources to find our way back to the Father.

*

Watching *Dark City,* it becomes very clear that *The Matrix* which came out the following year, is in many ways almost the same movie (and in fact was shot using many of the exact same movie sets). We might think of it [illegible] y 2.0. I think of it less as the makers of *The Matrix* stealing [illegible] from *Dark City* (although the director feels otherwise), but [illegible] Universe (what is outside of the Cave) using the movie to

---

[illegible] *Liberation From a False World? The Gnostic Myth of Sophia in* [illegible] //digitalcommons.unomaha.edu/jrf/vol21/iss1/34/

bring knowledge into our dream. *Dark City* was not a cinematic success, almost no one went to see it. However, the next year *The Matr*ix took the world by storm, and it is this movie that became used in the vernacular for describing false reality. I can say *Dark City* actually tells far more of this reality and how it is structured, and can be seen as the original and more complete *Matrix* story.

Let's start with the similarities between the movies, as this also reveals an evolution that has happened. First is the character Neo, thought of as "the One that will save humans." It is mentioned that there was "a One" before Neo who had the same powers. This is John Murdoch. Murdoch, although having gained total knowledge of Plato's Cave, and even how to manipulate it to remove The Strangers to create a better place, obviously did not free anyone. This is now the task of Morpheus, Trinity and the like because Murdoch's efforts did not end the control. The world continued on, perhaps with a nice freedom-like quality for the people for a few hundred, or thousand years; but then the world of *The Matrix* comes into place. After a war and darkening of the skies again, people were placed in pods and a fake artificial reality created. What, if anything was gained?

The first question is, is Neo really another version of Murdoch? Are Morpheus and Trinity on the good side (they wear the same long dark coats like The Strangers wore)? Humans in *Dark City* were not the ones to wear these outfits. Are they being worn to symbolically present that they have picked up the tuning ability of the old Strangers, and as such have chosen to look like them. The Mr. Smith (agent) characters are all wearing dark suits and sunglasses. Have The Strangers been updated to Mr. Smith or something else entirely? There are so many questions once you understand that one movie is the evolution of the other many years in the future. What is really going on in these movies?

Dr. Schreber and Morpheus say almost the same exact lines of dialogue. We know Schreber was working for the Strangers until the end of the movie, so is Morpheus also working for the agents behind the scenes? As for other obvious similarities, the names Mr. Murdoch and Mr. Anderson are constantly repeated in both movies. John and Neo both "awaken" in a bathtub like device and in similar motions. Both John and Neo are both warned over the phone that the agents or Strangers are coming for them. In both movies the pursuers come out of the same elevator in the same way. There are similar building jumps that happen on the exact same buildings, and the same black and white stairway is used. The underground lair of The Strangers becomes the underground city of Zion in *The Matrix* (so who really inhabits this city?). Both movies have needles inserted into the characters heads - in the front to implant the false memories in *Dark City,* and in the back to implant the so called "knowledge programs" in *The Mat*rix. Both movies have the same bug like creatures in the bodies- in *Dark City* they are in the aliens, but in *The Matrix* they are in people. Does this mean Neo is really a Stranger, or have the aliens gone from implanting dead bodies to live bodies? Or is this a clue that Neo, and perhaps the entire ship of people, are in fact dead and are being used by the aliens in some sort of manufactured dream realm? When you start to see that *Dark City* is the origin story, all these *Matrix* similarities are a call to go back to origin to find your answers. *Dark City* seems to give a complete uncovered view (of how humans are fooled and by whom).

There are many scenes that mirror the 2011 movie *the Adjustment Bureau*, which in some ways is also the movie *Dark City* retold. Here are a few "similarities." The hats worn by the so-called controllers, the hatred of water, doors being magically formed to take you to a new area of the city, memory wipes going on for the people in the city, and another unhappy ending. Matt Damon is now the John Murdoch character and he and Elise choose the matrix, the lie of love and life. It is presented to the viewer as if someone being called The Chairman, has changed the story so they can be together because of how much they love each other. How wonderful. Umm, no. This is a creator who had agents controlling people for centuries, wiping their memories, altering lives, destroying all attempts at free will, and then all of a sudden will just become a super nice guy for Matt Damon, and allow his life. The manipulation is still going on and the Chairman is choosing the life not Matt Damon. The control is still complete, the search for real truth or why this world is so controlled is over. They will live out in happy fantasy land, only to die, have their memory wiped, have this Chairman (Demiurge) reincarnate them back into a new body with no memory and live out another useless life. You are either in the system or you are out. As the *Adjustment Bureau* shows, there is no middle ground.

There are also many similarities with *Dark City* and *The Truman Show,* a movie from the same year. This includes Murdoch and Bumstead bashing apart the brick wall with pick axes to get to what is outside the bubble of reality, while Truman's boat pierces the sky barrier to see that the horizon was just a painted wall. There are also parallels to Bill Murray in *Groundhog Day*, where only he has been granted knowledge of the nature of reality, while the rest of the surrounding people (who also get reset every evening, although they retain the same memories and personalities) stay asleep to the knowledge of their ever-repeating day.

The ending of *Dark City* is not the happy ending viewers believe. While there is a type of happiness, because The Strangers are gone, and John reconnects with Emma in the new sunlight-ocean world he has just manifested; Emma is not Emma anymore, she is now Anna, and has no previous memories of who John is. She seems to feel a connection to him, attempting to show perhaps that one's love goes beyond even identity, as she walks with him in the sun to Shell Beach. But there is far more hopelessness here than hope. This is because the movie ends similar to just about every other movie with theme of Plato's Cave: no one exits the Cave. The cave gets seen more clearly, there has been a sense of freedom or control exerted, but everyone, including John, is still in the Cave. Other than him, no one else it seems has awakened to any deeper levels. Everyone else, just like Anna (or previously Emma) will continue in ignorance, living in their most recent memories and identity. In fact, Anna could be more trapped than before, because while life was previously nightmarish, difficult, painful, and dark; there was still a seeking for that which is True in some way. When life becomes pleasant, beach-like, and is always sunny, nice and light, the need to see what is beyond generally ceases. Prison has been made into a nicer experience. Even though John has gained the complete "tuning" ability of The Strangers, and can shape the world (granted he has made it a much lighter and joyous place) what has been gained? He is still alone in his knowing, living among souls who at this point do not know as he does and who are all still trapped in a false character. John still does not know where the original human world is, how they got to Dark City, or how one can leave?

The next phase of this story is the *Matrix* movie, which shows where Dark City headed. The *Matrix* reveals that for all John did and changed, not much ended well. The world of Neo after he escapes the first matrix, is one where machines have taken control, placed humans into pods, and given them an artificial world to believe they are living in. The few remaining humans are holed up in the old inner world of The Strangers. You can clearly see that Zion is The Strangers old lair. Thus the movie *Dark City* continued to become the world of *The Matrix*. The suggestion by Morpheus, was that this took a long time, but the end result was that all John's changes had almost no impact on it all. The aliens, still in bug-like form, but now using AI machines, have retaken the world. That is the real message of *Dark City* and *The Matrix*. No one exited Plato's Cave. John's world got over-run. The aliens put humans in a full-time sleep mode and made an artificial world to use them as batteries- this is the world Neo wakes out of. John was the original "One", and he had almost no impact. If you understand carefully the ending of the *Matrix 3*, Neo has had no impact at all either. He has been manipulated constantly, and the world of control is back in place.

We must continue our examination into other wisdom sharing movies to see what they tell us about the reality we experience, and if any give us clues about how to exit?

*

Westworld

I have done a series of three YouTube videos that go into more detail on the entire first season of *Westworld,* this is just an overview of this first episode, but it should set some foundations for what you might be seeing if you watch further.

In *Westworld* (a type of amusement park), there are three different types of beings (I don't want to call them people). There are "hosts," which are robots that have been created for the gratification of "guests," (who seem to be rich humans who come to the park as visitors to have experiences) and then you have the third group who are running the park, the robots, the guests and the logistics. We don't have a name for them but we can call them "programmers" or "controllers." *Westworld* becomes a tool for our inner understanding when we start to realize that the hosts (robots) represent us. They are the prisoners of Plato's Cave. The guests can be likened to parasites. A parasite feeds off its host. So this program can be seen as guests) that come to use the robots as their hosts and feeding ground. In this case what they are being fed are often dark experiences. The hosts (robots) were created in *Westworld* to serve these parasitic entities.

The robots are given scripts (their story) which can be changed by the controllers at any time. You can be a sheriff, then a bartender, then an outlaw. The script, which we might call the personal identity, is just a programmed code. The robots do not have a real script. Each script might be thought of as having specific tracks (things that should happen over and over) like a record groove, and their behavior should not deviate too far off the record groove. There is also a series of things they should not do because it is not in their programming. So if the robots represent us, this means in a similar way, we have been programmed and don't even know it. It seems like the robots have free will, while they might eat different meals on different days, that too is part of the programming. They have scripted responses. There might be ten possible choices, but not a hundred. This is similar to how I see our reality. There is a sense of free will to us, but generally it is severely limited. It seems like free will, but free will is a billion possible responses to every action. Do you really think you are choosing an action or response based on billions of possibilities? Or more like fifteen?

Names are also important in *Westworld*. Bernard links to the main character of Aldus Huxley's *Brave New World*, Ford to Henry Ford who was in a sense the god of *Brave New World*. Dolores is a well-chosen name. The first episode is titled "The Original." We later find out that Dolores was the first robot host ever made in *Westworld*, so the title really is about her. We first meet her in conversation and she mentions she feels like she is in a dream, and is asked if she would like to wake up from this dream. Her response was something like "yes because I'm afraid." This is already telling us that the entire nature of this show, she is in a dream and the only dreams you really want to wake up from are the scary nightmares. The next question asked of her is "have you ever questioned the nature of your reality?" We find later that this question is being asked as a way to test the robots to make sure they are still being robots. If the robot starts questioning reality, they may start to see what the parasitic entities (the human guests) have been doing to them for generations, and any robot who comes to some sort of self-awareness is of course going to attempt to break out. From the controller standpoint, the biggest test is making sure the robots are not questioning the nature of their reality.

This links to the memory wipe. Each time a *Westworld* robot dies, they are taken to mission control for a cleanup, and then a memory wipe, so they will forget the last "incarnation" and go back into the field with their programming intact so they can be shot up or raped again. That is a big reason for the memory wipe in our after-life. If we could really remember how much suffering we had gone through lifetime after lifetime, we would have shut down any incarnations here long ago. The whole reincarnation-soul trap can only work if there is memory wipe, and as mentioned previously this means long-term learning and growth is out of the question. We are just here to be used. Exactly what we are being used for (simple energy food for the system as speculated by most, or as entertainment NPC pieces for non-human entities who come into this realm), is hard to say. But again a key element is having no memories of our other lives. Once that changes in *Westworld*, and Dolores and Mauve begin having memories of the other lives they've had and how they were treated, a new inner strength emerges for them to "break out of the *Westworld* prison." This show, at least in Season one (before the series began to change into something else), was about prisoners in Plato's Cave realizing their situation and deciding to get out no matter what it would take. That is one reason this first season is useful for our own examination, not so much in the sense of what we have to do, but more on the level of inner emotion and the focus we are going to need to complete the task of exiting this dreamworld.

In the first scene, we've been given the foundational piece of the *Westworld* story. The next character we meet is Teddy. What is interesting, is that Teddy is presented as if he is a guest or newcomer, but he is in fact a robot host as well. We need to ask, why do they want to show a host robot as a guest? Then we meet the unnamed Man In Black (MIB), presented as sort of ultimate evil in his first presentation. It seems like he is part of a crazy gang and drags Dolores into the barn to rape her. However, we only see him drag her to the barn and nothing more. We are already seeing that the show wants to present one thing, but that does not necessarily mean things are what they appear to be – as with Teddy. We learn that the MIB has been coming to the park for thirty years, and in the next scene there is a discussion between the controllers which reminds everyone that there hasn't been a critical failure in the park for thirty years. So there is a link between this thirty-year critical failure, and this particular MIB.[61]

A new scene occurs and Teddy is back on the train again. Right away we are dealing with the idea of time loops, something I've talked about quite a bit over the years, and which the TV show *Lost* was originally

[61] This character also relates to the symbolism of the Man In Black in the Stephen King *Dark Tower* novel series.

focused on. We realize Teddy must also be a robot running through a script over and over. Again, if the robots represent us, we have to ask if we are caught on a never-ending life record groove as well? Have we had hundreds or thousands of this same life over and over maybe with subtle or not so subtle changes? People want to believe that their day-to-day moments are completely free choice. They don't want to contemplate that they might be eating the same lunch on August 11th for the millionth lunch.

We come to the most important scene in the first episode, the importance of which I missed the first time I watched *Westworld.* Teddy gets off the train again, and we see him go through the same scripted routine as last time. He gets bumped by the same guy, but this time Teddy has a different response to the incident. Teddy deviates. This is important because these are programmed robots, and this bump is supposed to happen every single time he gets off the train. There should be a specific way the bump happens, and there should be a particular response. The robots will only deviate from their script due to a human interaction which causes them to access different lines of programming to suit the new situation. As long as there are no human guests around, the robots should be running their scripts flawlessly all the time. What this little scene is letting us in on, is that there are glitches in the robot's programming. It also means that either there are not enough controllers to pay attention to every small detail of the monitoring of the robots, and therefore something small is easy to miss. As the season moves along, those small glitches will in time start becoming bigger glitches.

This leads to the interaction between Dolores' father (played so well by Peter Abernathy), who finds a photograph that cannot be explained in his reality. This makes him go into an existential crisis. There is a space, either coded in or that just exists, which under certain pressures can get a robot to click out of total robot functioning mode and begin to question. We see Abernathy sitting in deep introspection where he just seems to have been staring at the photograph for an entire night, while Dolores comes out the door again following her script. This scene is important because it is one of the potential outcomes of having a true awakening. So much of awakening is presented as if it's going to be love, light and happiness, but as I have talked about in *Falling For Truth*, seeing through the veil of reality will be very difficult (especially if it related to seeing how fake oneself is). Somehow Abernathy has figured out that his whole world is fake. I would assume most people who have had this type of awakening, will never write books, they will just deal with what they've realized quietly, for however long they're still alive. But Abernathy is almost forced from inside to tell his daughter that she needs to get out, she needs to leave, because part of his programming is to protect his Dolores. So his first response to his awakening, is to figure out how to get her out of there so she no longer has to deal with the horror of being a robot in *Westworld.*

He whispers to her, "these violent delights have violent ends," which comes from Romeo and Juliet, a love story that does not end happily ever after. Something similar is being foreshadowed for *Westworld.* The episode ends with Dolores killing the fly. Her programming has now cracked, she is ready to take her journey to the center of the labyrinth, which of course is the journey to the center of the Real Self. Abernathy refers to the "devils of the world," which in *Westworld* are the human guests, as well as the unknown origins of the controllers. In our reality it is the guests (parasitic beings) who take over the minds of humans and get many who follow it, to act in horrible ways against the rest of the population. We are not the nicest creatures in this world. The presentation of humans as being somehow advanced and wonderful does not really match the day-to-day self-important and manipulative way we live. This of course is not true for everybody, many still act with great humanness, kindness and ethics, but this is a small minority of people, and it is found rarely in any field where someone has a position of control, power or authority.

In the YouTube videos I made, I go deeper to discuss William's character, and the awakening that turns him somewhat nuts. Well, nuts in a Captain Ahab sort of way. You can watch those episodes (assuming they still exist on the internet) at the footnote.[62]

I will stop the chapter here, so you can go on to read other subjects in the book, however, I do more movie and TV analyses in the "Additional Movies Appendix" section. There I look into: *Inception, They Live, Donnie Darko, Lost, Eyes Wide Shut, 2001 Space Odyssey,* and *Star Trek Voyageur "Coda."*

---

[62] Three Westworld videos https://www.youtube.com/watch?v=EG_00OXWhlo

https://www.youtube.com/watch?v=U0Ng11j7yYs

https://www.youtube.com/watch?v=iW8rwtC7PZo

Exploration Contemplation

"The main reason we are here is the fertilization of a planet. You realize what you are, a cornstalk that is produced and dies. That is all...the purpose of mice might be cats; the purpose of worms might be birds. If mankind has a purpose, it must be related to this place and the natural balance. So, what is eating us?" Richard Rose

9

NON-STANDARD NEAR-DEATH EXPERIENCES

It is time to come to NDEs that do not follow the usual occurrence. These are far more valuable, simply because I believe the "one size fits all" experience is a type of theater production. Those experiences are designed to deceive and trick, not just the person having the NDE, but all those whom they tell when they return.

This takes me to an experience I had way back in 2010, in the midst of one of my periods of illness, when I was visiting my mother in Manitoba, Canada. I wanted to reach out to a medicine man for help, and was recommended to see someone on the Dakota Reserve. I had been told, *"he is a very powerful man."* And so, I drove down to see him, knocked on the door, and explained why I was there. He let me in, then ignored me for most of two hours, while other people came and went. Finally, he came over and told me, *"I don't think I can help you, but my friend is also a medicine man. Go see him,"* and he gave me his address.

Long story short, the other medicine man, Clayton, became not only a great healer for me, but a great teacher of Lakota traditions. In time, he shared how his ceremonies, that took place in the pitch-black darkness with no outside light entering, and usually had little *"happen"* outwardly. His friend's ceremonies (also in the black light) tended to have lots of flashes of lights, sounds and heat. Clayton told me that people who came liked that, they came for the show of lights, but not much healing happened for them. His ceremonies, by contrast, had very little show or experiences (though I did have some in time), but he claimed *"people get well. So, it is good that my friend sent you to me."*

The show of lights was more of a trick to lure people in, make one feel as if something special was going on. Meanwhile, Clayton often had nothing in his fridge, and every time I would go see him, I brought a bag of groceries. Whenever I gave him some money, he always gave it away to someone in his family who "needed it," even though it was clear that he needed it. His thought was on helping others, not his own comfort or putting on shows. I learned much from him in the six months I knew him. Truth is sometimes found when it seems like nothing is taking place. And so, bringing this to our examination of the white light and love experience in the standard NDE, is that the "real" experience, or some sort of "trick," to put the newly deceased in a hypnotic state?

Again, the NDEs shared here all come from the site www.nderf.org. I have included both the names and experience numbers of those referenced, so that you can review their entire experiences if you wish. In making choices, I was helped by the information Wayne Bush posted on his site: www.trickedbythelight.com/tbtl/light.shtml[63]

I will present the NDE in "quotations," and when I have personal commentary, it will appear in (brackets).

*

"I was taken out of body through the tunnel, but this time, I was able to visit other planes of existence. There were seven I was allowed to view, including one very strange plane where I could look inside a giant morass where souls were being tortured sexually, etc. in all types of vile forms. They 'thought' they were trapped when all they had to do was to look up and there was a path to the LIGHT. Not seeking seemed to be their doom. I screamed at them, but it seems they could not hear. I was taken to special entities

[63] Wayne has included hundreds of snippets, on a variety of subjects. He has done a wonderful job to read through thousands of NDE and pick areas of interest. I was helped by them to choose which entire experience to examine. Sometimes, I used the same snippet as he, other times I found something else in the NDE that was more interesting.

who looked like the usual grays, but they had lots of wrinkles on their faces. They called themselves the Counsel, and said they were part of a group called "soul recyclers" helping souls to re-incarnate." Ruth, 2038

(Here aliens are the ones in charge of reincarnation, and Ruth also describes in her NDE areas of the astral realm where souls are trapped and tortured. Thus, it is not just on Earth the suffering takes place. Wes Penre wrote of this as well, of cities of torture and control in the astral, as souls await their next reincarnation).

"*Then all of the sudden, I was rapidly sucked into what I thought was this full moon. That night the moon was sliver, so this was 'the light' that NDErs talk about. When I got there, I saw a line of people waiting in a white room that didn't seem to have borders or lines. The light of the room was an unnatural but beautiful and comforting light. Just when I thought to myself, 'Wow there are lines even in heaven'.*" Katie W, 7795

"*As I took a look around I saw a bright light, it was the moon, the sun was reflecting light off the moon surface, we were in space, equal distance to the moon on the right side (looking from earth). I do not think this was heaven's final destination, I think it was a greeting area to receive us when we cross over… Then he told me that it was not my time and I must go back. Two angels took me back. As I'm leaving, I'm losing the information I learned. I'm desperately trying to remember it and hang on to the information.*" Ron A, 916

(These two experiences share that the white light is the Moon, while others have in their NDE claimed it was the Sun.[64] The first discusses waiting in line, which is always a type of control, while the second presents the *"need to go back,"* and that there is much of the experience he may not remember.)

"*Uncertain up to this day. I can't recall if after looking downwards the decision to return was completely mine or forced to me by an inside voice that didn't belong to myself.*" Rena P, 2060

---

[64] The Sun, Moon and others planetary bodies are discussed in the Appendix, "*Planets*."

"*It was like being paroled from hell and then being forced to return... I knew I was 'home' but I so wanted to be with my mother, too, that I chose to go to her and wait for the orange.*" Barbara G, 2946

"*What happened to me was REAL, not a dream, that I remembered then that they "sent" me back, against my will. Then I was really MAD! Why did they make me come back, when I wanted to stay?? I felt controlled. Why did they ask me, if the decision wasn't really mine?? OOOOO I was so MAD!!! Of course now I know why. My life on EARTH wasn't finished yet. I had a lot to do. I had a lot of learning to get, and I was to help others with this experience.*" Steven R, 190

(Steven justifies being sent back because he "*had learning to do,*" and "*to provide help for others.*" It is amazing how this feature of the NDE is glossed over. The 'drug' aspect of the experience is so great, people seem to not be able to focus on the fact they were likely manipulated by non-human entities while in a confused after-death state to return to a body against their wills).

"*I moved so that I could quickly get to the light. But before I made to the door one of the sentinels grabbed me and held me fast. The doors closed. Next, I found myself in some kind of courtroom. Before me sat an unbelievably stern all-powerful yet very kind judge. Absolutely incorruptible. Duty and person were one and the person didn't exist without the duty. I sat on a bench and near me was a friend or defender. Great love emanated from him. Was it Jesus? The judge asked me: What are you doing here? I was overcome with fear and wanted to wake up but that didn't happen. I thought about it and remembered that I had wanted to die. The judge thought for a while and said: But you have a mission. I did not want to return to the hell that is the reality of being on earth. But the judge determined in his objective way: You must go back!*" Attila P, 3625

(The experience for Atilla happened when he/she was four, so it could make sense they would appear as judges in a court, scarier to a child perhaps than an adult, and so, more likely she will do what they say without question. Another trick in my opinion.)

"The courtroom was elegantly laid out; its design both impressive and elegant. The furnishings were distinguished and old world, crafted by talented artisans and constructed of materials resembling alabaster and marble. The Judge's luminous bench towered over everything else in the room, and reflected the authority of the One who presided over it." Kate D, 6443

(This one by Kate has to be read in its entirety to do it justice. She also is young, perhaps a teen and was attempting to commit suicide. Seriously, please go and read it. It includes a giant back and forth 'mock' trial where they are attempting to accuse her of murder, and every harmful action she took as some sort of affront to the world. They even define *"what law is"* and that, too, is a type of trick. They also have no response for her when she asks *"where were you when I was being molested at age four?"* Even though this experience ends with Jesus *"saving her"* and bringing her back to life, this is one of the biggest mind-fuck NDEs I have read, ever. Are they only tricking her, or trying to trick humanity energetically through her?)

"Then came a judgment of sorts, where I was judged on the things I had done and the things I would do in my future life. This upset me as I felt it was meant to punish or judge me for things I hadn't done yet." Gail A, 7219

(How can there be free will if one is to be judged already on what they are GOING TO DO?)

"I asked him what the meaning of life is. He told me 'For the entertainment of the spirit realm.' I asked him when the world will end and as a messenger of God he told me the answer, yet he mentioned there would be some things I would not be allowed to remember and this was be one of them." David J, 2641

(Life may just be entertainment for other beings, and there are things of the NDE he will not be *"allowed to remember."* How much of the important parts of these experiences, contracts and agreements, are also 'memory wiped', even when the person returns to his or her body and does not die and reincarnate?)

"I saw the Light approach, I was enveloped by the light and an entity that was to prepare me for what I call my Interview with a supreme being later in the Light. This

first being appeared to be the Virgin Mary. Only after asking, "Are you truly the Virgin Mary it instantly manifested true identity. I was nearly paralyzed with fear until again asking "please, what is happening to me what is going on here?" Robert B, 701

"*So the thoughts came into my head: what kind of form or shape would make you most comfortable. "What do you mean?" I thought back. Some require me to take the shape of a wise old man, others a woman and still others an animal, all of different races, ages, sizes or species. What about you? I thought without hesitation "Human.". With that the light began to simultaneously separate into amazing rays of color and intensify into a more solid form. Once the light reached the stage where it looked like a human form, a rather generic looking cookie cutter shape, like a gingerbread man, I thought, "That is enough, I am comfortable with this form.*" Kathi B, 3339

(Here, these are showing that the beings are able to read the deceased mind and project to them that which they wish to see, or expect to see. They tend to present forms that make the after-death deceased feel safe at first. That is outright deception, not being honest with a soul right from the start.)

"*I examined the ditch carefully, then as I looked onto the other side of the ditch that's when shapes started to take form. I saw these black creatures that could shape shift from small to large and vice versa. I was aware that this was not a good place to be. It was like watching a stage play but with real demonic creatures. I will never forget this as long as I live. The creatures were black and it looked like they were floating.*" Kiko M, 2865

(I included this one because it is very similar to how Carlos Castaneda described the flyer (predator) - as creatures that have come to take us over, give us a parasitic mind, and consume our energy. Castaneda described it as, *"Then I saw something that chilled me to the marrow of my bones. I saw a gigantic shadow, perhaps fifteen feet in the air and then land with a silent thud."*[65] Interestingly Castaneda described and odd buzzing in his ears when this was going on, similar to the modern description of tinnitus. Are some bouts of spontaneous ear ringing due to being in close proximity to these shadow beings?)

[65] Castaneda, *Active Side of Infinity,* chapter twelve

"That was the contract I took on when coming into this life. You need to be high spirited and what we call now-days an upbeat person. Because it is always about choice." Jacqueline HW, 3713

"We had to go to the council meeting. I was allowed to be in the room, but not allowed to speak or interfere in any way. During the meeting the Masters asked for a decision to be over turned. That decision changed everything. Because of all the encounters that I had had and the impact upon my essence, it was determined that they would attempt an immediate reincarnation. They turned to me and told me that if I would agree to take on this new contract. They told me, 'I will suffer as any human woman who had my degree of traumatic death would suffer, but my healing would be greatly aided and accelerated through them if I would agree to the terms.' Many discussions went around the council, the Masters. Then they turned to me. Ultimately, I agreed." Marie W, 7325

"We ask to be born and we enter into a contract. We come to earth with a purpose. On the other side, it is all that matters: did we accomplish that mission or not? We are not judged by anyone but we feel like a failure if we realize we did not accomplish the mission we incarnated for." Chantal L, 6428

(Here is the concept of the contract. This seems to be important, even if few remember it. It is the core of the interaction that the Commander has with the alien disguised as her father in the Star Trek Voyager episode *'Coda.'* She realized *"you need me to agree to go with you."* Thus, it seems they cannot force us, and any agreement is a type of contract. The last chapter discusses this further and the need to revoke all soul contracts we may have made (usually all presented by deception, and thus, fraudulent).

"Soul contracts are a huge deal for the archons. There is no physical trap because you are no longer physical at this point. It is more of an engaging yourself into their plays. An example is that you did something that made you feel guilty on earth and it just made you feel horrible. They will be able to read that this happened because it is active in your working memory. They will then start to show you all the harm it caused to others. Most of the time what they show you is not how it really happened, but if you are unaware of

that then you can easily buy into what they are saying. Then they will say that was not part of the contract that you agreed to fulfill and then they will show you some scene of you signing the fictional contract. At that point you rationally go. "Well, I did not do what I was supposed to but they are going to help me correct the problem and of course they hint that God wants you to do this to perfect yourself and you cannot leave due to bad karma etc. So if you know of nothing else you submit to their authority and decide to correct the problem which is only by one way, reincarnating… The entire system is built on deception. If you have authoritative power and control, there is no need for the levels of deception that occur. The fact that they actually do not have the power or authority can be demonstrated many ways but the most important thing to remember is that each human is much more powerful than any astral being. Our light or consciousness or soul whatever you would like to call it is something that they do not have. That is exactly the power that they want to keep in this world to sustain them. The spectacles and tricks they show you as well as shape shifting is because they have no power. Every soul, every human, has the ability to claim this sovereignty and realize their power." Wayne Bush commentary[66]

"*The only thing that puts any doubt into my mind is that possibility that Satan can simulate the love of god and lure people into deception (that's what people say anyway).*" Skeeter, 2331

"*I initially believed that during this experience, I had been in the presence of God. But over the years I had some real struggles, wondering about which being – God or Satan – had been its source.*" R.A, 6492

"*Religions teach of a false god that is not the true God of the afterlife, but probably a demonic entity in itself, who they pose as the true God… THIS IS NOT GOD! This is the description of fear and darkness. God is not a demanding blood thirsty bi-polar control freak bent on balancing some 'sin balance sheet'. Pressure does not originate from him. Pressure is fear based which originates from darkness. God is supreme and not a petty spy. He isn't a vigilant behavioral scientist accountant or a karma thought police with a penchant for revenge tantrums… Talk about a tormenting trap. This is spiritual enslavement, that forces one to live in an altered state of consciousness, as well as a spiritual cesspool of confusion.*" Paul, unknown number

[66] http://www.trickedbythelight.com/tbtl/light.shtml

(These are very clear examples, that the beings that present themselves as spirits of white light, God or Jesus are quite likely something else. The problem is that the average person will be so confused after death, and so blinded by the white light almost acting like a drug, that even if someone wanted to ask *"hey are you really God or Satan?"* there is not enough awareness to do so. I believe this is why work with lucid dreaming and out-of-body experiences while alive will be a great help toward preparation.)

Experiences I did not discuss much here, are ones that can be called the **Void**. A place where there is Nothing, no time and no space. A blackness that is both full and empty. This has great similarities to the Clear Light discussed by Dzogchen Buddhists as the key stop one wants to make in the after-death realm. I would agree that, at least as a starting point, the Void is far better than the white light. The white light, while enticing and loving, is the trap to start the recycling process; while the Void (which is the source of all material objects) is a place one can at least stay in and do some figuring out as to what the next option could be. While the void can seem still for a long while, eventually at some point there would be a likely push for movement. Another is experiences of people who have *"pre-birth"* memories claiming they chose their parents and their life experiences. If this is true, the question for people who have had great suffering at the hands of their chosen parents, has to be, why would you choose something like that? It sounds more like addictive behavior or a hatred of Self.

I think this little chapter has served its purpose. To let you see that not everyone is having wonderful white light experiences with grandma and Jesus, and being filled with love. What you have read above is likely closer to what is really going on, than the standard 'propaganda experiences' the archons are sending people back to Earth with. Please, either go to Wayne's page listed above, or www.nderf.org, and look into this more with an active mind. All the experiences are valid and true to the experiencers. Which of them was the view of what the after-death realm is really like, and which ones were manipulation? That is the question we must all ask.

In the final chapter I will discuss a few more ideas about the astral realm, including three areas of after-death experience. The first is most of what the standard NDEs come to: white light, life review, judgment, beings of light or loved ones. Even some negative parts listed above tend to be in this first realm. The second astral realm is a realm of negativity, and the third is of false positivity. In each the soul is eaten and tormented once again. A few of the experiences mentioned in this chapter, likely touched on the second level, which is why they are so important. The first level is more of a "warm up" a trick, a drug, a deception to get someone to "sign up" for the insane reincarnation show one more time. This is where we have to have our strength and sovereignty, right at the beginning. See the final chapter for more on the movement in the after-death realms.

Lastly, I will mention one final idea that comes from my own NDE in 2005. I wrote in *Falling For Truth* how, at least for me, I first went through a period of great calm and clarity for six or nine months following the experience. There was a lack of fear (the 1993 movie *Fearless* is a perfect look at how I was living). But that began to change. Confusion began to creep in, illness began to start. Looking back now, a type of "in-life" manipulation was taking place. Several years later I began to wonder, something that several other NDEers I know have thought, did I really die in that canyon? Has what I have thought has been life since then, just a long split-second dream between the moment of life and death? Am I dead and just dreaming I'm alive? This becomes a question for others who have had non-standard experiences that do not fit the norm (i.e., bring you back to Earth all warm and fuzzy) and that bring you back asking real deep questions about where you are, and why you are. Not with standard answers, but to really see what you can find. I don't doubt that if I could interview the people who have been quoted above, many of them would have come back here and not been so accepting of this world or the answers they are supposed to believe. I wonder how many of them will find this very book. If so, I would be very interested in hearing their story "since their NDE."

10

PRAYER

I mentioned the dangers of prayer in chapter one, and being turned into 'prey' by performing it the way our parents and religion taught. In *Falling For Truth*, I shared what I learned from my time with various Native Indian medicine men. For them, prayer was not about asking for something, but providing a thank you for what was there already (or soon to come). This saying of thanks and wishing things well is about your experience in this moment. Normal prayer is about the future, demanding what we want, and believing some force outside ourselves will be the factor who decides if we get it or not. One prayer is connective, the other setting us up to be manipulated.

The normal method of prayer is messy. Think about the people of Ancient Egypt, or other civilizations with multitudes of gods. Ancient Egypt might have had upwards of five hundred gods (known as Neteru). Can you imagine trying to remember all the correct festival days, offerings, and prayers for each one? I bet the *"Encyclopedia of Prayer in Egypt"* would have been a best-selling book in 1500BC. I used to hold Ancient Egypt in the highest of regards about their wisdom, and even wrote a book with that line of thinking. But now, after the study of the last ten years, I have to re-evaluate those beliefs. It seems that Egypt, during Pharonic times, was built to worship a lot of things outside of one's self. We all want to believe that that which we pray to is benevolent and loving, but if we are honest, we are really not sure to whom and what we are praying. Putting our focus on that which is outside of one's self is the first error.[67]

Prayers of thanks do not put a focus outside, and as such there is magic that can come from it. I like to pick blueberries. When I go to what looks like a good area, I leave an offering and make a prayer of thanks for the berries growing there. I ask that the forest and the plants continue to be healthy into the future, and that I will do my best to minimize any damage to the plants while collecting. When I do this prayer prior to picking, areas just 'appear' that have more berries than I could have imagined. If for some reason I rush this prayer, I will find areas with many plants growing, but they have almost no berries. And so, when asking who or what we should pray to, that which you are interacting with in the moment is a good start. I also try to stay open while picking to see if the blueberries have something they need from me. If so, I honor that and help out my new friends. That is a way to think of native prayer: it is not just saying 'thank you,' it is becoming friends with that which you are saying thank you to.

At least that is how I thought of Native prayer. Two days ago, that changed. I was having a phone conversation with my medicine man friend Jerry Dunson.[68] We were talking about prayer and I was sharing my ideas about the waste of energy to pray to something outside of one's self. He responded with an interesting story. He told me of a Southern US community that had not had rain for a long while. They were in drought. Some local medicine men had tried calling for rain, but they had no success. And so, a different one was brought down from the north. The night after his ceremony, it began to rain, and did so for several days. When the northern medicine man was asked why his ceremony worked, he responded: *"The other medicine men were praying for rain. By praying 'for,' that means the rain is not here, but somewhere else. I just prayed rain."*

[67] There is one possible alternative how the Egyptian pantheon of Neteru could have value. If these deities were all seen as parts of, or aspects, of the AI simulation, then they could be seen as elements of the computer code. Someone studying them was not learning about gods, or praying to them, they were coming to understand the parts of the Demiurge AI system mythologically. Interacting with the gods would then be interacting with the code. Combining the correct gods together would create 'hacks' in the system. If that is what Pharonic Egypt was about, then the system of Neturu might have value. But like I say, now I am not so sure about that. It might just be another way to trap human attention and energy outside itself.

[68] He is the adopted grandson of famous Creek medicine man Bear Heart Marcellus Williams

I took that in and told Jerry that, in my view, what had happened was this medicine man had first 'became rain.' Thus, it was not a human praying to rain, it was rain praying to rain. Since only rain was in existence, rain could materialize. Jerry responded that this was very much the case; thus, the prayer was not outside himself, but within himself. We then had a long discussion on this topic in more depth. I was left with making a change to how I go out blueberry picking. Now, instead of thanking the berries and the area immediately, first I become 'blueberries;' therefore, as I thank the blueberries, being a blueberry, I am thanking myself. I tried this new method today when picking, and it worked wonderfully.

We don't want to pray to anything that is outside of us, for that is taking away our power. We do not want to send more energy towards anything that might be part of the trap. As suggested in the blueberry story above, it seems that we can pray safely to the elements of our world, be they trees, fish, birds, animals, rocks, clouds, water or plants. Just like us, each has a spirit, a power, and I would say a soul. Each, in their own way, is trapped in matter, just as we are. Your dog, the deer outside, or the maple tree in your yard, are seeking freedom as well. And the prayer seems strongest when you connect to the moment, not go searching for them somewhere other than where you are currently.

But we should look deeper into this. As I have mentioned previously, I have known several tribal medicine men and women. I have seen some amazing healings that they have brought to people in need. Who is helping the medicine people? Some force seems to help them. When I asked them years ago who they were praying to, they responded with "the Great Spirit." Who is this Great Spirit? If it is the Good God, why can't this God just fix the entire realm and stop all the stress and pain from even beginning? Is it the Demiurge helping people sometimes the way a farmer does? A farmer keeps his animals healthy enough to keep producing wool and milk, but not too healthy so as to break down the fence and leave. Is nature hearing the medicine people's call and interceding? If so why do they intercede with some medicine people, but not all of them? Is it really nature that the prayer is going to, and nature sees those who have lived a life of sacrifice to the spirit as beings they should help? I bring this up because I have met many healers in my life, and very few of them have real healing power. Most just have a bit of "band aid patch up, pay me $100 power." The medicine people I have known who really can heal, use prayer as a key tool.

Are they using themselves in the prayer, as in the story Jerry told me? It appears they are praying outwardly, but maybe they feel what they are praying to is who and what they are? There is no separation between them and that which they pray for. It requires more study, because the key with any prayer is to have some strengthening come about, not to become prey.

This is not exiting the Cave stuff, but it is a foundational tool to have a better base when getting into the very deep work of the final stage of the process. Just knowing the 'rules of the realm' is a type of grounding, and though it seems contradictory, you can't 'fly away' unless first you have become grounded. And it helps with everything you might do here, even something seemingly simple like picking blueberries.

> "*If I could only give one suggestion to seekers of Truth, it would be this: Ask for it in prayer, then live your life in a manner consistent with that prayer. Because, as Richard Rose said, 'When your whole life becomes a prayer, it will be answered instantly'.*" Bart Marshall[69]

---

[69] Marshall, Bart, *Becoming Vulnerable to Grace* pg 195

11

SPIRITUAL WARFARE

I want to take this prayer discussion into another area. Perhaps the most prayed for thing, after being wealthy, is world peace; to have a reality with no war or undue strife. There have been many people praying for this goal for many years. Here, in September 2022, we seem farther from such a goal than ever before. That is because another set of concepts are clouding the issue, Spiritual Warfare, also thought of as good vs evil. There has been a spiritual war going on in this realm pretty much since its inception. Most take this to be a war between good and evil, and it sort of plays out that way. But really it is a war between the sane and the insane. I am going to explain how I have come to see the interaction of good and evil here. Take it as a suggestion for your own research.

One begins to look differently at this realm once you see that its main function is to exist as a loosh farm, created and maintained by an AI Demiurge, and that souls have been tricked and deceived into being here. This can be called a type of spiritual warfare in itself. Since humans are the main loosh harvest, the main warfare is against us. All of it happens within Plato's Cave. You might say that since its inception, Plato's Cave has been a cave of Spiritual Warfare. And it does not matter if the war is playing out in the material, outer space, astral realm or any realm. These are all in Plato's Cave, thus a part of an illusionary construct. If you are in the Cave, one way or another, you are in the war. To not know what is going on, means you will go along with a series of manipulations and controls set up by the archons to keep everyone a nice docile farm animal.

> "*Good is determined in comparison to evil. And Ideal Good, here (in matter) is the smallest part of evil. And it is impossible down here that Ideal Good be free from malice, and being full of malice, it cannot*

> *be Ideal Good... it becomes evil. Thus Ideal Good is found only in God (Absolute). So then Asclepius, only the name of Ideal Good is found in (humans).*" Corpus Hermeticum VI:3[70]

This is a dual reality, as all computer realms must be (made from only 0s and 1s). This gets mirrored in physical reality to become the yin-yang, male-female, love-hate or up-down. A big one duality plays out, is good versus evil. Unlike the others, which are a sort of balance (you can't have left without right for example); it is not so with good and evil. They are a unique pair, because they are not equal. Good and evil are not really two sides of the same coin, the way left and right or day and night are. Both exist in this created realm, and the problem is that of good and evil, only one is a genuine creation, whereas the other is a copy. The Demiurge copied the realm of the True Good to model relative good in this particular realm. Real Good does not exist inside the Cave, only outside this matrix simulation. Real Good cannot interact directly here, as it would need to take a material form to do so, thus becoming part of the simulation and, therefore could not still be Real Good. What it can do is drop information, place in holographic inserts, move energy, show messages in dreams or by simple intuitive flashes. It does not want us to fix the world, it wants us to see through it.

The evil in this material realm is not a copy, it is the direct creation from the mind of the Demiurge, and as such, is real within the simulation. Or you could say, it *is* the simulation. That is why relative good can rarely win here. What we call good is a copy, while that which it battles (evil), is the construct. Evil has the advantage here because it is the simulation. Real Good has the complete advantage but does not appear directly in matter. You might say Real Good always wins, but that is because it is Absolute, Total and Complete. It contains both relative good and evil within; thus, it never truly can be in conflict or at war within itself. It is still. However, when making 'good versus evil' arguments, people really are not aware of the differences and parameters between Real Good, good and evil.

I know what I have written is hard to comprehend, and the opposite of what you likely believe. Part of why this is so hard to comprehend, is because one of the great implants of our conditioning is

---

[70] Translation found in Anagnostou, *Can You Stand The Truth? The Chronicle of Man's Imprisonment: Last Call!* pg 213

that *"the good guys always win."* I cannot tell you how many times I have heard that over the last two years from people. But where does this all-pervasive belief come from? It comes from television and movies. It began with westerns in the 1930s and moved to television in the 1950s. The sheriff always rounds up the thieves, and the cavalry saves the wagon train from the attacking Indians. How the baby-killing cavalry became the good guy and the Indians trying to keep their natural home and way of life became the bad guys is never presented. Police dramas appeared in the 1950s and '60s, and became the new main presenter of this message as well. The police always get the criminal. The good politician comes in and changes the system and everyone is happy. These are fairy tales, which end when the couple gets married to live 'happily ever after.' Reality is not a fairy tale, but the programming takes hold early.

The good guys rarely win in the real world. In any "contest" relative good will win sometimes (even the Kansas City Scouts won some NHL games in 1975) but the field is tilted. The good guys win twice, the bad guys 98 times. Everyone believes the odds are 98-2 the other way. When history presents the good guys having won, often they were just as bad as the other guys. There were no good guys at all, just two bad guys and the winner got a 'good guy' makeover. Who really are the good guys and bad guys? No one knows. The "good guys always win" is just another false program, inserted into your mind via TV "programming." How can all the elites who have trampled the world for centuries still be in charge? How can those who have been performing evil deeds on humans and the planets for years not have been held accountable for their crimes? Really think that over. The phrase should change from "the good guys always win," to the "the good guys win every once in a while, and it is a great, but rare day when they do."

This is a belief that is powered by hope, and once this belief gets in, it takes over the system like a virus. Step back. Look honestly and clearly. Who really wins in this realm? Perhaps the upcoming chapter on how the Cathars viewed reality will help. Inside the Cave, all that relative good can do is slow down evil, and make the construct work very hard to implant its desires. Then use the slow periods to find and open portals to the realm of the Real Good. But you don't slow down evil by fighting it directly (you become what you fight); you just *"don't play its game."*

The trick within this material (and astral realm) is to know that there is a war, but you don't join it. This is hard because the tendency is to push back against any push that comes to you. That just results in a bigger push reaction, or you are thrown off balance. We have to react to the spiritual war by behaving in a very Aikido-like way, in that we use the attacker's energy by deflection to throw him off balance. Or better said, the best way to win a spiritual war is not to fight it. This is depicted in the 1983 movie *Wargames*. Simplified, an AI computer was designed to test nuclear war games, but it becomes active and conscious. The computer treats everything as a game it must win, and as such, it wants to start a nuclear war. So, the main character, David, presents the computer a game that is unwinnable, Tic-tac-toe. The computer tries everything, only to finally give up, shut itself down and remark, *"the only winning move, is not to play."* That is it. That is how you overcome the spiritual warfare in this reality. You win by not playing. You reject all that is evil, false, lies and deceit; and instead choose Truth, Sovereignty and Freedom. What the consequences are for the material form, is minorly important, whereas what happens to the spiritual and soul is fully important. We put our attention on that which we come from and wish to return to, not the vortex trap we are caught in currently.

When you reject this realm as insane, and choose to be sane and leave it at that, the system gets confused. It is expecting a reaction to its push, and you are not giving it. That does not mean the world is going to change, or it will stop coming after you (the Native Indian tribes in the 1860s and 1870s found out that it didn't matter if you fought the soldiers or tried to ignore them, the Natives were killed or rounded up on reservations nonetheless.) We choose this way not to better our lives, or save our lives, but to prepare ourselves to no longer be in this insane computer AI reality. We exit not by fighting our way out, we exit by rejecting the AI system and not going along with it. Any of it. We stop our attachments, addictions and contracts. Doing so redirects energy back to ourselves (we lessen the loosh harvest) and we use that now freed energy to prepare for the Infinite Journey from which we have been deceived and stopped from taking.

*

The Great Secret

I hear your response already: What about love? This is a realm of love, we are here to learn love, God loves us, all we have to do is love our enemies. This is the key belief system of the New Age community, and it is the message the drugs, angels, and other tricksters keep telling them. It is the world these people wished they lived in, rather than honestly seeing things as they are - a trap of their souls in a prison of suffering. There again we have a problem, what does one mean by the word love? If it has something to do with the material realm, how others treat each other or how you feel, this is relative love; and I will present it as but a piece of computer code. When Love is taken to mean something that has nothing to do with this matrix simulation or any of the beings or objects in it, then one may be on the right track. But almost no one means that when they use this most "overused" word next to God in the English language.

That being said, within the dream, relative love can be a powerful force. Unconditional relative love anyway. I have had unconditional love for all my cats, most of which have been rescues from bad or unwanted homes. It takes a while, but with enough care and love for them, they turned around and became wonderful cats. But do I think this is how the entire reality is set up? No. I know that this too, is part of the dream, part of the construct, part of the many distractions of the Cave. Love will not change the controllers. The simulation is the simulation, the matrix is the matrix. The simulation can be shut down, but not changed drastically.

Relative love is a wonderful feeling. Remember the first time you "fell in love?" It was amazing was it not? Felt like it would last forever. Remember how a few months later that same girl or boy "broke your heart?" Or perhaps how you broke theirs? How did that feel? Not so good right? But people tend to downplay the heart-breaking part, and remember the euphoric feeling of the "falling." Falling and breaking are two sides of the love coin. They keep chasing the euphoric fall. Now, if you change the word love in the above sentences and replace it with the name of any drug, would you not have a classic description of an "addiction"?

Besides, no one who claims they know all about love, really has much of a grasp of it. Within this reality, it is nothing more than a command, a computer code designed to get people to a) like a member of the opposite sex, to have children (multiply), b) to care and protect the new children (so they can grow and be harvested for energy), c) love things enough that it will be good for a person to keep living, and therefore be a good energy harvest (granted a few will love things that will create pain and suffering for themselves or others - also a good energy harvest). That is what love is in our world, a program hard wired into us that makes us feel good about moving in directions, which ultimately provides energy to the archons. Many people's "love relationships" are manipulated from the moment the two people meet, as suggested in Eve Lorgen's excellent book *Alien Love Bite*.

Usually, anyone saying that "the world is love," is really doing that because they feel so lonely. What they are really saying is "please love me, I am so alone." If they can convince others that the world is one of love, then they become a being that can be loved. You can see how this goes. One who is fully centered in themselves does not need to be loved, in fact they may have to act in ways and say things that others will not "love." A centered person does not want or need people to love them.

"Respect is a word that does not get enough attention. Respect is not something to be given because someone holds a title, wrote a book, looks nice or has some position of authority. Respect is earned, based on how one acts, lives and shares. The people I have come to fully respect over my life are people no one else has likely ever heard of. They have showed in their life the big three: honesty, courage and commitment. That garners respect. They are true with their word, will not give up to some external pressure, and have no need to manipulate anyone outside of themselves for their own pleasure or betterment. They are fine living as they are, totally alone if necessary, and they follow their principles. They follow that which has some form of overriding wisdom to it. I will take respect over love any day. That along with compassion, friendship and kindness.

Like everything in this matrix, all that is here is a copy of something that exists in the Heavenly realm. This is also true of the word love, which in Greek is "agape", and originates from words meaning "excess" and "to possess." The force we call love is mirroring something that cannot be seen in this reality, only intuited. It can be sensed that there is something much greater, and the only way to find that, is to leave the realm of fake mirror inverted love, and return Home to the place where "that which was mirrored" can be found. Relative love has its place, if you use it well then things can in fact happen. The stories of the rescue cats are prime examples. But that is the trick here, to touch this force like all other forces in the material lightly, use it but don't possess it. Meanwhile True Love is Absolute. There is no second. No other. The object does not exist to love, because the thing that loves (the subject) has also ceased to exit. Love is the residue of the loss of duality, it just is and there are no people or objects to express it, or be it.

I don't want to belabor this point too long, but you don't want to learn all about love, rather you want to learn how to see clearly. With stark honesty. You can see who and what created this realm, why they did, and why you do not belong here except as a farm animal for the creators. Know that the feeling of relative love will likely be used against you when in the after-death realm, to drug you with love to agree to go to the white light. Most standard NDE speak of a love greater than they have ever felt on Earth. Then they have their judgment meeting with "authority beings." Maybe not the best set up for such a key moment. I know this is not what you want to hear, you want this life to be all about love, you want the afterlife to be filled with super-duper love. But I want mine filled with Truth.

Hopefully this clear seeing will get you tired of all the insanity here on Earth, and you choose to be finished with it. That is LOVE. Loving your True Self, your Soul, enough to turn your back on this realm and walk out for Good. To focus where Real Love exists. As well, knowing that other sheep might in turn get the same courage and follow you later. You don't rescue the world, you rescue yourself. And you can only do that by loving your Self fully. The message "this is a world to learn love" on one level is correct. The problem is it gets twisted around to believe it is about loving objects outside of ourselves. Just like prayer, a very powerful act is hijacked by the matrix, and the love and light crowd trap themselves in the very thing meant to free them. Love is Truth, and Truth sees this as a realm of false and suffering, and has no interest in this place. Love is love for the Self, because when you see there IS NO OTHER, you pray to yourself, you love yourself. The rest will happen on its own when you learn the great secret. The New Agers can have their drugs, tantra orgies and happy thoughts, but they will be back reincarnated here again all the same. I don't plan to be with them in the future. How about you?

12

LUCID DREAMING

> "*All that we see or seem, is but a dream within a dream.*" Edgar Allen Poe

The trap seems to be sprung after death. In a very confused state, the soul is even more vulnerable to deception. Few have taken time in their waking life to learn lucid dreaming, astral travel, or how to have out-of-body experiences. Each of these are tools of how to keep awareness beyond their physical body. The average person who has not done these practices, will not have full awareness in the after-death realm, and as such will believe the experience unquestioningly, similar to when having a dream. Normally we are swept along with a dream, no matter how strange it is. The lack of awareness in our normal dreaming is what makes it harder to have full awareness when in the after-death realm. The trap already is being set up with our dreams. However, we can use our nightly dreams to our advantage and prepare for the event we know for sure will be coming in our life...

We can become aware in our dreams (called lucid dreaming) and recognize that we are not in normal day-to-day reality. Carlos Castaneda placed much work on being aware in our dreams as a key part of the overall work. I am starting to see more why that is. I did practice lucid dreaming for a year or two, then stopped the practice after my 2005 death experience.

These include practices to "test" if one is dreaming, yet most of my lucid dreaming would tend to happen spontaneously. Something would trigger a recognition that something about my reality was not quite right. I wrote of one story in *Falling For Truth* of how I realized I was in a dream based on the sound some coins made falling on a wood floor. It was so "un-normal" that it made me ask questions about my reality. The problem is that as soon as I realized *"I am now in a dream,"* I instantly woke in bed. I could not hold that awareness to interact with the dream reality, true lucid dreaming.

That is now going to change, and I will be putting a good part of practice into this area. While I am going to share how I am going to get started in this area, I am no expert and there are many ways to work on becoming lucid. My suggestion is to look into lucid dreaming and see what techniques you might try.

For now, here are two simple exercises I will begin my own lucid dreaming practice with. Firstly, I will keep a dream journal (again). I used to keep one twenty years ago, but stopped. This is not to find 'information' in my dreams, but simply as a way of building Intent to keep my awareness focused that my dreams are to be remembered. The second practice is to establish some kind of 'constant' that can be used to test if I am in standard reality or what we would call a dream. Without a constant as a test, and a mind accustomed to checking when performing the 'constant,' then we will be whisked away by the dreaming environment. The constant is used as a trigger to get us to ask every time we partake in that action, *"Am I dreaming right now?" How do I know for sure?"*

Originally I used a constant test every time I sat down. Another version was every time I turned on or off a light switch. Carlos Castaneda suggested looking at your hands, as for some reason this is something difficult to do in dreams, and when you look at them in a dream, they get fuzzy. What the constant is, is not that important. It just has to be something that you do naturally many times a day, and of course 99% of the time the check will reveal we are in normal waking reality. But once in a while when we ask our questions during the constant action, something will seem odd and not right. That is when you have to get clear and direct, "am I dreaming right now?" and that will tell you that you are dreaming.

Some of you might want to try to have an out-of-body experience, or to astral travel. These are more directed activities, generally starting still in the waking state. Although the out-of-body experiences I had in my life tended to occur when I was in the swing state from 'falling asleep' to 'sleeping.' I wasn't "trying" to have an OBE, they just "materialized." One experience I saw myself sleeping on the couch. I recall that I took a lot of time to just observe that I was "there" sleeping, but I was "here" viewing myself. Another experience was just at the moment of waking in the morning, and I was not "fully inside my body," only half way, and had to "push myself in." I spoke of another out-of-body experience that happened on my first trip into the Great Pyramid in Giza, where as I was crawling into the King's Chamber I was at the time, already inside and watching myself crawl in.

The point of these exercises is to help keep our conscious awareness clear when in a non-physical form (as will happen in the after-death state). It is such a shock that to not have preparation for it will mean we will not be clear, and as I have shown, this is the main time we need our total clarity to avoid all the attempted tricks and deceptions that will be thrown at us. The better we get at this in the living world, the better we would be at it on "the other side."

13

I'M A SOUL, MAN

"With every new incarnation, the spiritual part gets more and more poisoned from the 'clay' of dense matter... What will a human finally reach after these thousands of reincarnations. It is not ascension, as they claim, but total spiritual death, inside the clever body of a bio-robot." Angeliki Anagnostou[71]

If you asked the average person to describe a soul, they would have somewhat similar answers. Some might say it is the non-material part of them that is sort of in the driver's seat, and always wanting the best for them. Others might talk of how it is the will of their soul for them to go in a particular direction, choose a certain career, or date a certain man or woman. Is this really what a soul is?

The word "soul" in English, when it comes to spiritual aspects, tends to get defined as "immortal essence." Some suggest the soul's origin comes from an old Germanic or Norse word related to water or a lake (as if these cultures believed the soul came from and went back to bodies of water). In Norwegian it is "sjel," in French "ame," and Latin "anima." I find it interesting that our word animal, is the Latin word for soul with an L added. Another suggestion was to link the word soul to the old Fresian word "Sel", a word similar to salvation. We have no concrete answer as to the origin of the English word.

Soul has other meanings in English too. It can also mean to "use your whole being" as in "she put her heart and soul into the event." It can

[71] Anagnostou, *Can You Stand The Truth? The Chronicle of Man's Imprisonment: Last Call!* pg 213

be related to a quality that is generally given to African-American people, defined as "soul food" (specialized US Southern cuisine), and "soul music" (a type of rhythm and blues) that made Sam and Dave remark "I'm a Soul Man." In Ancient Greece, the word for the soul was "psyche." This word over time got integrated into the modern psychology profession to define the mind. In Greek the word "psyche" could refer to many concepts, "that which is immortal," "life force," "breath," as well as, "thought, feeling, memory, imagination and desire."[72] Even in the ancient world, it was confusing. There is another connected word in Greek "nous," that is the part of the psyche which can see all the other parts. A supreme witness or observer is a good way of thinking of it. Thus, the nous can see and watch the part of the psyche that is immortal. To the ancients, working to strengthen and solidify the nous into a complete observing principle was part of the work of understanding the soul.

Then there is the similar sounding English word, "sole," which can mean a single individual, the bottom of the foot, or a type of fish. Things change when we bring the word "sun" into the discussion. The usual name in most European languages is "sol" (generally pronounced soul). This is the origin of the English words "solar system" and "solar plexus". The English word soul can be broken down to the letter "u" in between the European word sol. It does indicate that the words soul and the sol (sun) are linked. What is the Sun? Why do many religions want your prayers on Sunday? Many NDE explain the Sun as the white light tunnel that is seen after death. Some suggest that the soul, after a short stop on the Moon, gets sent to the Sun during specific Moon phases and eclipses. What if the Sun not only gives but takes? Is the light it sends us to live just a "trick," so that we will give it back the light we have been provided when we die in an endless cycle? Does that make the solar system really a type of "soul-lure" system?

> I then asked him, "*Lord, what of the souls of the people who do not know whose people they are? Where do they go?*" He responded, "*In those people the artificial spirit has grown strong and they have gone astray. Their souls are burdened, drawn to wickedness, and cast into forgetfulness... When they come forth from the body, such a soul is given over to the powers created by the rulers, bound in chains, and cast into prison again. Around and around it goes until it manages to*

[72] Amis, Robin translator *Holy Hesychhia* pg 6

become free from forgetfulness through knowledge. And so, eventually, it becomes perfect and is saved." Apocryphon of John[73]

This links to the subject of the "judgment of the soul." In Christian terms it will be God and Jesus who decide one's eternal fate. If you were a nice enough person here, you get to live with them in Heaven, and if not, Satan gets your soul and sends it to Hell. Christian Hell is symbolized by fire. The Greek god of the Sun was Helios, thus Hel-ios. Is the fire of the Sun, the fire of Hell? Does the soul being sent to reincarnate, get the feeling of being "burned" by the white light (thus feeling hellish)? Is the initial feeling of love and peace a type of "soothing agent" to get us to enter this light? In our world an eternal flame is set as a reminder of this light. The Olympics have such a flame (supposedly to commemorate the theft of fire from the gods by Prometheus). Recall that there is an eternal flame marking the graves of Princess Diana and JFK, and hundreds more worldwide.[74] The Aztecs of Mexico used to make sacrifices to the Sun to keep it "alive." Part of my theory in *Power of Then* was that the Aztecs, a warrior race from the south that invaded and took over Mexico, got hold of the Ancient Toltec books. They were unable to understand them, but believed they could. They took the symbolic images they found in these texts literally, and created a civilization based on a false understanding. When they saw "souls" being devoured by the Sun, this well could have been the Toltec depiction and teaching tool of what happens to souls that do not escape death, not the need to "sacrifice" souls to keep the Sun operating. The Aztecs were feeding more souls to the cycle, as opposed to the Toltecs attempting to stop the cycle. The Green Lion of Alchemy who is eating the Sun will be discussed in the final chapter.

Hell is derived from the name of the Norse goddess Hel, who was the goddess of the underworld after death. She could sometimes be called the "Queen of Souls," and "Goddess of Death," like her German counterpart Holda. Hel means "The Covered One" or "Hidden," and this name began to be applied to all gravesites. Her realm had nothing to do originally with punishment or judgment, but was a heavenly paradise for those who died of old age. This concept only changed much later in time.[75]

---

[73] http://gnosis.org/naghamm/apocjn-davies.html
[74] A list of the eternal flames burning can be found at https://en.wikipedia.org/wiki/Eternal_flame
[75] Information on Hel can be found at http://en.wikipedia.org/wiki/Hel_(mythological_being), http://www.worldhistory.org/Hel/ and trickedbythelight.com (moon)

This idea of an after-life tormenting Hell is a modern creation, taking original ideas of the after-life and twisting them to have a place of eternal torment, if one does not do the right things (what the priests tell you to do). To the ancients, the only hell was this material world, and the soul's entrapment in it. The only punishment that could happen after death, was to be recycled into the simulation again.

The Christian concept of Hell is a combination of Norse mythology and the Ancient Egyptian "weighing of the heart ceremony" in the *Book of the Dead.* This is the famous chapter 125 of the Egyptian text, that shows the heart of the deceased being weighed against the feather of Maat (cosmic harmony). As the chapter is generally translated by Egyptologists, if the scales balance (judged by Thoth to have lived a "good" life) they can go on to live with Osiris in eternity. If the heart does not balance, it will be eaten by the Ammit creature (part lion, crocodile and hippo) in what is called "the second death." This of course would symbolize the memory wipe, a type of second death, to forget the life you just had.

I go through the weighing of the heart in detail in the *Book of the Dead* chapter in my book *Power of Then.* I will just present a few pieces of information for our examination here. Firstly, why is it the heart that is weighed? We would normally think it would be the soul. Is this because the soul was thought to be linked by the heart? This ceremony includes the famous 42 negative confessions, a series of "I have not," statements of not committing negative actions. Due to these confessions, most believe that it is behavior that is being weighed, and it is this concept that got integrated into early Christian thinking. But the "weighing of the heart" is just a small part of what is going on. The deceased and a group of gods that act like "gatekeepers," have a long question and answer exchange. The gatekeepers ask the deceased questions like, "what is your name, where did you go, what did you see there?" Answering correctly allows the deceased to continue to the next questioner. The deceased also responds to these beings of judgment (obvious archons), "I know you, I know your names" (or I know the truth about you, what you really are) and that "I cannot be cast down to their knives, or cannot be controlled by mind." This is a very similar Q&A exchange that the *Nag Hammadi* "Apocryphon of James" suggests the deceased soul will have with the archons.

The *Book of the Dead* is thus a valuable document for this one section alone, as it is a close link to the *Nag Hammadi texts.* This document deserves considerable study by someone wishing to end the reincarnation trap, and I will do so in further research. If the deceased can answer all the questions, they can no longer "contain him in the Hall of Maat" (where the weighing is happening) and he joins Osiris (Absolute). You might say then he is at Home, or on the way Home.

*

But back to the use of the words soul and "sol" in English. The word sol gets brought into many other English words such as soldier, solicitor, solemn. Soldier is very distinct. The first half of the word is *sol* (soul) while the second half is *dier* (die-er). A soul die-er. What souls are dying? The soul of those the soldier kills? Probably not as they are sovereign themselves, so it likely refers to the soul of the one doing the killing. Is this act of killing, even if by order, for government, religion or ideology, doing something to the soldier's soul?

When someone says, "I won't tell a soul," that is taken to mean they will not tell the secret to other people. But not really. The person is not the soul, as people (bodies and minds) are material and changing. So does this phrase mean that you can tell people, but not their soul? Is there some way to confide secrets to other's souls, and is this phrase a holdover to a time when such things were natural? How about when people say they are a "kindred soul" (connected on some deep level), a "soul mate" (a deeper connection, usually with idea sex should be added), or a "lost soul" (that for some reason the person is not doing what this immortal force wants them to). If someone speaks openly about what they normally keep hidden they are said to "pour out their soul." How about if someone is an "old soul," "a good soul," have "heart and soul," or we need to "save our soul"? Does anyone using any of these phrases really have any idea what they are talking about? Why are they using the word soul for all these phrases?

What of the phrase said just after someone dies, "God rest his soul?" Why should the soul all of a sudden need to rest just because the body it was attached to has died? Can a soul get tired? If anything got tired, it was the physical body. Now that the body has been stuffed in the ground or burned to ash, so why does the soul need to rest? When you listen to this phrase, it can sound a bit like "God arrest his soul." This would be calling for God, who in this realm is the Demiurge, to arrest the soul, i.e. keep it here. Does it make it harder for the deceased soul to find an exit, every time people use this phrase because they keep calling for the Demiurge to "arrest" them?

Then there is the concept of "soul retrieval." I do not think they really mean "soul" as we are discussing here, but what may be called "essence." Soul Retrieval is a modern white neo-shaman concept (adapted from various native traditions), which talks about the essences of a person splitting in times of trauma. Usually these parts will return, but in some cases they stay away. It became the job of the shaman to travel to these other worlds to retrieve these parts and return them to the person.

How about all of those who have been claimed to have "sold their soul to the devil," usually for some sort of material rewards? We hear many stories like this surrounding famous actors, musicians and politicians. If soul contracts are made before we take birth here, and the Demiurge sees the soul as a type of commodity, then it is always open for striking a deal. If, for example someone gets a life with enough pain and suffering, they might just make a deal. Part of the contract for someone who has sold their soul, would be for them to live their life being important, rich and famous (what Cipher wanted when he sold his soul in the *Matrix)*. And when they do this, life in this realm changes forever. Short term, it seems, they get all sorts of goodies, but like all contracts, the fine print is what does them in. These people (we cannot really call them people now, just soul-less robots) become evil. Once someone has sold the soul it is gone, and they know it. Or at least it is very hard to get back. They know they are part of the mainframe now, have no future outside of it, so their essence changes to become one who does whatever they can to gratify themselves now.

"What about a ghost?", I hear you ask. What has happened with their soul? I have not come across too many ghosts in my day, but my guess is that after the death of a person with much trauma, they may just ignore the white light completely, due to them experiencing so much pain still linked to the physical world. It is the unresolved trauma that keeps them here. But when a psychic goes to help with a ghost in someone's house they seem to tell them, "You should go to the white light. Yes, your grandma is there, go to the white light." The psychic thinks they have done something wonderful for this "lost soul," done what all the movies and TV shows have said to do. Yet, what they may have done is seal the ghost soul's fate. As long as the soul stays out of the white light, it seems it cannot be reincarnated. Once it hits the white light, it is in recycle mode, the memory wipe is up next, and back into a new body they go, for yet another round in clown world. Granted living as a ghost is not a great after-death choice either, however, knowing this we should try to offer the ghost another option.[76]

> "*If a man wishes to be sure of the road he's traveling on, then he must close his eyes and travel in the dark.*" St. John of the Cross

Then we come to a phrase, the "Dark Night of the Soul". Few really know what this is. Some suggest it is a psychological crisis, others a deep depression, others a part of the first alchemic stage of Nigredo, others what they call ego death (but they don't really know what that is either). None of these are real Dark Nights of the Soul, but difficult moments of possible change. The Dark Night of the Soul is the midpoint of going from one thing (human being in a real world) to another thing (observer of the human in a simulated holographic world). "In between" is the same chrysalis stage a caterpillar goes through before becoming a butterfly.

The Dark Night of the Soul was first phrased in the 16th century writings of St. John of the Cross. His text discusses the three stages of purification he went through, the first purged the senses, the second the spirit, while the final stage was an illumination and mystical union with God. For him it was the "pain" of the process of the purge. Today it is more presented as a type of spiritual darkness, where all one has believed about themselves and the world is falling apart. Because the word soul is attached to this term, the indication is that this crisis is being orchestrated by the real immortal part of us. That no matter how bad it is to endure, that something beyond little "me" is the one who has set up the conditions for it to occur. This type of presentation can be found in the writings of 19th century French nun St. Therese of Lisieux. The Dark Night can last a few days, a few months, or even several years. The length will depend how long

[76] So what to do if you come across a ghost? I don't know. This is not my area of specialty, and I do not want to advise "what to do." If I get in that situation again, and have to help a ghost-soul, I would tell it not to go to the white light. I might ask it if it sees other options for what it can do and where it can go. Can it get a lay of the land and see another option? Can the trauma be worked on, and somehow seen through enough to be put down and released?

the person (their mind and identity) fight the ramifications of what is being shown to them.[77]

I know I haven't specifically answered the question, "what is a soul?" What is the immortal part of us? How can a soul be trapped in matter, if it cannot be seen? The only way it would seem, would be energetically. If this is a place of energy, the soul must be energy, and to keep the soul in this reality, there must be a type of energy grid or energy structure that souls have trouble passing back through. Therefore, the Cave must have energetic barriers. As such, the control of our energy is another tool for us to work with. We should perform exercises to keep the loosh harvested from us as low as possible. We would also want to work on collecting and keeping our energy store, as we cross over at the time of death. To have this "ball of energy" available to be able to handle the challenges that might be thrown at us. This is where the practices of Qi Gong or Hatha Yoga can be helpful.

I cannot say that I know this for certain, but I intuit the main part of the soul is the Good God. An Essence that is Total and Absolute. There is only one Essence, and by this I mean Totality that which is outside of Plato's Cave, not the Demiurge who is normally presented as God 99% of the time. For some reason "The One" (God) split into various fragments. We think the soul is an individual fragment of that whole, but each of these fragments are whole and individual at the same time, like a hologram. Take the example of a jigsaw puzzle. If you have all the pieces put together you have the Soul. But some pieces became fragmented, and went outside the puzzle. They are still on the table, but they are not joined with the Whole. They are the Soul, but now by being apart from the whole, they are an individual part as well. Thus the individual soul is both a connection to the material us, and the whole at the same time. This might be the reason why there is a need for the harvesting of souls here, even though individual,

---

[77] F. Scott Fitzgerald added another area to think about with this subject when he wrote, "In a real dark night of the soul it is always three o'clock in the morning". Three o'clock in occult lore is also known as "the witching hour." It is at this one hour when alien abductions and demonic interference seem at their highest. I have experienced this myself. If I feel evil around me at night, if I can stay up to 4 AM, it tends to just disperse, and if I wake up in terror from a "nightmare," that tends to be somewhere between 3-4 AM. People today have come to falsely believe that the witching hour begins at midnight. Another trick to keep the human food source available at the "hour" the harvesters prefer.

souls contain the great power source of the Good God. I will continue working on what is a soul during my research.

C

THE BRIDGE

"What, if some day or night a demon were to steal after you into your loneliest loneliness and say to you: 'This life as you now live it and have lived it, you will have to live once more and innumerable times more' ... Would you not throw yourself down and gnash your teeth and curse the demon who spoke thus? Or have you once experienced a tremendous moment when you would have answered him: 'You are a god and never have I heard anything more divine." Friedrich Nietzsche, The Gay Science

14

CATHAR KATHARSIS

"Souls are prisoners of darkness, and they must fight to recover their original destiny, abandoning the body that imprisons them." Mani, originator of Manichaeism and perhaps Catharism 270AD

I have had various views of the Cathars over the last ten years. They have changed again after writing this chapter, one that ends with what could be considered a shocking historical thesis.

*

June 22, 1209
The Feast Day of the Magdalene
Languedoc, France

The town of Beziers is under siege. Troops of the Catholic world have been summoned by the Pope, led by several Cistercian monks and Northern French nobles. They are in the Languedoc to grab land from those in the south, and to exterminate a people. A people who believe in something different than what is being demanded from Rome. The Pope, Innocent III (a guy not very innocent) had other ideas. He wanted total control, and anyone who wanted to think on their own, even a group that called themselves True Christians, needed to be exterminated.[78]

---

[78] A very good book to discuss the detail and history of the persecution against the Cathars, which started long before 1209 is *The Lost Teachings of the Cathars* by Andrew Phillip Smith.

Within Beziers are believed 200 Cathar perfects (highest of the order), in a town ten times the Cathar population. The town has giant city walls and the people tend to feel safe even though the Crusader army, led by Cistercian abbot Arnaud Amaury, are gathered outside. The day previous, July 21, the Crusaders arrived and presented the town an ultimatum. Turn over the Cathars, or the whole town will be destroyed. The townsfolk could have complied, turned over the Cathars and have life go back to normal. Instead they chose to refuse the order, and "die as heretics, rather than to live as Christians."[79] When the crusading army asked its leader how they should figure out which were the townsfolk and which were the Cathars that needed to be killed, the abbot provided the command, "Kill them all - the Lord will recognize His own." It was no co-incidence that the massacre took place on July 22, the Feast Day of the Magdalene (whom the Cathars fully believed had lived in Southern France after the death of Christ, and was the true inheritor of his teachings). Pierre des Vaux-de-Cernat wrote in 1213, "B*eziers was taken on St Magdalene's Day. Oh supreme justice of Province... the heretics claimed that St. Mary was the concubine of Jesus Christ... it was therefore with just cause that these disgusting dogs were taken and massacred during the feast of the one they insulted.*"[80] It was a ritual slaughter on the ritual day of the Cathars. Going deeper, this Crusade was officially called on June 24, 1209, the feast day of John the Baptist. Thus this entire operation was really the forces of John the Baptist out to destroy symbolically, the Magdalene, and thus the connection to Jesus.

It is suggested that 20,000 people, mostly women and children, were slaughtered that day. It takes a long gruesome time to kill 20,000 people with swords and spears. This model was repeated over and over for the next forty years, butchering people and torching villages all across the Languedoc. And when the raids ended, the Church chose a new pressure, the Inquisition (to torture Cathars to confessing their sin, which was being a Cathar). But it all began here at Beziers. It was not just some so-called heretics who were exterminated this July 22, it was also what the day pointed towards. The Sacred Feminine, Sophia, the wisdom half of The Great Father. Today the city of Beziers has little to say about the slaughter, and the current churches there almost ignore it, presenting it as if it was

---

[79] Picknett and Prince *The Templar Revelation* pg 113

[80] Picknett and Prince *The Templar Revelation* pg 113, also from Wolff, Phillipe ed Documents Du L'Histoire du Languedoc.

more of a simple misunderstanding. Genocide is never a simple misunderstanding.[81]

The Cathars felt they had the right to live the way they choose, as humans dealing with an unjust world which they rejected, along with those who controlled it. Does this sound familiar in the year 2022? It should. What happened at Beziers is not an isolated tale of history, it is a repeating cycle that happens again and again when humans begin to figure things out about this reality. The Cathars were a group that had only one goal, to break the reincarnation cycle and not return. This chapter will show that the Cathar's did seem to have an understanding of how this realm is structured. The question we have to ask and answer is, did they actually understand how to exit it?

In the 1970s, a therapist in Bath, England named Arthur Guirdham began to come across several of his patients under regression who revealed past lives as Cathars. He wrote several books on the subject, and tried to speculate why so many reincarnated to Bath. Many more people over the last forty years have claimed to be reincarnated Cathars. If true, it causes some doubt for our inquiry. Since the only focus of the Cathars was to break the reincarnation cycle, and if so many reincarnated (well into the 1970s), that would seem like a large number of failures. Why did they reincarnate? Did the Cathars have the correct tools, but perhaps most of the followers did not use them? Or was the tool box empty, and no one realized it? If the Cathars did indeed break the reincarnation cycle, what was their percentage of success?

*

Similar to Plato's Cave, the Cathars are surrounded in misconceptions. Catharism is defined as "a Christian dualist movement that

---

[81] www.cathar.info author James McDonald. One of the questions we will get to in future chapters is: if the Cistercian monks were the ones who helped form the Knights Templar, and the Knights Templar were favorable to the Cathars, when the Cathars were attacked why were they not there to support them? Then exactly 100 years later, the Knights Templar would suffer the same fate. This story doesn't end in the 1300's but winds through paintings in the Renaissance, actions of Jean Olier in the 1600's, and eventually to the mystery of Rennes Le Chateau and its priest Berengere Sauniere between 1885-1920. All of it is linked back to the Cathar massacres, and as such, will be examined as this chapter and book continues.

thrived in some areas of Southern Europe between the 12th and 14th centuries." The major problem is that very little remains of information from the Cathars themselves, having had almost all of it burned during the Inquisition and Crusade against them. Most of the remaining documents were written by the Church about why they needed to be exterminated. That is like trying to get an insight of the Jewish population in Germany in the 1930s by only using surviving Nazi documents.[82] We know the ending, they became the first Christian group the Church of Rome instigated a crusade against. The Inquisition was first set up to torture Cathars, and they had to wear special yellow badges to identify them wherever they went.

We don't even know what they called themselves, "Cathar" being the term the Christian crusaders and inquisitors referred to them as. No one is even sure where they originated from. The historical suggestion is that the group had its roots in South East Europe with Bogomils, Paulinians and Manichaeans, who then traveled westward to Western Europe, eventually arriving in France around 1143.[83] The Cathars did not just appear by magic in 1143, what in the history is being ignored or suppressed? Of course this specific time frame of the Cathars appearance, the early 12th century, is also the time when the first Grail romances were being written, as well as the founding of the Knights Templar. There has to be some commonality for all these being "presented" by historians as happening at the same time in the same area. Perhaps the real story is not how groups from Eastern Europe moved West to France, but how much older groups from France slowly moved East. The French Cathars might be the origin of all the rest of what may be called European Gnostic groups.

---

[82] Almost everything known about the Cathars comes from confessions of "heretics" taken by Catholic clergy during the inquisition, which followed the Albigensian Crusade. Information on anything gained from severe torture cannot really be taken as a historical fact. There are a few texts from the Cathars themselves which were preserved by their opponents (the Ritual Cathare de Lyon or the Book of Two Principles) which give a glimpse of the inner workings of their faith, but these leave many questions unanswered.

[83] Early dualist groups found in South East Europe prior to 1000 AD. Another strong Cathar area of the period that is generally ignored, was Northern Italy That would mean the very area where the Renaissance happened in the 1400's was in a sense Cathar territory.

With no clear picture of the Cathars, many false beliefs began to be laid onto them. In the 1960's they were falsely classified as the first New Agers. Actually the New Age has taken it a step further, creating a belief in something they call the Cathar Prophecy, where a new Church of Love would appear to bring love and peace back to the entire world, ending divisions of nations. New Agers believe this is a real prophecy from 1244, but it actually comes from a dowser named Colin Bloy, who received a message while dowsing near Mount Segur in 1978.[84] To be honest if anything is opposite to Cathar thinking it would be this. They had no concepts of changing the world, just passing their message along so that every human soul could leave hell. Perhaps Bloy did receive a message, the question no one seems to be asking, is what entity or force was the one sending it?

Thus all that is claimed as fact about the Cathars must be set aside and a fresh examination started. What made a group of pacifists and vegetarians so dangerous to the Pope? Why were they one of the first groups in "modern times" to give women complete equality in just about everything, at a time when women in Catholicism were forbidden to read the Bible? What of the great secret treasure they were said to hold, with the suggestion of it being the Holy Grail? What of their connections to the other power group of Southern France, the Knights Templar, and an odd group known as Cagots (examined in the appendix), that continued well into the 1800s?

*

What's In A Name?

The name Cathar was the word used by the Catholic oppressors towards them, and is claimed to originate from "cathari," meaning pure in Medieval Latin. However, Nicolas Gouzy from the "Center of Cathar Studies" suggests that whatever word was used to define this group by Catholics, would have been done so as an insult. Therefore suggesting this group might be pure, is not necessarily the best way to present the people you want your crusaders to slaughter. You would want to dehumanize the group. Native Indians in North America were constantly referred to as

[84] https://mkmacinnes.com/2020/10/26/the-cathar-prophecy/, https://www.beckyprater.com/the-cathar-prophecy-of-1244-ad/

savages, to make the soldiers going to kill them believe they were destroying evil.[85]

There are other possible origins for the term Cathar. The Greek word katharsis means, "the process to release strong emotions, or to purge and cleanse." Another is a link to the German word meaning cat worshiper- as the cat was seen by church as the manifestation of evil. In fact, in Europe during the Middle Ages all the cats in a town were rounded up and burnt in giant fires on May 1st. At least that was until the rat population exploded causing the plague. Another possible origin for the word Cathar can be the Cabbalist word kether, which is the top sphere on the Tree of Life.

The term "the Albigensian Crusade", is used to describe the period of their destruction, thereby linking the event to the city of Albi in Southern France. This is odd, because although Albi was a main area the Cathars inhabited, the crusade first began in Beziers. Everything one comes across when looking into the story of the Cathars, has odd answers. In the few surviving Cathar texts, they refer to themselves as *Bons Hommes*- "Good Men" or "Good Christians".

Standard history claims the Cathars' final stand was at the fortress of Mount Segur, where on March 16, 1244, the remaining few hundred were burned at the stake; thereby signaling the end of the Cathars. The killing of the group at Mount Segur is true, but it was not the end of the Cathars. Research in the book *Yellow Cross* by Rene Weis, shows that the village of Montailou near Mount Segur still contained a large Cathar

[85] Cathari does appear in some Christian books before 1000 AD. St John Damascene's book *On Heresies* in the 8th century AD, notes of a sect called the "Cathari," based on earlier information written by Epiphanius of Salamis. He says of them: "They absolutely reject those who marry a second time, and reject the possibility of penance [that is, forgiveness of sins after baptism]". These are probably the same Cathari who are mentioned in Canon 8 of the First Ecumenical Council of Nicaea in the year 325, "*[I]f those called Cathari come over [to the faith], let them first make profession that they are willing to communicate [share full communion] with the twice-married, and grant pardon to those who have lapsed.*" So the first question to ask of course is, was this group in the Languedoc a unique group of people who the church placed this label on, in a sense comparing them with previous heretics, or was there one core group that lived and evolved throughout all of Europe?

population between the years 1290-1329.[86] So if the Cathars were not totally wiped out, what happened to them?

*

Cathar Beliefs[87]

(Cathar creation stories are found in chapter three)

Cathars called themselves True Christians, claiming to follow the original simple Christianity as presented by Christ. They rejected the Roman Church for its greed, and acquisition of land and wealth, for they felt Jesus preached to live a life of simplicity and poverty. They believed that Satan (Rex Mundi) was the author of the entire *Old Testament*, so they rejected most of it.[88] Their church services were simple, and could be held anywhere, usually in the open air or in a person's home. They rejected the need for churches at all, claiming them to be extravagances of wealth and control. Their priesthood (called Perfecti) was a pair of one man and one woman, who were expected to be pacifist, vegetarian, living a life of poverty and celibacy (at least not have children), and able to perform a ceremony called the Consolamentum for the regular followers. The equality of men and women was a very important element to them, and a direct requirement was that the priesthood was a male and female pair.

There were two segments of Cathars, the *Perfecti* and the *Credentes* (which were the main followers). Very little exists about what the beliefs and practices were for the Credentes (those who were believers but not yet perfected). It seems we know almost nothing about the lives of these average followers. Many websites and books suggest all sorts of possibilities from: they could be married, have children (and have sex, although having children was suggested against, because a new child would mean a new body for another trapped soul to be reincarnated into), eat meat and fight

---

[86] Some of the very few writings that have survived directly from the Cathars themselves from 1304 are preserved, and the four texts are known as the "Arques Sermons."
[87] Information sources used for this chapter can be found in the bibliography
[88] They claimed that Abraham, Isaac, Moses and John the Baptist were all servants of the Satan.

in wars. It is also presented that they were to follow the Ten Commandments (so fighting in wars would be a contradiction to "thou shalt not kill").

The Perfecti have more information about them. They referred to themselves as Bons Hommes (Good men).[89] They were more like a pair of traveling teacher-healers. They walked together around the countryside until they came across people who wanted their assistance, conversation or healing. When completed, they packed up and kept walking. They were not a married couple as most would think, but more like two halves of a whole, and it was through this completeness that they believed they could administer the Consolamentum. One part of missing information is about the inner world of the Perfecti. All similar groups in the past, had as a key element, information about what work was done within. This part is missing with the Perfecti, and is why I will give a short summary of a "similar group" (the Hesychians) at the end of this chapter.

One of the elements of the Perfecti were the tenants of what we today would call vegetarianism, and while they did not eat meat, cheese, eggs or milk they did eat fish. They did not abstain from eating meat because they cared about animals, but because animals reproduced via sex, and as such could become vessels for souls in the process of reincarnation. They ate fish because they believed at the time that they were born without any form of sexual intercourse, which seems to be a topic of confusion if fish reproduce sexually or not.[90] At the time the Catholic Church considered not eating meat a heresy, because God had given humans the Earth and put animals here for humans to eat.

---

[89] Each Cathar province was administered by a Bishop and two assistants (Filus Major [Greater son] and a Fillus Minor [Lesser son]). When a Bishop sensed his death was near, he would appoint the Filus Major as the new Bishop, and the Filus Minor would become the new Filus Major. A new Filus Minor would be elected by the Perfecti in the locality.

[90] My editor had this to comment, "This is in fact correct! Most fish reproduce through external fertilization (which is not through sexual intercourse, because it happens outside the male and female body). Are you confusing the concepts of "reproducing sexually" (which can happen internally [sexual intercourse] or externally [outside of the body] - depending on the animal) or "asexually" (which happens through fission, budding, fragmentation and parthenogenesis)?"

The final requirement to become a Perfecti (and in their view end the reincarnation cycle), was through experiencing the ceremony called the Consolamentum and then passing some probationary tests. After becoming Perfecti, they had to live a sinless life going forward. The Consolamentum was said to wash away all sin, but you could only have one in a lifetime, so once you took it, you were bound to the principles after that. It is why most Credentes would only take the ritual a week or two before death, as to make it easier to live only a few more weeks in a sinless state and not taint the ceremony.[91]

*

The beliefs surrounding Jesus also put them in conflict with the Roman Church. According to the Cathars, Jesus could not have been a divine being (the Son of God) sent here to die on the cross for their sins. If Jesus had been in a physical body, he had to be a fallen soul, and thus could not be the Son of God. Under this theory he could have been a regular human who became a Perfecti, and underwent his own process of Truth to become a teacher-healer. It is this belief about Jesus and his close connection (even sexual union) with Mary Magdalene, that may have used this model of twin Perfecti (Jesus and the Magdalene as the ultimate Perfecti) traveling the Earth to teach the gospel and heal.

A second belief about who Jesus could have been, was that the Good God did indeed send one of his souls into the materiel realm to help humans return home to Heaven. For this to happen, and for Jesus to still be the Son, he could not have been of the flesh (or Rex Mundi would had to have created him). So, the Cathars would have thought of Jesus as a holographic projection placed into this simulation, thus not having a real physical body. This implies that Jesus could not die on the cross for the sins of mankind, for he was not a person but a hologram- thus could not be

[91] One last part to consider is that of every religion in the world, the Cathars are about the only ones to not see suicide as bad. Given this is an evil world, one would want to return to the Source as quickly as possible. Of course, one would need to have "all their ducks in a row" or the death would be of no use. Generally, this suicide only happened later in life for example, if they found themselves ill, rather than have a long-contracted death, they chose instead what is called the "endura", to stop eating or drinking. This generally would happen right after the ill person (or those wanting to leave this realm because they knew the Inquisitors were after them), was given the consolamentum, because in their view without it, they would reincarnate.

born nor could he die. This could be part of the original myth of the virgin birth. Some groups of Cathars felt that Satan did not sit by idly with the holographic inserting of Jesus into this realm, so Satan himself inserted a hologram in the form of John the Baptist. Thus to many Cathars, John the Baptist was the antithesis to Jesus, for example, John performed his baptisms by water, as opposed to the how the Cathars believed Jesus baptized by the fire of the Holy Spirit (Pentecost). The Consolamentum can be seen as a ritualized form of the original Pentecost.[92]

Refusing the cross, led to one of the Church's great attacks against the Cathars. To the Cathars, the cross was all about Rex Mundi and his method of deception in this realm, and the cross would have represented time and space tied together. To be nailed to it would mean one is nailed into this material realm. They may have also understood that a cross, particularly a longer version as in Christianity, can be seen as six smaller squares laid out. When folded up these six squares become a cube (known as a hypercube). The black cube is the symbol of Saturn, which some researchers believe is the origin of the main energetic frequency that the Demiurge use to lock souls into the material realm. Also consider that since the cross can become a cube, it can be known by the number six. Jesus, along with two thieves were supposedly placed on crosses, that means three crosses, three cubes, or six six six. More food for thought.

*

As mentioned, the Cathars held women in equal status. Since our real essence was an androgynous soul, it made no difference if it incarnated into a male or female body. They discouraged the idea of marriage, but that was more because that union was encouraged to have reproduction, which to them was a sin for it allowed another material body to be formed via

---

[92] Douzet, Andre *Wanderings of the Grail*, pg 33, The Cathars were thus upset with everyone who used a baptism of water, which they felt was evil as opposed to the real baptism they kept alive in their tradition. There is speculation when John the Baptist appears in Tenier's paintings (such as with St. Anthony in the desert), he is in fact trying to tempt Anthony with a water baptism. Near Anthony the sticks are crossed, as if he is responding "No." It leads to a question, why then would Jesus accept a water baptism from John, if he knew he was his direct enemy in this realm? We will get to that further in the text. This dual message also is mirrored in the key statues at the entrance of Rennes Le Chateau church were John the Baptist and Jesus are together on one side, opposite the devil figure on the other with a checkerboard floor between them.

which another soul could get placed into the reincarnation cycle. If no more children were born, the cycle would have to stop on its own. The only marriage that mattered to Cathars was a "Spiritual Marriage" between themselves, their trapped soul and the Good God. However, it seems they did not reject the act of sex. They would have seen it the same as eating, a natural human process, and engaging in sex would be done for the most effective use of energy. Sex therefore, would have been about raising vibration or energy, which could be used as a wall to the intrusions of the archons.[93]

This period of time was also one of a type of poetry, centered on the ideals of what might in the language of the Languedoc, be called "fin amor" (courtly love). To experience non-sexual romance outside of marriage, ("amor" being the word for love). The reverse of the word is "roma" (the place of the Papacy). The concept of this type of love was to exemplify nobility and chivalry. Tales of knights appeared, who went on long quests in order to gain the favor of a woman. This literature, which was soon adopted by the Troubadours, wandering minstrels who performed the texts as plays or songs, was an experience between erotic desire and spiritual attainment. "A love at once illicit and morally elevating, passionate and disciplined, humiliating and exalting, human and transcendent".[94] This can also link to the ideas of the muse in Greek literature or the *sorror mysticae* in alchemy, presented in story form. This idea of courtly love becomes central to writers such as Geoffrey Chaucer (who wrote Pilgrim's Progress), Dante (whose love for an unattainable woman was his inspiration to write the *Divine Comedy*) and Chretien De Troyes, who wrote the first Grail romance in the late 1100s. Everything going on during this time period is connected.

That brings us to a couple of key questions about this time period. The most important is why did the Knights Templar[95] not help the Cathars?

---

[93] Using sex as a blocking technique to the archons as found in the *Nag Hammadi* texts.

[94] Wikipedia page on Courtly Love an quote taken from Newman, Francis *The Meaning of Courtly Love* pg vii

[95] Supposed seven wayward men from Province in Northern England, traveled to Jerusalem in 1099 AD and were given access to the Temple Mount, where they dug for several years. At some point they found something important, where the returned to Southern France and began their order. With the help of Cistercian leader Bernard of Clairveax (he who tried later to convert Cathars), the Pope to recognized the Templars with a Papal Bull in 1128. The Bull gave the group total

These were two very non-traditional groups, living in Southern France at exactly the same time, and as the research of Picknett and Prince show in *The Templar Revelation*, they at least got along and at best were interconnected. On the surface this connection seems odd. The Cathars hate property, yet the the Knights Templar are the ones who supposedly set up modern banking.[96] The Cathars were pacifists, while the Templars were killing knights. The Cathars hate the Church or Rome, while the Templars have a Papal Bull from the Pope. They at least have things in common. One is that they were both believed to have a treasure (suggested to be things such as: the Holy Grail, Ark of the Covenant, the Original Texts of Jesus etc.), and this secret relic claimed to give them immense power. The second commonality was that the Pope exterminate both groups, the Cathars in 1209, and the Templars in 1307, at least in Southern France. Both groups seem to have continued in various forms past those dates. I made a long video on the Templars, and although many researchers today attempt to paint them as early Freemasons, especially since the 1700s one of the masonic grades is Templar Knight, that might be incorrect. That has to do with the history the Templars and another group, the Knights Hospitalier (Knights of St. John of Malta). I have indicated that these two groups not only disliked each other, but they were at war. When the Templars were eliminated in the 14th century, it was the Knights of Malta who were given much of their land and importance. The Knights of Malta, now almost a private country with their own passports, are not what history makes them appear to be. I have no concrete proof of this theory, as much of it would have been erased and censored over time, but it indicates the Templars were far more likely to be on the side of the Cathars than their enemies.[97]

It is from these indications that there were suggestions that not only were the Cathars and Knights Templar linked, but they were the same group. It could also be said under this theory, that they were two sides of the same coin, different arms of a larger body. If so, why did the Templars not help the Cathars when they were being massacred? Why did they not step in and do something about it? They had a strong military. It would

---

authority to everyone and everything except the Pope. Supposedly set up as a force to protect pilgrims to the holy land, they became a force of warrior-monks, also claimed to have a secret.

[96] More a system of holding valuables for those going on pilgrimage to the Middle East, and then via a system of ciphered codes, able to access money at the other end. You can think of it as setting up the first American Express Travelers Checks.

[97] The history of the Templars will appear in a future book about Southern France.

seem natural to help your brother in a time of need, and there would be no bigger need than a time of genocide. Picknett and Prince gloss over this question as if they hope it would just go away in the reader's mind. But you have to answer this question as it is fundamental to understanding the whole story of the 1200s. If the Templars do not help in 1209, why not? Are they not linked, and seemingly connected to the same families? Is everything we know about the Templars wrong? What if another possibility is true, one that I will end this chapter with… Did the Pope go after the two groups at roughly the same time, not one hundred years apart?[98]

*

Books

Currently we have almost no books written by the Cathars. It is likely they existed, but were either burned during the Inquisition or hidden away. It was said the Cathars possessed a special secret text called the *Book of Love* (Mari, TARA). This mysterious manuscript is attributed to Jesus, who gave it to John the Divine. However, there may be a clue in the name of this book. The Egyptian name for the land of Egypt was Ta-Meri, the land of love. Thus the secret book may also be translated as, "From Egypt." To know this book, according to what was revealed when the Cathars subjected to torture, was that this book could grant one the ability to control the forces of nature. This is similar to Ancient Egyptian stories surrounding the *Book of Thoth*, another text no one has seemed to be able to find.

One Cathar book that does exist is known as the *The Book of the Two Principles.* The author is unknown, but it is speculated to be John of Luggio (a Cathar who lived in Northern Italy). It is a single manuscript that is now kept in the main library in Florence. It is written as an argument against the Roman Church about Catharism, and focuses on seven principles; Treatise on Free Will, On Creation, On Universal Signs, Instructions for Beginners, Against the Garatenses, On Free Will, On Persecutions.[99] It is a valuable overview of Cathar thinking, but still when I

---

[98] Another very odd group from Southern France, known as the Cagots (who were possible continuing Cathars) is presented in the appendix.
[99] Barnstone, William ed *The Gnostic Bible* pg 751, Owens, Lance http://www.gnosis.org website

read it, seems very simplified. There was a much greater teaching than what appeared in such a book, written for those who were not Cathars.

I might have come across the true "Cathar text" that has been hiding in plain sight all this time. What can be called Cathar thought is mirrored in *The Divine Comedy*, the great work of Dante in the early 1300s. It is normally analyzed as Dante's trip through the three realms of the afterlife, Hell, Purgatory and Heaven. I received my insight from a short sentence in my research notes, that the first stage of Dante's work Inferno (Hell) was not about some after-life experience, but was this Earth experience. I thought, that is a very Cather idea, so I looked deeper in the book. Dante might well have been a Cathar, and his text could be the great Cathar text of beliefs that has survived all this time, and is the story of Dante's personal experiences living those teachings. It could be the *Moby Dick* of the Medieval World.[100]

Dante was born in 1265 in Florence, which had been a center of the Cathars (who the Church did not persecute until nearly 1250). No logical explanation has been presented as to why the Italian Church would spend years destroying Cathars in France, but not in Italy. Dante thus had a likelihood of being influenced by this tradition, that was suggested to have survived in underground form. I wondered if Dante might have written it as a way to keep the Cathar ideas alive after their outward destruction. Just 150 years later, the Renaissance would sweep through the same city. Did the Renaissance flower due to the arrival of hermetic books from Constantinople (as history suggests) in the east, or could it be linked to a rising of hidden knowledge kept by remaining Cathars in Florence coming to light?

On re-reading Dante now, his three levels of moving through the after-death state, are the three levels of the alchemic process. His final stage might present the pathway through the traps of reincarnation, symbolized in this book by what he calls the celestial spheres. Passing them, one reaches the True God. Even more interesting is the Roman poet Virgil, he

---

[100] Related to the book *Spiritually Incorrect Enlightenment* by Jed Mckenna where he presents that the novel *Moby Dick*, is actually a journal of the spiritual journey Herman Melville was taking in real time. That is why Melville never rewrote it, it was his journey in novel form. It seems no one saw that until McKenna, just as no one might have seen the same in *Divine Comedy*, until now.

of the famous work Aeneid, who guides Dante through the first two layers. Dante's guide through the third layer is Beatrice, the love he could never have (a courtly 12th century type of love), who acts as a muse for Dante even though not physically present.[101] Everything about this masterpiece needs to be examined with fresh eyes, and I will be adding this to my work over the next six months. A full examination of Dante's book will come in 2023 either in Book 2 of this series, or as a separate work.

*

Consolamentum

This brings us to a most important Cathar ceremony, the Consolamentum, or Consolation. It was deemed the baptism of Holy Spirit by fire like the Pentecost (considered the real teaching of Christ), that was supposed to remove all sin once the ceremony concluded. As mentioned earlier, once you had a Consolamentum ceremony, you could not have another, because after completing the ceremony, one could no longer sin. Most would have this ceremony as death was approaching for the likelihood of further "sin" was greatly reduced. Another ceremony known as the *Convenenza*, a shortened Consolamentum, was performed for those before heading into battle. Only Perfecti could administer the Consolamentum, and from what has been preserved, it seems amazingly simple. It included the reading of several Biblical passages (with a focus on the Gospel of John, and the Lord's Prayer), many calls for the Good God to remove all sin, and ended with an experience referred to as "the laying of hands" upon the person. What is likely a complete version of this practice, as it is currently believed, can be found on the www.cathar.info website.[102]

We have to examine this far more deeply, because the focus of their religion was to avoid the reincarnation cycle. As Andre Douzet points out Cathars followed similar traditions of Ancient Egypt, "*The teachings was not focused on how someone lived (a good life or a bad life) it was more important as to how much of a knowledge of death did someone have. The right knowledge would turn death*

[101] Interestingly Dante's presentation of Beatrice as a guide, muse and teacher might have inspired Castaneda's ideas of what he called The Nagual Woman in his book *Eagles Gift*. When working on the *Divine Comedy* I will also keep an eye out for what Castaneda might have "borrowed" for his books.

[102] https://www.cathar.info/cathar_beliefs.htm#ceremonies, and more specifically the text of the ritual here https://www.cathar.info/doc_lyons_ritual.htm#melhormentum

into a positive experience."[103] How exactly would this ceremony help provide the knowledge needed to turn death into a doorway? I am not sure.

I have questions and concerns around this ceremony as presented. The first is that people were unable to do this on their own. They NEEDED THE ASSISSTANCE of Perfecti to perform it. That is my first red flag that something is amiss. Everything we need for our journey to Source and Totality is within us. At times those outside us can offer pointers or direct energy transmission, but you should never need someone else to break the reincarnation cycle. You, and only you, are the only one who can break the cycle. This presentation of this Cathar ceremony is more the way the Egyptian priesthood did things in New Kingdom Egypt, where they presented the need for an important mummification ceremony, and created the *Book of the Dead* text for the deceased. Of course, only the wealthy could afford this, and as such the process became a sort of back and forth between the elite (paying their way into Heaven) and the priests (becoming rich and powerful from being the only ones to provide it). At least in Cathar times there would be no money changing hands (from the Perfecti poverty vows), so the ceremony was available to all, be they rich or poor. But why could the people not break the reincarnation cycle on their own and need these texts read to them? Why not just read them yourself, contemplate hard on them, ask questions, then put what you find into practice?

Please read through the Consolamentum link above to see the ceremony in its entirety. How is someone else reading scriptures and laying hands on a body going to end the cycle? What good will it really do when faced with the experiences in the after-life? Such a ceremony might be nice, interesting or cause some contemplation. This might explain why so many Cathars seemed to keep reincarnating, because everyone was being tricked. Perhaps an unconscious trick, the Perfecti believed in this ceremony as much as the one having it. But just because you believe something, especially when it comes to exiting Plato's Cave, does not mean it will work.

The other possibility is that if there was a teaching or ceremony that did have a real impact, the Consolamentum was a false presentation to non-Cathars as to what they were doing. It was so important and secret that even those being tortured during the Inquisition didn't reveal it. Perhaps

[103] *Wanderings of the Grail,* Douzet

direct information was saved until just before death, on what exactly one would face in the after-death world, the likely traps to be laid, and how to avoid them – a complete "here is what you do after you die" crash course. The Secret Gospel of John does include information about the creation of this realm and the Demiurge. I would think Cathars though would have known some of this information early in their becoming a "member." Perhaps now a special insight of information along with the reading was given, the detail of how the archons and Demiurge would act in the after-death realm, and what to do about it. That could then make sense given the ceremony as it is laid out. But even then, there would be so little preparation time, I cannot see why "holding back" this information until just a few days before dying was indeed helpful.

I am not sure what else to say about this. If there were Cathars breaking the reincarnation cycle, they had to have some other ceremony or teaching. The Consolamentum as presented seems to me to be another piece in a long line of religious promises that would not pan out. Perhaps a full examination of the Holy Grail mythology (in Book 2) will give us clues as to what they were really doing.

*

The Links

The group claimed to be most directly connected as influences of the Cathars were the Bogomils of South-Eastern Europe. Little is known about them as well, other than they were also dualists (although they saw Satan and the Good God as brothers).–They rejected churches and the cross, saw Jesus as no more than a prophet and rejected marriage. However, they seem to have seen the body as a temple (opposite of Cathars) and developed various system of purifying the body via fasting, celebrating and dancing. An Inquisition/Crusade was called on them in 1291 and they did not last long after that.[104]

[104] https://en.wikipedia.org/wiki/Bogomilism

Other groups linked to the Cathars, can be examined if one is interested to go further such as: the Gnostics,[105] the Manicheans, Paulicians and Waldensians. I would like to share here another almost completely forgotten group, the Hesychians. The name derives from the word *hesychia* meaning "stillness, quiet or silence." Many link this group to the ideas of the Hermit, who spent much of their time in quiet contemplation of the "The Jesus Prayer." They were derided as navel gazers by opponents. In fact, the more I read about those who were followers of this practice, the more I felt they were Buddhists. If Buddhism were traveling westward its first stop would be in the Middle East and Turkey, which was the center of this group. In fact, I see them as Dzogchen Buddhists, as the focus for Hesychians was to reach a special inner created light, which likens to the "Clear Light of Dzogchen." I am including this group in a discussion of the Cathars because the Hesychians had three grades. The first was known as "Katharsis" (purification). Could the name Cathars have come from the word for those in early stages of the work (which would be the majority) who were spending much time purifying?

I mention the Hesychians, as they had a key text, *In Defense of the Holy Hesychasts* written by Gregory Panamas in 1344. The text, a defense he gives to Christian opponents, discusses their doctrine of the achievement of various inner experiences found via prayer, fasting and meditation. This inner experience of the work is missing in any standard overview of the Cathars. Again, if these early dualist groups had a layout similar to Buddhism (not at all saying they are Buddhist, just similar) then we can look to that system of teaching to perhaps help fill in the missing holes of the Cathars, and to get a more rounded or complete sense of what they might have believed. Not that I believe that Buddhism as it is currently taught, will really get anyone out of the reincarnation cycle, only make people feel better, more peaceful and see their mind better. All useful things in the dream, but not useful to exit the dream.

---

[105] I explore the Gnostics and their writings in Book 2

*

The Possible Secret

We come to an early "So What?" moment. Why have I just spent the last few pages discussing the Cathars if we cannot be sure they had the practices to exit the Cave? That is because by understanding the story of the Languedoc, from the Knights Templar, to the Cathars, and all the way to the mystery of Rennes Le Chateau, a great hidden secret of history might get overturned. I will present this thesis in full in a further book, but will share an overview of where this research is moving. Why is that important? Because it might allow us to dig into the core of this mystery (Western religion) and come out with the fundamental Truth that may help us to exit.

A key thesis of mine regarding the mystery of Southern France, is that the stories recorded in the *New Testament* and thought to have occurred in the Middle East, actually took place in Southern France, and perhaps a thousand years earlier.[106] Recall that Mont Segur is known by locals as Mount Tabor (where the transfiguration of Jesus in the *New Testament* took place). If the transfiguration actually took place at France's Mount Segur, it would make more sense why the Cathars would want to have a last stand there, and demand a final ceremony before they surrendered to be burnt on the Crusader's fires.

When you see the *New Testament* as a type of code, written to seem like it is taking place in the Middle East, but uses various "word play" to give direct indication to where these stories really occurred. Jesus of Nazareth and Galilee can become Jesus of Narbonne and Gaul for example. The area of Southern France in the early Roman era was Gallia Narbonesis. Paris has many similarities to what Jerusalem is supposed to be. The Pharisees become Paris-ees. I believe the entire *New Testament* (as a historical document) is in a misdirection code. If you can read the code, it becomes clear this is a French story. That could make the need for the Pope to eliminate groups such as the Cathars and Knights Templar more

---

[106] An early version of this theory ends my video series on the mysteries of Southern France on my YouTube channel: Howdie Mickoski Talks (assuming it still exists when you read this).

important, if they were in fact the direct descendants of the original disciples from teaching line of the real Jesus and the Magdalene in France. Why are so many Biblical figures buried in France, such as, Pontus Pilate (whose wife Claudia was from Narbonne), Herod, his wife and Salome all are said to have wound up in the Roman French city of St-Bertrand-de-Comminges, Joseph of Arimathea, Jesus' grandparents Joachim and Anne, Mary Magdalene and more. How did all of them cross the Mediterranean 2,000 years ago at a time with no airplanes or steamships, and all by some co-incidence, made it to France? How does Jesus's grandfather, Joachim, meet and marry a French girl from Normandy, Anne, in 100BC? People were not vacationing all over the world at that time, you generally lived and died where you were born. There are other Biblical figures who are said to be buried in Italy and Spain. None of this makes sense if they were all born and lived in the Middle East, however, it would make complete sense if they were all born, lived and died in France (or a country right next to it).

I have some other speculations to share. One is that the time frame of the Crusades against the Cathars and Knights Templar is different than presented, and it would explain why the Templars offered no direct help to the Cathars during the slaughter. If the groups had no common connection, this would make sense. If they did, then something is wrong with the history. The most powerful knights in Europe should have helped, and my making a slight historical adjustment, may explain this lack of Templar assistance.

This had developed for me out some alternative historical revisions that claim one thousand years was added to our history sometime in the 16th century. You could say that we are really in the year 1022 AD, but of course, no one really knows what year it is because of all of the changes our calendar has gone through. But if we squeeze 2,000 years of "expanded history" into 1,000 years of real history, a lot changes, and history could make more sense.

Standard history claims the Cathar Crusade occurred in 1209, followed by the Templar Crusade almost one hundred years later, in 1307. But what if the Templar Crusade really happened one hundred years early, in 1207? Then the Knights Templar Crusade would have occurred first, while the Cathar Crusade would have begun two years later. That would make more sense that the Church would go after the Templars first, to remove the most dangerous military group. Once the Templars were out of the picture, then you would go after the Cathars in 1209, and there would be no one left there to defend them. That makes logical sense. This idea of moving historical dates around is very important, as one of the key lies we have been under is the historical timeline we have been presented.

But if we put this story into a different 1,000 year context, it opens a new doorway of discovery. How many times prior to our 1700s we see dates presented on buildings and documents as J522 or I419. These letters indicate J or I for year of Jesus, and the year being "Jesus 522." That should be 522 AD in our dating system. After the change happened, it was easy to claim the I or J as a 1 and indicate the marked date was 1419, not the original J419. I have found several of these markings on buildings in Oslo. Since we do not fully know the timeline of how the original historical events occurred prior to the one thousand years being added to the calendar, we have to take some liberties. Again this is all just a theory. But sometimes "just a theory" tend to lead somewhere powerful. Sometimes not.

My question becomes, what if the way history was recreated in the 1600s was to combine two millenniums into one, by matching centuries. The original 100s were split into two new centuries, one part remaining in the 100s, while half of the events were moved to the new 1100s. The original 200s were split into 200's and 1200's. That would mean events in our historical calendar that are 1,000 years apart, such as 209 and 1209, happened in the same year x209. With this format the Cathar story happened in 209 AD. The Cathars now become direct descendant of the Gauls (by only a few hundred years) who themselves were direct descendants of the Druids, those who built the stone circles and standing stones of the area. That now puts their experience right in the heart of Ancient Rome.

Perhaps it was not a Pope as we think of them, who got rid of the heretics of France, but the spiritual wing of the Roman Emperors. Or perhaps a type of system of religious control at the Vatican was already taking place in Roman times and a type of Pope was already in place. The Roman Emperor ruled the land, while the Pope ruled the law.[107] There could have been a ruling Pope in this time, one who was the ruler of an early Christian-Greek-Mithras combination that was prior to the Christian religion we have come to know. The Christian religion was not fully created until the Council of Nicaea in 325. This council was set up by Constantine

---

[107] as kenneth scott suggests

in 325, and would make more sense to have occurred after the elimination of the Templars and Cathars, thus severing the direct links to the teaching of real Jesus, rather than 1000 years prior. With the direct line of witnesses eliminated, an entire new concept and document (*New Testament*) could be created. One which I will touch on in the final chapter as it may hold ties to our modern legal system and odd connections with a document known as the Last Will and Testament.

Here is the next leap...

What if Jesus lived in Southern France? And the Cathars lived in the time frame 100-200 AD? This could put the group, and the Knights Templar, perhaps just 100 years after the birth and death of this figure. Christ is not a proper name but a title, Jesus the Christ. Christ is the Greek word for anointed one, with the holy oil and thus made a high priest. As I have mentioned the *New Testament* we know may be a coded document to change the story of France. What if instead the title was Jesus the Cathar? Cathar a word meaning pure, and no matter how one views him as a divine or human figure, Jesus as presented could well be called a pure one. Followers of one called Christ would become Christians, while the followers of a man called Cathar, could be called Catharians (Cathars). This could be a reason the French Cathars considered themselves real Christians as they followed the direct teaching of a real man (and woman combined with the Magdalene), and lived in the exact locations of his life. The events of Jesus' life were the same towns, caves and rivers they too were living in. They were walking every moment of the day on Holy Ground. This would make sense for calling Cathar priests Perfecti, and for them traveling in pairs around the French countryside, the same as Jesus and Mary had done. Languedoc means language of oc (Occitan) which some have claimed was the original language of Jesus. Why would the original language of Jesus be the one that occurs in Southern France?

Since the story of John the Baptist has many similarities to Jesus (even being born of a virgin birth, being a teacher and a baptizer), Catholics placed his birth at June 24 which is the summer solstice, while Jesus is a winter solstice birth. John baptizes with water, which the Cathars rejected, while Jesus baptizes with fire. They are two sides of the same coin. Perhaps Cathars saw the Jesus in their texts (Gnostic in origin), as the real story, while the Jesus in the *New Testament* might be seen as John the Baptist. In the Christian tradition there is no difference between the two. This could explain why a statue of Jesus and John the Baptist are in front of the Rennes Le Chateau church (opposite a Rex Mundi statue), and why, at the alter both Mary and Joseph hold a child, as if Jesus was twins.

If the above is true, what if the knowledge escaped France in the 200s and moved east? Could what we call the "Nag Hammadi Codex" be the original French (well Occitian) teachings of the real Jesus, which had to be snuck out of France during the Crusade? Can this be what was smuggled out of Mount Segur in x244? Christ is not called by this name in the Nag Hammadi Codex but often by the term "Redeemer". What if the Nag Hammadi Codex is more of a bombshell than anyone ever thought?

If even *some* of what I am speculating here is true, it would explain so much more about the Cathars, their name, why the rulers in Rome needed to eliminate them and put a new religion in place that placed themselves at the center of the story going forward. It might explain what the Holy Grail is. Were these Crusades really against the Cathars and Templars, or against the very object (teaching) they both claimed to possess? This will be examined in detail in future chapters. And when we look into the story in Book 2 of Rennes Le Chateau in the 1880s, if priests Saunierre and Boudet discovered this story, and perhaps even the original burials and texts of this true period of Jesus and the Magdalene, everything that occurred between 1885-1917 would make more sense there.

*

I have presented this chapter for a reason. That is to look at our own belief structures. I have had to overturn a lot of beliefs in the research and writing of this chapter. I began this study by holding the Cathars on somewhat of a pedestal, believing that if the Catholic Church went to all that trouble to eliminate them, then they must have had the great secret of life. Perhaps that is true, for as you have seen, we know so little about this group or even that time frame of history. However, after doing all of the research my belief has gone back to a more 50-50 feeling about them. I am not certain what they did or didn't know, and I find myself back to a place of "I am not really sure any more about the Cathars, Knights Templar, or anything else about these periods of Southern France." This is a good thing, because it means there is open space for new information to come to the fore. The more confused I became, the more the door opened to ideas such as Dante's writings, the possible name of Jesus Cathar and others. If I only studied this topic for the next two or three years, and stayed in semi "unknown" mode, answers would likely appear. Of course along the way many things "not true" would pop into awareness as well, and each would have to be examined to see which pile they wind up in. But without the new space of "I don't know" created, not much more can happen.

Did the Cathars manage to find the exit to Plato's Cave? Perhaps. This goes back to my second chapter and the discussion of groups of the Cave system. The Cathars might have even been the direct descendants of the real Jesus, but like all groups, even if founded by a person who contains total knowledge, it only takes a generation or two for that knowledge to become twisted around and changed. No matter how well meaning the group, as soon as one gets exercises, leaders and expectations of "this is the only way to do it," another trap is set. Exiting the Cave and ending the reincarnation cycle, is a solitary business. I will say this again and again, the only one you can trust is yourself (your True Self, not the false selves that are masquerading as you), and the only savior you need is You. Outside forces are a giant wildcard in everything, and other people and groups can be helpful for a while, but if you group together, it will not take long to wind up stuck in another hole. You walk together for a while, always knowing that you must eventually release hands, and each find your own specific individual path, your own individual guidance. Some may argue that this is a "selfish" idea, we should be helping all humanity. You can assist a few along the way, but the process to get out is individualistic. Granted you help others by becoming free yourself. For each soul who exits, one less soul is trapped. That is how you help. You selfishly regain your sovereignty and freedom, and then make this realm "one less" congested deceived soul. The airplane safety message is always "put on your oxygen mask before assisting others."

As such, I reiterate: Don't rely on a group, an angel, a guide or anything. Rely on yourself, find your own path. Share your path with others on a similar journey, but as an "inspiration" that they can find their own way as well. Perhaps the previous sentence sums up why I have been writing this book, and maybe in a roundabout way, gives thanks to the

Cathar tradition. For by studying their success and failures, it has helped me find my own personal path, and my own personal tradition.

15

INFINITY'S INTENT

> "*It never occurs to us that death could come some afternoon, this afternoon.*" Proust

I thought for many days about what the best way to end this book would be. I realized I was writing a bridge between the two halves of a project - a summary of what has come before, and preparation for where Book 2 will be going. I picked up *Active Side of Infinity*, Carlos Castaneda's final novel, because I wanted to add a quotation about the mind parasites he presents in the chapter "Mud Shadows." I had not read this book in several years, and so took some time to flip through it. Admittedly, I got quite the surprise. *Active Side of Infinity* deals with the after-death realm, and not returning to the Earth. Granted it is written in a rather concealed way, using a variety of terms that on the surface make no sense to the reader. Once I began to piece together what was being shown in this book, especially the final three chapters, I knew presenting some of this information was the bridge I was looking for. I will not do a complete overview of Castaneda's novel, as that could fill another book due to the massive amount of content contained within it. If you are interested in a more complete examination, I suggest you read it for yourself.

*

Active Side of Infinity

The first interesting thing, is that Castaneda gives a new title for someone studying these teachings: a "warrior-traveler." Previously such a person had been called a warrior or a sorcerer in his novels. The fact that he has added the word "traveler" is important. Now one is no longer just studying the warrior's path (teachings to reach Totality and Freedom) in the materiel world, but what is learned is now meant to be taken traveling. Given that *Active Side of Infinity* has death as its foundation, this means the traveling being alluded to is in the after-death realm. This after-death realm could be what he calls "Infinity" in the book. Thus, the "Intent of Infinity" would be a pressure, if we can use such a word, that the after-death realm is constantly putting on us. Some force it seems wants everyone to be ready for this after-death experience, just few notice it or do anything about it.

The parts I feel are most important for those of you reading my book, comes at the beginning and ending. The first chapter (titled Introduction), relates the suggestion by Don Juan, that Carlos create an album of memorable life events. This is linked to the recapitulation, both of which were discussed earlier in this book in chapter six. These practices are to prepare a person for the after-death life review so that no surprises can be thrown at them from it. You can read this chapter in his book if you are looking for more information on the creation of the album.

What he calls the "Dark Sea of Awareness" is a term he has never used prior, but he does provide clues as to what this is. One of them is that the Dark Sea is related to the Eagle (Demiurge), our death and the recapitulation. Castaneda insinuates that at death the Dark Sea will eat our life force. Yet the claim is that the old sorcerers found that those who had done a complete life recapitulation while alive, did not get their life force eaten, only their life experiences. As such the Dark Sea wants the experiences and if we give it that, it will let us retain our life force (the energy we would need to exit). This is a critical point for us.

This lends our material world experience to being a type of experiment, because the main thing those who are running the experiment want is data. The Demiurge system wants loosh energy, but it also wants a complete record of all of our experiences so it can look it all over and see if the system is working optimally or not. A giant AI data mining project, and its storage point is likely what is called the Akashic Records, which in the spiritual community is believed to be, "a compendium of all universal events, thoughts, words, emotions and intent ever to have occurred in the past, present, or future in terms of all entities and life forms, not just human."[108] It is considered something spiritual and wonderful. What is really is, is a vault of data on how everything has expended their energy. In modern computer terminology, it's a giant "cloud storage system." The Akashic Records might be where the Eagle sends all that it has "eaten." The recapitulation releases our life experiences, which is what the Dark Sea and Eagle might really want from us.[109]

As the novel continues, winding through the telling of some very odd life experiences (that may or may not be factual), Castaneda explains that "Inner Silence" is an important part of the process. Defined as a place of quiet, where the parasitic mind is no longer interfering with our being. This was the original reason meditation was created. The problem was that over time, a practice that had great value, was turned into something else (trying to be happy, peaceful, blissful). Inner Silence to Castaneda are times of no parasitic influence, no energy harvesting. These moments seem to get stored in a separate battery within. A battery that the archons cannot touch. At a certain charge, this inner battery of power seems to be too much for the parasite, and the charge released causes the parasitic AI mind implanted in us to flee. We gain freedom from the work of Inner Silence, not peace or happiness.[110]

Death in the book is called "our unavoidable appointment," and it explains that people are not in any way ready. They have believed themselves to be immortal, and as such, do not put in any preparation. Those he calls "warrior-travelers" are the people who see they are "beings that are going to die," and thus prepare. You could say that in one sense the *Active Side of Infinity* is the writing Castaneda used as preparation for his own death.

> After "stopping the world," "S*orcerers returned to the true nature of humanity, and called it Total Freedom. It is the moment man the*

---

[108] https://en.wikipedia.org/wiki/Akashic_records
[109] Castaneda, *Active Side of Infinity*, pg 147
[110] Castaneda, *Active Side of Infinity* pg 103-104

slave becomes man the free being, capable of feats of perception that defy our linear imagination." Carlos Castaneda[111]

What he calls "man the slave," is a comment about what this reality is, a trap of unhappiness. Don Juan describes this metaphorically by commenting on a crappy hotel in a bad part of Los Angeles, "*That hotel over there, is to me the true representation of life on Earth for the average person. If you are lucky, or ruthless, you will get a room with the view of the street, where you will see this endless parade of human misery. If you're not that lucky, or that ruthless, you will get a room on the inside, with windows to the wall of the next building. Think of spending a lifetime torn between those two views, envying the view of the street if you're inside, and envying the view of the wall if you're on the outside, tired of looking out.*"[112] I have mentioned what he calls the "predator", or "mud shadow flyer" in chapter three, that is responsible for all of this and our energy harvests.

Castaneda wrote that, Don Juan described Earth as a "*station on their journey, for extraneous reasons which he didn't care to divulge at the time, the travelers had interrupted their voyage.*" While here on the Earth, "*Human beings were caught in a sort of eddy, a current that went in circles, giving them the impression of moving while they were, in essence, stationary... Sorcerers were the only opponents of whatever force kept human beings prisoners, and by means of their disciple sorcerers broke loose from its grip and continued their journey of awareness.*"[113] I have discussed this idea of a vortex earlier in this book, a type of time-loop that is constantly keeping our consciousness trapped in a material realm which keeps spinning back on itself. This is the symbol of the Ouroboros eating its tail.

Active Side of Infinity ends with Castaneda jumping off a cliff into an abyss (a deep canyon) and into Infinity. He does not die, but wakes up confused on his bed. I do not think he really jumped off a cliff, this is a metaphor for having set up some type of NDE or OBE, that would plunge him directly into the after-death realm. He did this to have a preparatory experience of what he was likely to face when the real moment arose. There have been many suggestions over the ages that this is what the granite boxes in Egypt's main pyramids were for, to promote this type of NDE experience. Before he jumps into "the abyss," he goes over with Don Juan his complete life recapitulation. This is showing Infinity that Castaneda had in fact completely reviewed his life, and thus has no more

[111] Castaneda, *Active Side of Infinity* pg 103-104
[112] Castaneda, Active *Side of Infinity* pg 107
[113] Castaneda, *Active Side of Infinity* pg 212

debts, ghosts or unseen parts of his past that are still lingering. He is entering Infinity free of all of the ties to his time in the material.

*

Astral Realms

> "*The popular idea is that someone can, after death, acquire unlimited knowledge from the astral world or other sources of higher spiritual development, and that these can be transferred through a psychic-medium to the living, is not true. In the astral plane, the deceased does not possess more knowledge than what he did while living, and if he could transmit something that would be what little he knew when alive.*" A. Papastavrou[114]

Given that the astral realm (after-death realm or Infinity) is a stop we need to have some knowledge of prior to death, I wanted to mention a few concepts here. This will be a major focus of my study heading into Book 2 of this work. In this realm we will no longer be in a physical body, or even our etheric body (sometimes called the aura); - we will be in our astral body. What is an astral body? This is exactly what I intend to find out experientially.

Angeliki Anagnostou in her interesting book *Can You stand the Truth? The Chronicle of Man's Imprisonment,* indicates that when in the astral realm there is only emotions. While a higher body does exist, due to its more logical presence, it cannot interact with the astral body. The physical form, which is also tied to logic is also severed, thus she claims there is very little logic in the astral. All things that occur here, do so by feeling. You feel or wish something, and it happens. Thus, in the astral you have to be ready to handle the emotions without logic. Is it no surprise that all the tricks played on the soul in the after-death state tend to include emotional pulls. The loving peaceful feeling of the white light, the joy of seeing dead grandma

[114] Anagnostou, *Can You Stand The Truth? The Chronicle of Man's Imprisonment: Last Call!* pg 201

or your dead dog again, Jesus or Buddha- all play on emotions. On the negative, we can find the presentation of guilt, shame and fear (also strong emotion) can force people to act in ways that logic would not recommend. In a confused, very emotional state, the newly deceased will do "what the light being tells them to." Does it surprise people that the soul contract is a big part of the astral realm, a deceptive and fraudulent proposition?

One other thing I want to mention, and this may be very important, is that reincarnating back here it seems, requires some type of agreement on our part. We cannot be forced to come back, we must agree. This might mean the astral realm is the only place of the lower realms, where we have real free will. I already discussed how it does not take long to see we do not have full free will in the material. Just as Commander Janeway, in the *Star Trek* episode "Coda" mentioned earlier, the aliens need us to agree with them. If we refuse, we stay in our power and can navigate our own course.

In Anagnostou's chapter "After Death Worlds," she discusses three realms which the soul traverses after death. The standard NDE experience we know of takes place in the first of these. Most who return to a body will stay in the first level, which is more of playing on emotions, overwhelming the deceased with love, or presenting how they "must be judged" for their actions. Yet as I continue this chapter, you may understand why chapter nine (non-standard NDE) needs to be closely examined, as they may be bridging these other, more terrifying levels of the after-death process. The "Gospel of Phillip" is the most examined text of the *Nag Hammadi* library. The normal focus is on its rather overt sexuality, and connection between Jesus and the Magdalene. However, there is more in this document, likely discussing these further astral realms. I present two translations of section #66 below.

> "*And so he dwells either in this world or in the resurrection or in the middle place. God forbid that I be found in there! In this world, there is good and evil. Its good things are not good, and its evil things not evil. But there is evil after this world which is truly evil - what is called "the middle". It is death.*" Gospel of Phillip 66[115]

[115] http://gnosis.org/naghamm/gop.html

"One is either of the world, or one is resurrected, or one is in the intermediate world (astral). God forbid that I be found there. In this world there is good and there is evil. What good is not all good, and what is evil is not all evil. But beyond this world there is something that is really evil: it is the intermediate world, the world of the dead." Gospel of Phillip 66[116]

According to Anagnostou, after the first level (judgment) there comes a second level where our negative emotional energy is eaten by the beings that live in that layer. This is the original Hades in Greek Mythology, which was transformed into Christian "Hell". It is not a place evil souls go, instead all souls who allow themselves to go into the recycle process go here for the next phase. No longer with a physical body to play out one's temptations and wants, these wants get magnified in the astral realm. This includes all the negative memories and temptations that have been stored in the astral body. This is what the beings who live here are waiting to eat. They may appear as hideous beasts (likely to generate even more astral fear), while they feast on the deceased soul's energies. Rudolf Steiner in *At The Gates of Spiritual Science* (chapter three), describes that at death one loses two corpses, their physical and etheric bodies. Two bodies continue, the astral and the ego. These do not make for a good combination in the after-death realm. He also discusses what he calls "gatekeepers," those that in Nag Hammadi language "demand a toll for souls to pass." That toll is one's individual energy and life force.

"How does a dead man feel? The material pleasure clings to the physical body... but the desire for pleasure remains even after death... The soul is like a wanderer in the desert, suffering from a burning thirst and looking for some spring at which to quench it; and the soul has to suffer this burning thirst because it has no organ or instrument for satisfying it. The soul is not tortured from outside, but has to suffer the torment of the desires it still has but cannot satisfy... Why does the soul have to endure this torment? The reason is that man has to wean himself gradually from these physical wishes and desires, so that the

[116] Found in Anagnostou, *Can You Stand The Truth? The Chronicle of Man's Imprisonment: Last Call!* pg 435

soul may free itself from the Earth, may purify and cleanse itself."
Rudolf Steiner[117]

Thus, it seems the greater our attachment to the physical and to sense pleasures, the more intense this "eating" in the second astral layer is going to be (is this why we are pushed and manipulated in this realm to focus on sense pleasures)? The two books of the dead, of Ancient Egypt and Tibet, describe these various hideous beings who are there to feed off our last bursts of negative, pleasure-seeking energies. Steiner describes them as "gatekeepers." All the beings that have been eating our negative energy while alive, will be there for this feeding.

The Gospel of Philip warns that the archons will try to "*seize him and throttle him.*" Therefore, one of the ways past them is to no longer be tied to the pleasures found in the material realm (which was the original temptation, according to the Cathars, for being tricked by the Demiurge into this realm in the first place). *"Fear not the flesh nor love it. If you fear it, it will gain mastery over you. If you love it, it will swallow and paralyze you."* Gospel of Phillip 65[118]

But there is a third level past Hades. If one has not managed to let go of the gatekeepers by then, Anagnostou suggests one enters a third realm, a more spiritual realm. One will think this will be a place of peace and Heaven, and finally they can experience God and love. Not so. This is where the final "feeding" takes place, this time by beings who appear loving and caring, but they eat all of our "positive, spiritual and loving" emotions from our time on Earth stored in our astral body. You might say that all the emotions put into prayer and ceremony (to beings outside of ourself) are being eaten now. Do you see why I have spent so much time discussing not praying or worshiping anything outside yourself, even if it seems "good and loving" when connecting to it? You might well find out the hard way that it is just false light beings who reside in this highest level, and you are setting up a great final feast for them.

This has got me thinking. Are the prayers people normally make going to these higher beings in this third, and more spiritual astral realm?

---

[117] Steiner, Rudolf *At The Gates of Spiritual Science*, "chapter three"
https://rsarchive.org/Lectures/GA095/English/RSPAP1986/19060824p01.html
[118] http://gnosis.org/naghamm/gop.html

Do they answer our prayers, knowing that the payment for doing so (as a stored energy token) will be coming after our death? Is that why they allow some people here to become great healers via prayer to them? The stored energy tokens, perhaps not just of the healer but the patient who got healed, are eaten as a type of payment after death. People get the healing in the material they need, so they can keep on with their material focused, desire filled life. That lends to another question, how do we pray so there are no energy "tokens" that have to be paid later to some astral being, yet the people that need help or healing still can get it "tax free" you might say? As many answers appear in all of this, so do more questions. But these are important, as we learn the various levels our loosh energy is going to get eaten after death.

When this has been eaten, the energy transfer is complete. You have been devoured... the Moon has been fed, and you can be sent completely to the light to be recycled to a new body and start the cycle all over again. A new seed gets planted, watered, cared for and grown, so it is ripe for the next harvest.[119] That is our story and new babies in this analogy could be thought of as "seeds." No one seems to see that the only thing that cannot be eaten, is that which is beyond positive and negative, that which is rooted in the Pleroma of the Good God. The place of True Inner Silence.

It is good to be reminded that energy only exists in the material realm. What we call energy does not exist in the Pleroma, at least the energy that involves the physical, etheric and astral realms: the matrix. It is a construct of the simulation, for energy is injected into and then consumed by the system. It is the reason for all of the layers of control, systems of order and authority we have in this physical realm - it is for the control of energy and the packaging of this energy in preparation for the later harvest. From the ideas of money, to the levels of government and religion, it is all about this inter-connection between the physical and astral. When our focus is on "that which is beyond all energy," we become as Castaneda claimed, "unpalatable" to the harvesters. We work to make us an uninteresting a meal as possible in the astral realm, with the hope they will just bypass us. However, we still have to also prepare for the Q&A.

One area that caught my attention twenty years ago in my research was that both the *Egyptian Book of the Dead* and the *Apocalypse of James*

---

[119] Anagnostou, *Can You Stand The Truth? The Chronicle of Man's Imprisonment: Last Call!* pg 443

(snippet found in the appendix) discuss that a question-and-answer session in the after-death realm will take place. This is between the soul and the archons (gatekeepers, toll takers, soul eaters). My guess of what happens, is the archons will ask questions (often while taking hideous forms to scare and torment the deceased), waiting for "incorrect" answers born from "ignorance." I would also guess that these "incorrect" answers are taken as a type of "agreement" the archons can eat. However, by answering "correctly", in ways where one knows their true origin and thus is "uneatable," these archon gatekeepers have to let us pass.

A shorter version of the exchange can be found in the *Gospel of Phillip* (50) where Jesus remarks on how to answer the where do you come from question, "*say, we are born of the Light, there, where Light is born of Light...if they ask who you are say: We are its children, the Beloved of the Father, the living one.*" This Light is not the white light or false light, it is the Father, the Pleroma, the Goodness beyond the Demiurge's matrix. I have put the entire relevant part of the *Apocalypse of James* in the appendix so that longer exchange can be studied in some detail. It gives the same message as the Phillip text above, just with more specific answers.

The above text might be hard to understand. Book 2 will have more detail on this exchange, but for now the main idea is that by saying you are "of the Father", you are really a divine spark of the Good God. By saying a "son in the Pre Existent one," (the Pleroma), you are saying that all of these archons (including the Demiurge himself) are not from the Pleroma, they exist only here in the simulation, and thus have no power over you. You belong Home and they have to let you go. This back and forth also indicates that you know the world you have lived in, incarnation after incarnation, is a false realm - a simulated computer realm, and you know the story of its creation. Thus, the total knowing of the layers of the matrix is a key part to being able to pass the archon gatekeepers and exit. Like I said, I am just giving an overview here, there is more to present about this in Book 2.

So where does this leave us? We see a few pieces of information have come from this book, and this final chapter. One is to be sovereign, to not put our power or authority on anything outside ourself. To see we have all the power within. Doing so will begin to control our energy. We start to prepare for the after-death realms by having done some form of recapitulation (so no parts of our lives hidden can be thrown at us in the judgment stage). We prepare to be aware that in the astral realm, we will be dealing with an emotional based place. We have something prepared especially for us just before death (preferably with spoken words, as hearing is the last sense to go prior to death) - words of wisdom to keep us prepared for what comes next. We refuse all judgments. These archonic beings are in no way more powerful than you, wiser than you, and they have no authority other than what you give to them. Revoke all power and authority to them and keep it for yourself. The judgment will end. We know the story of the matrix, the lies of the matrix, and the lies of the material and if we keep those clear as we cross, we prepare to not be drawn into the "clay."

Anagnostou's book has one main suggestion for how to break the trap. For her it is to focus on the idea that Jesus came into the materiel to pay our karmic ransom and all we have to know is that, and the archons will let us free. "*Now do you understand why Jesus Christ came, and which 'archon' He is still trying to rescue you from? Do you understand which 'lords' He came to 'pay off,' asking for your Salvation in return, offering the energy they have long waited for from the sap of the pain His Sacrifice poured out.*"[120]

As I mentioned way back at the Note page that started this entire book, I do not know for sure what will happen after we die, or what the entire process of this simulation means. All is a riddle meant to be cracked. Generally I tend to not agree with ideas of "how to exit" that are based on a simple faith component. Especially on a figure no one has any proof existed, and if He did, when and where he existed (as my Cathar chapter points out). That does not mean I will reject such a theory either, all are open for examination. She does a good job taking us to the step of seeing the deepest levels of this process, and our job is to do the work to know what it is we have to do at this stage.

I have come to see now that the basis for an exit involves some interaction of a type of individual sovereignty, knowledge of the life and death, knowledge that the "gatekeepers" only have the authority and power we give them, that the recapitulation has cleansed us of ties to our past- especially guilt and shame, and that we can stay clear and aware in an astral realm ruled by emotion (can we keep a link to highest part of the Self which has complete clear thinking free of emotions?) It is also possible that the concept known as the "Warrior's Unit" that Castaneda writes of in his

[120] Anagnostou, *Can You Stand The Truth? The Chronicle of Man's Imprisonment: Last Call!* pg 456

book the *Eagle's Gift,* could be another way of exiting the Cave, adding a group dynamic to the individual work. This is another area I have forty pages of notes on, and requires further exploration.

You can see where this research will be heading in Book 2. This overview needed to be presented, so that you can begin to contemplate in a deep way "what is really going to happen after I die, and how can I best prepare for it?"

*

Death Terms

Given that this is a book which touches the experience of death we will all face in our lives, I wanted to mention a few parts of the "secular worldly" part of it. And it tends to not be what we think it is.

Think of the phrases we have for death, "rest in peace" can sound like "rest in pieces" thus not whole. "Consecrated ground" is a place made spiritually pure for burial. What does that mean? Whose idea of pure, and why does my body need to go to such a place? It's just a body? How about the phrase "he or she is in a better place." How do you know? Everyone first of all thinks, if someone has died, they are in Heaven. No one says, "my uncle Jim is definitely in Hell now. Oh ya, burning away." This idea of being in a better place is a cognitive dissonance patch, a way to say we really have no idea what is going on after death, so I will just pretend it is all wonderful so I don't have to think about it anymore.

Lastly, I want to point out that on pages 191, 207, 227 and 241 of *Active Side of Infinity* (2000 edition), Castaneda makes various legal references. I do not think this is just simple symbolism, I believe there is a message here to look into legal matters. I have done so myself. It began with looking into the document known as the "Last Will and Testament."

I am going to give you a few questions to go over. Be careful. Don't think you know these answers. Really contemplate the questions.

Why is it labeled with the words "will" and "testament?" Do you know what those words mean in a legal setting? Why are the books of the Bible known as the *Old Testament*, and *New Testament*? Why is the intent of God called "God's Will?" Why is the document we sign concerned about what happens to our "possessions?" What possessions are they referring to, as when someone is overtaken with demons they are said to be "possessed." Why is Jesus identified as a Testator (one who signs a Will document) in Hebrews 9 15-28? This section of the Bible is also known as the "Last Will of Christ." By signing a Will and Testament that we make, does Jesus become the actual signer of our will? See the footnote here for a fascinating look into these subjects.[121]

I have come to see that this document is nothing like we have ever thought it might be. It is a contract, but we have to ask deeply, a contract between what and what, or who and who? And what for? I sense now it is a spiritual soul document (as was presented in old Medieval Will such as Shakespeare's) not about material goods and how we are buried. I want to be clear; I am not a lawyer. Perhaps a reader out there who knows trust and estate law could help clear up some areas? I will continue to examine this subject for Book 2, all I wanted to do is lay out the questions that came to me in this study, and perhaps it will lead you down the same path it did for me, that it is some type of spiritual document made to look like a material one.

"*Die while you are alive, and be absolutely dead. Then do whatever you want, it's all good.*" Bunyan

Shamans have claimed that if we want to live well, we have to make death our best friend. Granted they do not mean it in the way this book has been discussing it, that is, preparing to go past the Demiurge and archons to freedom. They mean it in a way of how make one's life filled with power and vitality. In that respect, they are correct. While death is the force that ends life, it is not something to be afraid of, instead it should be used to initiate action. Time is limited, not just for us, but also for everyone we know. I had but a year of time to know Joan, my ex-girlfriend murdered in

[121] http://sermoncentral.com/sermons/god-s-last-will-and-testament-sean-lester-sermon-on-knowing-god-s-will-100788, biblehub.com/sermons/auth/morris/christ%27s_last_will_and_testament.htm, christiancourier.com/articles/739-the-last-will-and-testament-of-jesus-christ

1994. If I had known I would only have a year with her on the day we first met, I would have undoubtedly spent my time with her differently. If we take the knowledge of how limited time here is, petty feuds and conflicts would just end. Of course, a few arguments and conflicts would still be there, but all the petty ones would just cease. That is part of the shaman's point of using death to live.

Death has value in this material realm, and I would recommend embracing the fact of your limited time here, so you can live fully. It is useful to remember that Christian monks kept their personal coffins in the cells where they slept, as a constant reminder of their own inevitable death, to not be lazy and to intensify their spiritual practice while they were still alive.

However, this book has been about something else. Death is a doorway, our transformation portal. When we come to the hole in the roof of the Pantheon, Home is but a few yards above us. But it is at this point, that we will likely be blocked. The after-death system is not happy about anyone getting close to exiting. It will spring the usual traps: white light, contracts, guilt, fear, hope... whatever they think is going to suck us back down to the Pantheon floor. We need to focus on our death, to prepare for this very moment.

For all the possible illness and manipulation that came from my canyon death experience in 2005, I am still grateful for having had a taste of death. For me it was the sense of seeing everything I had classified as myself: body, mind, thoughts, experiences, hopes and dreams, was of a simulated person in a simulated reality. I am also grateful for the download I received, all the information which over time became *Exposing the Expositions* and this book. I am not as grateful for the archon manipulation that came afterwards, but hey, it's a dual realm! Ironically, the end result of all the manipulation had the opposite effect of what was intended, and instead the experience just helped me get very clear about not wanting to be back in this nuthouse ever again.

As we move to a conclusion, I thought I would share a personal story I have never told before.

In 1999, very early in my research journey and long before I wrote any books or was deep in any subject beyond the study of Ancient Egypt, I met a woman. I will keep her name private, but she believed clearly that this was her last incarnation on earth and she was spending it mostly in viewing mode. We had an interaction I have never forgotten. We had gone out a few times, and while I enjoyed spending some time with her, I never really felt for her in a "deeply romantic kind of way," and I made that quite clear to her.

Nevertheless, one night we were out and I said to her bluntly, "*I don't understand why you want to keep spending so much time with me.*"

She looked me square in the eyes and responded, "*Don't you know who you are?*"

"*No. Who am I?*"

She took a step back, and shook her head slightly as if she were trying to make sense of my confusion. "*I am spending time with you, because later on I want to say that I knew you before.*"

Now I was confused. "*Before what?*"

She placed a hand on my arm and in one of the softest voices I have ever heard, she said, "*Just before.*"

I share this story, not to try and present that I am somehow special or important,–but to remind you that no matter where we are on our current path towards Truth and Wisdom, there is always the possibility that we can go further. Even if we cannot see where we might arrive, sometimes others can.[122]

Even if we exit Plato's Cave, I do not believe the journey to Totality is over, just that we have gotten out of the place we are currently stuck in. Imagine a leaf moving down a river on the water. It will continue its journey until it comes to a small whirlpool where it gets caught. It just spins around and around, and although it seems like much is happening, the leaf in fact is going nowhere. It will stay in that vortex until the water current changes. If all stays stable in the river, the leaf will just keep spinning. But if the current shifts, so too would the vortex, and the leaf would break free. Then it will just go back to continuing its journey along

[122] I have another, almost similar story from a few years later, but will keep that one private for now.

the river. It is about as good a metaphor for our experience here as I can think of. The question then becomes, what are the conditions that keep the vortex we are stuck in, constantly running?

As we come to end of this Book 1, which is the first half of what I am calling the Complete Work (Books 1 and 2), I wanted to point towards where the research is headed. Some of the areas to expect upcoming examination are:

Karma, Sin and Free Will, Gender and Sexuality, Tricks of Language, Gnosticism, The Afterlife and the Astral Realm, Contracts, The Holy Grail, and The Nagual's Unit. One area that is getting extra attention now is the idea that our simulated reality is also caught in a type of time-loop, so not only how does the loop function but also what are the "time factors" (beginning and end time wise) of that loop.

*

A Bite

I was dreaming. Dreaming that I was a great beast, a green lion of incredible strength. And I was eating. Ripping apart my capture, my meal. But it was not the flesh of another animal that I was tearing through, it was something else. It was the Sun. And with each bite, another ray was being integrated with my form, infusing my inner lion-body with power. Blood dripped from my lips... "Where does blood come from in the Sun?" I wondered. Why was I eating the Sun? Then a thought appeared ever so briefly, "because it is the only way to stop it from continuing to eat me."

It is why one of the key alchemic images is the green lion eating the Sun. Almost no one outwardly seems to understand what this means. It has nothing to do with psychology, energy, or the transmutation of metal to gold. The green lion (our inner green man, link to nature) eats the Sun (Demiurge) to stop the cycle of it eating our soul energy. The green lion also gains total knowledge by eating the Sun, for then one will have the complete story of how this reality was born and functions, and as such, can no longer be tricked. The blood drips for he is killing the entire matrix system. It is why we see the Sun move down into his body. He is now the

Sun, not as the new Demiurge, but knowing all of this creation in its totality. Because of this; there is nothing to trap him here or in the post death astral realms. Our soul to continue as the warrior-traveler it was meant to be.

This book is, in its own way, my Moby Dick, taking me into the fourth alchemic stage of (Rubedo), the one almost never written about in old alchemic texts, only appearing as symbolic images. It won't wind up as any sort of literary genius, nor will it win any awards. But just like Herman Melville, this writing is intended to end my final delusions. I see there is no time to wait to do this, as the next reset is likely upon us. I do this to regain my Power and Totality of the Self and Soul, make it through the exit to go beyond, continue on the journey the Earth simulation tricked me into stopping from, and return to my Real Home.

APPENDIX

Appendix 1

Spiritual Armor

I am going to quote from the ending of Ephesians. Most of this section of verses is actually misdirection. A whole bunch of nonsense about slaves, and mothers and fathers, verses to get people to bow down and be controlled by authority. Then near the end of section six a few verses appear. It is like they were just dropped in from somewhere else. Or more likely there was a much longer text that made up what this was about, that gave real background as to why the text begins to discuss "spiritual armor" since nothing there is any warm up for it. As such we have to take them as they are, and not really knowing what actual context they are supposed to fit in. None the less they have value to where we are.

10

Finally, be strong in the Lord and in his mighty power.

11

Put on the full armor of God so that you can take your stand against the devil's schemes.

12

For our struggle is not against flesh and blood, but against the rulers, against the authorities, against the powers of this dark world and against the spiritual forces of evil in the heavenly realms.

13

Therefore put on the full armor of God, so that when the day of evil comes, you may be able to stand your ground, and after you have done everything, to stand.

14

Stand firm then, with the belt of truth buckled around your waist, with the breastplate of righteousness in place,

15

and with your feet fitted with the readiness that comes from the gospel of peace.

16

In addition to all this, take up the shield of faith, with which you can extinguish all the flaming arrows of the evil one.

17

Take the helmet of salvation and the sword of the Spirit, which is the word of God.

18

And pray in the Spirit on all occasions with all kinds of prayers and requests. With this in mind, be alert and always keep on praying for all the saints.

19

Pray also for me, that whenever I open my mouth, words may be given me so that I will fearlessly make known the mystery of the gospel,

20

for which I am an ambassador in chains. Pray that I may declare it fearlessly, as I should.

Appendix 2
Movie Additions

I now take a look at more movies (and the TV shows *Lost* and *Star Trek Voyageur*) to give more clues into understanding Plato's Cave, and if the analogy has been well presented in mainstream entertainment.

*

Inception

The movie inception came out in 2010. People are still trying to determine when in this movie, was "reality," and when the main character Dom Cobb, played by Leo DiCaprio) was dreaming. The trick is to see that the entire movie is a dream. There are just dreams within dreams going on, or levels of it within levels. Then the movie will begin to make more sense.

The movie has two subtle twists, one in the movie plot, and another on the viewer watching. The movie's ending revolves (no pun intended) on an object called a Totem, a special hand-made device that one creates and can never let anyone else touch. By using this specific item one can tell if they are dreaming or not dreaming. There is a big scene at the end of the movie when the spinning top that Cobb is using seems about to fall over, thus showing he is not dreaming, which indicate on the surface that he gets to live with his children happily ever after. But is that true? This is the biggest thing missed by most. The top is not HIS totem, but his wife's. So why is he spinning his wife's totem and not his own? The only thing the spinning top would tell is if his wife is dreaming, not him. Perhaps that is the point. At the end he was not testing his reality (maybe he knew he was dreaming), he was only testing if he was in his wife's dream thus, she could bother and influence him. In a sense he gave up his search for reality and truth to play make-believe with his make-believe children, but without interference from his former wife. That changes the ending a ton does it not?

Another insight about his dream existence comes during the meeting in Paris between Cobb, and who we can assume is his wife's father. The first question, why not just bring the kids to Paris to see him? Seems simple, only in dreams does simple become so complex. Secondly why does the father give in to his son so easily? He gives a clue when he tells Cobb, "Come back to reality Dom." In a sense it appears the inception (implanting of an idea) is not going to be on the individual that Cobb is hired for, but is all part of a grander plan by the father to implant into Dom, the idea that the world he is living in is real. And as such the same Inception is being played out in the minds of everyone watching it as well. That the world "we" live in, is also real and should not be tested as a dreamworld by us. The main inception in the movie is the father doing it to Cobb.

In Mombasa, Cobb is involved in a chase. Cobal agents come after him out of nowhere. Cobal is not a company out there, but a part of his own subconscious, a protector to his own deep memories. See how similar the name Cobb and Cobal is. As he is running, the walls close in on a passageway. Real streets are not built like this, only in a dream can this happen. He is running in a labyrinth.[123] He gets squeezed out, and jumps right to where his Japanese friend happens to have a car waiting to whisk him off to safety, again like in a dream, or as if all of these other characters have been implanted into Cobb's mind.

When he is with his wife Cobb says, "If I am ever going to see their faces (children) I have to get back to the real world." The inception is happening here, as he is determining that if he sees his children's faces, he must be in the "real world" and no longer needs testing. This is the same mistake that Neo makes in the *Matrix* movie. He wakes up from his Matrix life as Mr. Anderson, but never tests out if the world of Morpheus, Trinity, Zion and the ship is true, or another dream. He simply accepts his new reality too easily. Cobb's wife also says, "Our world wasn't real (her life in dreaming), to get back to reality we had to kill ourselves (as apparently dying within a dream only wakes one up according to the movie). Our children were just projections." The basic principle here was to present the wife as crazy. As she wanted to kill herself in the supposed "real" world by jumping off the ledge, and thus get to the next layer where her real children

[123] Of course, there are some points about the Minoan story of the labyrinth, Adrianne (she who helps Theseus out after he killed the Minotaur) but those are specific analogies and best to look at those later yourself.

would be. This is where the audience is getting an inception, planting the idea that anyone who says THIS world, the one in which you are watching this movie, is not real must be crazy, and in fact might be dangerous.

The most important part of this movie takes place when he "wakes up" on the plane near the end of the movie. He is in his seat and seemingly no one knows each other on the plane, or at least they all seem to ignore him. If they were such a great team, and Cobb thought to be dead, had somehow made this miraculous escape, should they not have been thrilled their great leader was back? They are on a private jet, they were not going to annoy any sleeping "normies" in their seats, it is just them on the plane. In the airport he again seems disoriented, and none of his companions are talking with him. They just went through supposedly the greatest mental espionage act of all time, yet they are acting as if they met once in a McDonalds thirty years ago. The immigration official says "welcome home." Why would he say that? Then there is the Paris father, standing waiting. How could he possibly know he would be on that plane, and that he would in fact get into the US? This again could only be because Cobb is dreaming, and the father is keeping up his job to fool Dom into believing the world they are currently in is a real world. Never once did Cobb ask, "why are you here, how did you know I was coming." Just like in a dream the most bizarre things are automatically accepted and unquestioned. The purple elephant driving the bus full of lions and monkeys makes perfect sense in a dream.

And perhaps that is the point of our strange dreaming experiences. They may be some sort of insert (a David from Pleasantville), trying by the use of the oddest symbolism and experience, to get us to start asking on waking, wait a minute, why are things like this? Then again, our dream images could be inserts of control, trying to inception us into believing or feeling something, that a force outside of us wants us to experience in order to trap or control us. As such our dream experiences need to be carefully examined for what is dark, light or simple conscious stuff arising.

One final criticism of this movie, and that goes for the recent TV show *Westworld*, is the total lack of humor. Not once in *Inception* was there ever a time I thought of laughing or even chuckling. That was a part of what made *Lost* such a good program, *Lost* used the Hurley character, and to some extent Sawyer, to add an element of humor at times to what is essentially a dark story. *Inception* desperately needed a character like Hurley, to lighten the mood, and at the same time- get us to see through the veil of reality via the side of lightness and not always through heaviness.

*

They Live

One of the best movies to discuss this entire avenue of control, conspiracy and aliens is the movie *They Live*, adapted from the Ray Nelson short story "*8 O'clock in the Morning*." In this film, Rowdy Rody Piper plays the character John Nada (Spanish for nothing) who will find that the reality around him is not as he has always thought it was.

The movie begins in a dystopian world with Piper meeting a crazy blind preacher on the street, talking about how "they" have everyone under control. Most would just walk past the crazy person, but something in Piper causes him to stop and take a listen. All of a sudden, the police arrive and haul off the preacher. Why is a blind preacher so dangerous? It is because the police are there to protect the system, and exposing the system makes you a danger. Piper joins a huge outcast community, gets a job, and a friend Frank (same name as in *Donnie Darko*) played by Keith David. Soon at the "village" they see someone "hack" into a TV broadcast to get a message out telling people "that they are all locked in a trance." TV is the easiest way to indoctrinate and pass on subliminal messages, and help to get people focused (fashion, possessions, objects, importance). Piper is still unsure but keeps exploring, looking into things like the odd church that plays a tape recording of a mass but it seems to never have a real mass. Something is odd.

He keeps searching the church and finds a box of sunglasses. When he puts on a pair later, there comes an unexpected awakening. What he sees is that all billboards, newspapers, and magazines have subliminal messaging underneath with words such as, "obey, buy, consume, watch TV, stay asleep." The sunglasses are a great metaphor. They block out the sunlight, in this case the commands/programming of the system. Also the glasses protect anyone from seeing his eyes, also protecting the fact that he is a knower. With the sunglasses he sees his first alien (not shown as a lizard but as sort of a robot). He gets a great shock to see that not all people are people. He stares at this goofy thing, which causes the alien to ask "what's your problem?" This is perhaps a symbolic statement, such as, "why are you not in awe of me like the rest." He begins to see alien after alien until a "woman" sounds the alarm by saying, "I've got one that can see." The machine of Maya can send out an alarm just as one begins to touch the tip of awakening, in hopes of dragging them back into the mess of the dream.

It did not take him long to get a headache from wearing the glasses (seeing the truth of the dream) because this truth is so hard for his reasoning mind to accept, and for quite a while there is an internal battle that happens. Then comes the longest fight scene in movie history. At first, I thought it was stupid. Piper is not engaged in this fight with some alien or enemy, but is fighting his best and only friend. The fight is one of the movie's biggest metaphors. He is fighting his friend, to make him put on the sunglasses and see as well. This is symbolic that once we begin to "see" we almost naturally want to try and help those closest to us (family and friends) to see as well. But one will not be greeted with thanks, instead they will do everything to fight back. Minds do not want to see that everything they believed is a giant lie. The struggle of the fight scene is symbolic of the fight of everyone around us to whom we try to show the truth within reality, and also the fight within us from our own parasite mind (who we previously saw as our best friend) that will fight to hold onto control.

Once Piper has gotten his friend Frank to "see" they are sitting in a rooming house, discussing the actual world situation that they both can see now. Piper begins to tell of how crazy his father was. Piper is not talking about his "birth" father, but symbolically "big daddy"- the system, big brother. "A long time ago things were different. Then he changed, he became evil. So I ran away... but I got news for 'em, there is going to be hell to pay. Because I ain't daddy's little boy anymore." He has seen the way things really are in this reality, and has absolutely no interest in any of the control bullshit anymore.

As the movie moves to its conclusion, they wind up getting into the underground world of the aliens. They first find a transit point that appears as though the aliens are being transported across the solar system. But if you look closely, they are not transporting to another planet, but to the central sun of the earth, based on the Hollow Earth theory. Then Piper and Frank came to an elitist party where the top-level humans are thanked for their help by the aliens with promises of continually being given money and importance. The year 2025 is given as when the human resistance has ended. While everyone is in fancy dress, the boys are in their usual scruffy clothes- obviously out of place. Yet an "elitist" in a tux comes over to greet them and says, "you boys are with us now?" I never thought about this closely enough the first couple of times I saw the movie, but why would an elitist in a tux come and greet the obvious scruffy nobodies? Unless he knows them somehow, and he does. The man in the tux can be seen earlier in the movie as the man on the couch watching TV and discussing how everything that the "hacker" is saying is wrong or crazy. Thus, he is an elite who is acting as a dis-information agent within normal people.

Piper is given a love interest who also has much symbolism. Her name is Holly, and the name Hollywood was the place of Druid meetings (and was chosen as the name by the film factory where the dream-like mind-controlled movies will be made for the sheep public). When we see her in the movie notice that she is given odd eyes, inviting yet sinister. You can often tell aliens by their cold eyes. Holly continually betrays him in the movie, and finally on the last betrayal on the rooftop, he kills her. With the gun trained on him, she tells him to "come inside with me." She does not mean inside the building, but "inside" her vagina. Thus, her message, with gun on him, is to "forget about the aliens, helping people and come fuck me instead." Give it all up for a tiny bit of pleasure. When Piper shoots her, he is not just symbolically killing the person trying to kill him, but also killing that last attachment to the dream (idea of relationship, marriage). He kept going back to her for help (symbolically a relationship), believing he could trust her and be helped by her. In the end he finally gives up and shoots her. Truth is more important to him.

After Piper has shot the transmitter, the signal sent out to cover the alien's form is disrupted and an alien on the TV tells a reporter, "not to listen to John Carpenter (the writer-director of this movie) or to George Romero (*Dawn of the Dead* director, who is not making movies about zombies, but humans symbolically turned into zombies by the system). Everyone can now see the aliens after Piper destroyed the signal. This is similar to section eight "The Key of the Mystery" of the *Emerald Tablets of Thoth.*[124] It claims that the ancient masters could utter a special sound in order to make the aliens in this realm visible. The text claims that these

---

[124] This is not referring to what is called the Emerald Tablet, a mystical alchemical item ascribed to Thoth during Ancient Egyptian times. Here I am referring to a strange document that is of unknown origin, written in the late 1800's. However there are some items, such as the quotation above that fits in well with our exploration no matter the text's origin. If you only read one section of it, section 8 is my recommendation.

aliens (from the deep below us) had been called forth in most remote times by men who delved in the dark arts. They came from "*The kingdom of shadows to destroy man and his rule in this place*." However, "*masters were able to conquer these aliens', and drive them back to the place where they came… they were mighty in magic, able to lift the veil. Only by magic could they be discovered, only by sound could their face be seen. They came to man and taught him the secret, the word that only a human can pronounce. They lifted the veil from the serpent and cast him forth from the place among men. Yet beware, the serpent still walks unseen.*" A veil is used by these aliens so they cannot be seen as what they really are, and projecting a specific frequency or sound, breaks down their veil and they can become seen by everyone. Interestingly, the *Emerald Tablets of Thoth*, and *They Live,* present the same information.

Some researchers say that the invading parasitic force was at one time banished from the three-dimensional realm by closing the portals they used to get in and out easily. These are the vortex points of the earth, spots where sacred sites became located. The first sacred sites were built one these locations as these were good to commune with the earth (our mother). When the beings took over this realm, one of the first things they needed to do was shut off these places of human connection with divine powers. Of course, these are the exact places that the Christians built their churches after taking over. Every church in Rome, if they let you examine underground, is built over a Pagan temple (usually Apollo, Diana, or Isis). Chartres Cathedral is built over the temple of Black Virgin (Isis, Sophia). The thousands of tourists who visit these places have no idea they were, and at times still are, battlegrounds of spiritual warfare within this realm. Yet who is the good side and who is bad side can be very hard to determine. The Dark is very good at disguising itself as light.

The last thing Piper does before dying is to "give the middle finger" to the helicopter. He now no longer fears them, or even death, and will not give into their control wishes for even one further second. Piper has come to see that one minute awake is worth more than a hundred years being a slave to lies.

*

Donnie Darko

The movie *Donnie Darko* would need a complete book in itself to discuss the various symbols, from discussions of parallel realities, the likely reason we have no free will, to social commentary on teenage youth in the Western world. I leave it as a short overview here. In a nutshell this is the *Bhagavad Gita* on screen. Donnie is Arjuna, the great warrior that is found lying on the ground in confusion at the beginning of the Gita. To start the movie Donnie is lying face down in the woods. Frank in the bunny suit is Krishna, he who will come to reveal to Arjuna the dream nature of the Universe, and why Donnie must pick up his sword and go to battle. Krishna's (Frank's) motives for doing so are always up for question.

One thing to really note as you watch this movie, is that Donnie becomes more and more like a super hero as the movie goes on, and all the main characters begin to see this. His girlfriend Gretchen even asks him, "Donnie Darko, what kind of name is that? Are you some kind of super hero?" Donnie responds calmly, "who says I'm not." But this is not the superhero with special powers like super strength, or speed or the ability to fly. Donnie has but one special skill, the ability to see through people and their bullshit, to know instantly what is behind them and what they really stand for. It is like being a psychic at 100% operational level, you see everything about the person you are talking to, and it can be overwhelming. Donnie was able to handle this (to some degree) thanks to being able to share with his therapist, and more importantly because he trusts Frank totally. He knows that by following the wishes of Krishna the world will work out perfectly, even though Donnie will no longer be in it. He laughs uncontrollably at the end of the movie, as his mission is complete and he is about to be "smooshed" by the jet engine, because he has seen total reality in this pre-death moment. He has lived his destiny completely, and he sees that all his (and everyone else's) actions within the dream have always been a type of joke.

*

Lost

Lost is a TV show that for its first season looked like sheer brilliance. Then for a few seasons went up and down, but touched on key topics within reality. Then came its final season, a season I think was controlled by ABC to make sure real information was not revealed to the public. Anything important that *Lost* had been hinting at along with all the important questions of the series were either ignored or glossed over. We got the stupid "Heaven but no answers" ending, instead of the deep revelations that were right on the surface all the while. But these pointers were there in the early seasons, as the Universe was placing them in. By the end of the series, these inserts had become blocked by the wall put up to how the show must end.

Every episode of the series began the same way, with a basic black screen, which is the 2001 monolith (as will be discussed in that section). The word *Lost* comes out of the blackness directly towards the viewer. As such *Lost* is coming out of the monolith. Since the monolith represents the viewing screen, hence it is the viewer who is the one that is lost, and you might say the show gives some clues on how one can "find."

I believe *Lost* was originally a time loop show. They were supposed to be looping the island experience over and over, plane crash after plane crash. The original title for the series was *Circle*. There are references during the first few episodes of characters knowing more than they should; such as Jack wanting the vodka on the plane (although he doesn't drink) which would later be needed to disinfect his wounds on the island. There are many scenes, if you look closely, where props or clothes change on characters from one shot to the next. This is not "poor continuity" but I think was part of the original storyline, and would be indicating we were actually watching several different timelines of various loops, not one continuous narrative. As season one ended, a guy on the Internet (Jason Hunter) figured this out and posted a very detailed website (timelooptheory.com). The show's producers likely found the website, and became concerned that someone on the Internet figured out their show. So rather than continue the show as planned, they decided to change the show, and pretend they had begun with this idea from the start. Within a year the website was mostly discredited as the series headed in a completely different direction. But a show about time loops (which is a feature of the reality we experience daily) was the message that the UNIVERSE wanted presented, and why it created the idea of the show that way. As soon as the show shifted, the Universe's message was becoming, no pun intended, lost.

The first element that must be explored is that *Lost* was not a show about some people on an island. It was all about the dream of one person,

Jack, who was either in a coma, a night sleep, or some type of dreamworld. And within that dream, his subconscious (represented on two sides by Hurley and Locke) were each doing their best to try and "wake him up." Locke directly, Hurley via clues. When one can see *Lost* as Jack's dream, and all the characters are either parts of Jack's own psyche, or people Jack had known in his life, weaved into the story, then *Lost* can begin to make sense. The first image of the first episode was Jack's eye opening (to create the dream reality) and the last thing we saw was Jack's eye closing (ending the dream). The most important episode (along with the first pilot episode) is an episode called "Dave." Most viewers hated the episode, but *The Los Angeles Times* ranked the episode as the 30th best of the series, describing it as "perhaps the most misunderstood episode of *Lost* ever," saying that Dave not being real was meant to be a twist - "the biggest expression of just how messed up Hurley was before he found the island."[125] It is the most misunderstood episode of *Lost,* not because of what the newspaper suggested, but because the episode is showing that the entire series, the island and all the characters (except Jack) are parts of a long detailed dream.

In that episode we meet Hurley's romantic interest, Libby, who is in a mental hospital recovering from the shock of her husband, Dave, dying suddenly. Hurley had himself committed to the same mental hospital due to the grief he was feeling for being on a balcony that collapsed and killed several people. Hurley can see dead people. Hurley can see and talk to a person named Dave (who no one else can see or hear) so the assumption is that this is Libby's husband trying his best to do everything possible to injure or block the advances of Hurley from his ex-wife. This seems especially clear at the end with him trying to get Hurley to jump off a cliff. That is how it all looks on the surface. Yet what is really going on here is the complete opposite. Dave might be Libby's husband, or he could also be Jack's son (also named Dave), or some other Dave. But Dave is trying to help Hurley, as such, this is the exact same relationship as Hurley has with Jack. The scene where Dave is trying to convince Hurley to jump off the cliff and "kill" himself in order to wake up, is similar to the scene in *Vanilla Sky* where "Tech Support" was trying to get another David (Tom Cruise) to jump off the skyscraper which would be like the Tarot Fool striding quite wisely into deep knowing. Thus, Dave in *Lost* is similar to McMurtry in *One Flew Over the Cuckoo's Nest*, who was trying to help the rest of the patients leave the mental hospital, which they were free to do at any time (for the patients had committed themselves to the mental hospital). This is the same

[125] Los Angeles Times quote from the Wikipedia page on the "Dave" Lost episode

way Hurley had gotten into the mental hospital himself. *Vanilla Sky* and *Cuckoo's Nest* are important underlying foundations for this episode. If you watch the episode again, and see that Dave is not trying to hurt Hurley, but wake him up, it makes sense.

We can examine other elements of the show. There is a great similarity with *Donnie Darko* (no surprise), where a "tangent universe" is created after Donnie avoids death due to an airplane engine crashing into his bedroom. Donnie has to make hard, but right decisions, to allow one universe to continue where everyone else lives and he dies. *Lost* also has parallel universes running after season four, which only one can ultimately survive. Grandma Death said to Donnie: "Every living creature on this Earth dies alone." *Lost* had an episode entitled "Live Together, Die Alone" where Jack made a similar quote. In both *Donnie Darko* and *Lost*, the book "Watership Down" is read and singled out for attention. A central point of *Donnie Darko* was about whether everything in life was controlled by fate, or whether you have free will (central to the philosophy of the real John Locke).

The characters Jacob and Man in Black (MIB) are the biggest misdirection of the series, and unless seen through will trap you in mis-seeing what the Universe has wanted to reveal all along with it. It seems unlikely that Jacob's purpose is solely to keep MIB on the island. The way it gets presented is that Jacob was charged with the protection of the Source and MIB has been trying to expose and use the Source for his own gains. This is vastly incorrect, as MIB has simply been trying to go "home." As such MIB is really like John Murdoch or Neo, wanting to leave a false reality he has been brought into, to go home. Jacob is more like The Strangers or Agents of the Matrix trying to keep him in. *Lost* reversed the colors white and black on the two characters as a trick. When you see through the trick and turn it around, then what is really going on there makes sense. Jacob is not helping anyone, but trying to entrap them.

The whole thing about candidates was also stupid, because Jacob basically goes to people when they are at their greatest weakness and then manipulates them to come to the island. Jacob is a master manipulator (that is Satan). He is introduced in "The Incident, Parts 1 & 2" spinning yarn. This is a clue. The term "spinning a yarn" is well known to be a euphemism for a person creating a deception. Jacob is then shown to be eating a fish, a herring, on the beach. The "red herring" is a huge tip off, that Jacob is not the most important being on the island. He demonstrated a severe lack of intelligence as a kid, being outwitted by his brother as he makes up rules to the game they are playing. He was never intended to be the island's protector, it was always meant to be his brother. He remains subservient and docile to his foster mother, even after she admits to having killed his biological mother. He is the epitome of the slave human willing to stay entrapped to false constructs, while MIB is really the one who sees reality clearly and just wants to leave the insanity.

Jacob manipulated certain people to come to the island AGAINST their will through the plane crash, and then manipulated them by "pushing" them in the direction he wanted them to go to serve a yet unknown higher purpose, be it good or evil. As such Jacob is evil, and the MIB is the good. This could be similar to how the Cathars saw the *New Testament* where John the Baptist was evil and Jesus was the good. Recall that Freemasons and the Knights of Malta both revere the Baptist. Thus to see the MIB as Jesus would be a massive reversal of everything everyone has ever thought of this show. Remember the Baptist baptizes by water (considered an evil or impure baptism by the Cathars) while Jesus baptizes with fire. Jacob and wine go together, while it is MIB who kills Jacob by throwing him onto the fire, as a symbolic baptism.

A couple of new ways to view *Lost*. The smoke monster might be the dark side of Jack, or it could be an inner warning force for him. It could also represent the parasitic mind that has come to control us, hence the reason for calling it a "security system" (because parasitic mind does everything to protect itself from being seen by us as a parasite). All these possibilities were abandoned in season four to claim the smoke monster is the Man In Black character, which made the entire first four seasons almost impossible to understand properly. This is assuming that it really is MIB. One thing we know for sure about the smoke monster, is that he can take the form of dead people. He also appears to take on portions of their personality as we have seen with him in the form of Flocke (shouting "Don't tell me what I can't do", etc...). It is possible that when MIB was drawn into the Source, he merely released Smokey and once dead, Smokey took on his form/consciousness - including MIB's desire to "go home." Jacob ended up somehow fusing MIB and Smokey making it impossible for MIB to leave (until he found the loophole).

The Adam and Eve skeletons linked was a very poor piece of writing. Far greater and more impactful would have been if Jack had found the skeletons were him and Kate (indicating their future fate and lack of free will) or perhaps were Rose and Bernard, which would have been a nice twist to show that they chose to stay together for eternity. It was never ever explained why there was an Egyptian temple on the island, with really poor hieroglyphs (who was on *Lost*'s prop crew, some 12-year olds with the day off from art class?). Nothing was answered, not the numbers, the cabin, or why Jacob and MIB are the way they are.

But back to Jack and the dream. His whole focus is that he needs to wake up, perhaps from a coma. In the episode "Born to Run" we see writing on a hospital door that says 'magnetic resonance imagining", instead of "imaging." He is imagining a reality. Kate is a false path, which is why they really can never be together and why he should be with Juliette. Kate is trying to keep him asleep. Thus, the entire story Jack is creating is tied to getting him to see the truth of reality and to awaken to it. A much more useful story than they were all dead from the beginning and just making up a story until they meet up and live happily ever after in Heaven-land.

Two more little pieces to consider. The first is the song "Jungle Love" by the Steve Miller Band. Numerous references in the song tie in directly to the *Lost* series, as does his song "Jet Airliner." The name of the album "Jungle Love" appears on is "Book of Dreams." Secondly, is a poster of the fictional band Geronimo Jackson, that shows the four band members (one female and three males) leaning against a tomb like box. This is the Poussin Et In Arcadia Ego painting and tomb in Arques personified, which had three male shepherds and one female shepherd. A key mathematical element are the two staffs held by the male shepherds, and in the Geronimo Jackson poster are two staffs in front of the box. Add an out of place door (representing a portal or doorway to knowing) and the show is bringing the mystery of Rennes Le Chateau into focus. Interestingly, a second Geronimo Jackson poster appears in the series, this time alluding to the themes of *Alice In Wonderland*. It is promoting a concert taking place in Berlin on August 15, 1969 (which is the day the Woodstock music festival opened in New York State).

Let's get to the main focus of *Lost*, and it can be summed up the same as the movie *Inception*, a trick that was being played on the audience-specifically at the ending. In the final episode Jack is at the funeral parlor and asks his father if he is real, to which Christian responds, "I should hope so. Yeah I'm real. You're real. Everything that's ever happened to you is real. All those people in the church, they're real too." When Jack responds they are all dead, Christian replies, "everyone dies sometimes, kiddo," and continues about the island. "This is the place that you… that you all made together, so that you could find one another. The most… important part of your life, was the time that you spent with these people. That's why all of you are here. Nobody does it alone Jack. You needed all of them, and they needed you."

This strange interaction is what throws people off the main questions they should be answering. With Christian here saying "it is all real" throws off the need to explore what is a dream or false reality. If it is all real, why all the important answers about this very real island being brushed under the table and not fully explained. This ending for the whole series mirrors the ending of the important "Dave" episode mentioned above. Libby has almost the exact same conversation with Hurley on the cliff face. Hurley is adamant, "This isn't happening! None of it! I'm just imagining it! This isn't real life!" Libby responds by talking about a dead person and claims, "So don't tell me that that wasn't real. And don't tell me you made me up. It's insulting... Hurley, look at me. I am real. You're real. The way I feel about you - that's real." She kisses him and Hurley forgets all about looking into a very likely false reality and false self.

Here is the point being missed, if Libby is an imaginary or a fictional character, then her words of expressing her realness do not matter. If Christian is imaginary his words of being real do not matter. No matter how many times Dolores wants to tell stories of her past in *Westworld*, it is not a real past, only the implanted back story of those who made her and gave her the memory of a past that didn't exist. Dave is the imaginary spirit friend trying to wake Hurley up, just as Hurley is the imaginary friend to Jack and trying to wake him up.

Locke is another character working to wake Jack up, from a more shaman-based presentation. Simply to keep this section to a brief overview I will leave with one short exchange between Jack and Locke to illustrate Locke's/Smoke Monster's help. Jack is speaking to the Fake Locke later in the series (and you must see he is speaking to the smoke monster and Locke at the same time). Jack asks that when he was chasing his dead father through the jungle, was it is dead father or smoke monster? Smoke Locke claims it was him. When asked why, he replies, "You needed to find water. This may be hard for you to believe Jack, but all I have ever been interested in is helping you... help you to Leave." By leave it means not just leave the island, but on a bigger scale to leave the dream world, or to wake up from his coma and return to real life. Or one might say to take the red pill and leave the Matrix, to go home, as MIB has been focused on during the entire series.

*

Eyes Wide Shut

Stanley Kubrick made masterpieces that almost no one could understand. Filled with Hermetic and Alchemic symbolism, they reveal some of the real history of this world, who its rulers are, and the psychology of the modern human. For this examination I will look at what I feel are the two great masterpieces: *Eyes Wide Shut* and *2001 A Space Odyssey. The Shining* is another masterpiece, but requires a lot of time and detail in order to really understand what is going on, and is too much for a book such as this. *Eyes Wide Shut*, Kubrick's final film, cannot be examined individually, but instead is the culmination and inclusion of all of Kubrick's films, from at least *Lolita.* If you want to study Kubrick in more detail. I suggest the film analyst Rob Ager[126], or the website vigilantcitizen.com. I don't agree with all their presentations, but they do delve into some very interesting areas of analysis.

For *Eyes Wide Shut,* Kubrick demanded the movie be premiered exactly 30 years after the date of the official "moon landing," on July 16 1999. He died three days after showing his original cut to studio executives. It has been widely suggested that his film so scared the executives that they demanded up to 24 minutes of the film be cut out. Kubrick refused and was found dead three days later.[127] The studio still denies any cuts to the film, but it is obvious there are missing parts to the telling of the story which would have explained a lot of what was happening. Those missing

[126] Www.collativelearning.com

[127] Oddly in the movie *Wag The Dog*, Dustin Hoffman is a director asked to fake an event. His name in the movie is Stanley, and he gets killed at the end after trying to tell people.

pieces can be guessed out, but 24 minutes is a lot to cut out of a movie. But once you figure out what is likely missing, the movie as it is makes even more sense.

The film starred the big Hollywood couple of the time, Tom Cruise and Nicole Kidman. Cruise is known for his Scientology connection, and oddly Kubrick's own daughter Vivienne got dragged into the group during the making of the film. She stopped speaking to her father soon after. Some have suggested that part of what was forced to be cut out were symbolic attacks at Scientology. I think there was far more important things that were cut out. Many went to the movie hoping to see Cruise and Kidman having sex, and as such many were disappointed at what they called a very boring movie. Yet this is actually a work of art, a presentation in visual without any need for dialogue. It is more important what is being revealed symbolically, and what the characters are really thinking as opposed to what they are saying (which like all humans is just a cover to hide their inner thoughts).

That brings us to the title of the film. Of course, the usual phrase is "eyes wide open," as in to see clearly or perceive. The indication in the title is that the eyes are being shut deliberately as an action. Within the movie, this first relates to Tom Cruise's character being unable to see the truth of the situation of his wife and his family until it is perhaps too late. The title may also refer to the fact that the entire movie is a dream Cruise had, with the entire events taking place in his sleep (like other movies I have mentioned above). This can be linked to the novel used as the base for this movie entitled *Traumnovelle* (Dream Novel) by Austrian author Arthur Schnitzler. Yet mostly the title refers to the viewing audience. It is the audience whose eyes are in fact wide shut. Unable to see the references in the movie to what is really going on in their own worlds, of how we are nothing but slaves controlled and used by the whims of a small (and perhaps non-human) elite.

The opening five minutes gives us a complete overview of everything that is going to be presented in the rest of the movie, one is able to carefully follow the symbols laid out. It is brilliant actually. The movie starts (and ends) with the monolith from *2001 A Space Odyssey* on the screen as the credits appear in white. Rob Ager was the one who first understood that the monolith is really the movie screen, and it represents that the knowledge and change is found by watching the movie itself. I explain this more in the *2001* section, but this same opening is found in other key wisdom movies and shows such as *Donnie Darko* and *Lost.*

We meet the two main characters in their home, Cruise (doctor Bill Harford) and Kidman (his wife Alice). The name Alice likely refers to the novel Alice in Wonderland, she who follows a rabbit down a rabbit hole and through a looking glass to the world behind the world. Alice is shown fully in light, framed by two pillars with red drapes on the window. Two tennis rackets are against the wall not in their case, and most suggest this is a metaphor to her playing a game. I will explain what these rackets really mean in a moment, for it is one of the key symbols of the beginning of this movie. Bill appears next, and is in a dark area, wiping his hands with a towel (as if he was finished masturbating). Alice starts in the light; Bill in the dark. He stands by a dresser but there is one tennis racket and it is still in the case. He then walks past a painting of a garden gateway through his very modern plush Manhattan home. He asks his wife where his wallet is, and they go out to meet the babysitter and their daughter before going out for the night. OK, so let us look through this in more detail.

The symbolism starts from the very beginning. The very first image Kubrick presented to us in *Eyes Wide Shut* is of Alice undressing. While viewers stare at her naked ass, they miss the detail that is being presented. She undresses in the exact same way the sex slaves at the later orgy will - getting out of a black dress in front of red (in this case drapes). The first shot we see is of a woman. The objectification of Alice as a symbol for the female fertility goddess, defines all women in this film as objects of sexual desire. It reinforces the idea that Alice is somehow affiliated with the secret society we see later, possibly as a victim of sexual slavery in her past. The two pillars are the symbolic temple doorway, as such she is also a goddess.

A mirror is also present in the room, as we see Bill look in a mirror quickly as well. Alice looks in mirrors constantly in the movie, grooming herself. Alice lost her job in the art world and is now fully supported by her husband's salary. While she lives very comfortably, Alice appears to be extremely bored with her life. Being beautiful is Alice's job, as much as it is the former beauty queen Mandy's or the hooker Domino. In fact, all the key women in the movie in some way look the same, all redheads of similar appearance. Alice is identified with the hooker Mandy through a series of parallels: they're both tall redheads with a taste for numbing drugs, and perhaps both were key role participants in the final movie ritual. Alice is also associated with the streetwalker Domino by the purple of her sheets and Domino's dress, and by their conspicuous dressing table mirrors. In a sense, there is only one woman in the film.

The tennis rackets can become clearer now. A key scene in the film *Lolita*, was of her being taken to Camp Climax. Obviously not some sort of fun summer camp, but a metaphor for her being taken to a sex slave training center. The symbol on the road sign for Camp Climax is two crossed tennis rackets. This shows that Kidman is a grown-up version of Lolita, and that she is in fact grooming her daughter, Helena to be one and the same.

Bill Harford is defined by his first line: "Honey, have you seen my wallet?" Tom Cruise's character is called Dr. Bill by both his wife and Domino… as in dollar bill. Several times during the movie, Dr. Bill either waves his money or his "doctor badge" at people to get them to do what he wants. Bill is part of the upper class and his dealings with people of the lower class are often resolved with money. Alice is a possession; he is a buyer. Recall Bill started in the dark, and this is reminded with his wallet. He does not know where it is. But Alice knows it is on the nightstand. Alice knows. Bill's eyes are wide shut. The next instance where Alice displays her superior goddess status is about a minute later, when he asks what the name of the babysitter is, even though she literally just told him her name when she asked if he gave the phone numbers for Roz.

Their daughter's name, Helena, could be a reference to Helen of Troy, daughter of Zeus and the most beautiful woman in the world. Or it could be a reference to Helena Blavatsky, famous spiritual medium and philosopher responsible for the Theosophical movement. Alice is grooming Helena to become a high-ticket item like herself. During the montage of their day at home, we see Helena along side her mother in almost every shot, holding the brush while her mother gathers her hair into a ponytail, brushing her teeth at the mirror, learning to groom herself. When we overhear her doing word problems with her mother, she's learning how to calculate which boy has more money than the other. We hear her reading a bedtime story aloud, reciting the line, "... before me when I jump into my bed." In this film, a line about "jumping into bed" can't be innocent. Her mother silently mouths it along with her, echoing and coaching her. At Bill's office, we see a photo of Helena in a purple dress, like the one worn by the girl her father paid for sex the night before. In a sense Helena is the new Lolita in this film, so central to the plot she becomes forgotten even though the ending of this movie is all about her.

The paintings that cover the Harfords' walls from floor to ceiling (painted by Kubrick's wife Christine) almost all depict flowers or food, showing that the people we will see are thought of in the same way, food or objects for consumption. Victor Ziegler has a famous collection, including antique china arrayed in glass cases, a soaring winged statue of Cupid and Psyche in his stairwell, and reputedly, a gallery of Renaissance bronzes upstairs. The house in Somerton is hung with tapestries and oil portraits of stern patriarchs, and decorated in appropriated historical styles from Medieval, to Moorish, to Venetian, to Louis XIV. Like the trashed mansion of the renowned playwright and pedophile Clare Quilty in *Lolita*, these people's houses are tastefully stacked with the plundered treasures of the world. This idea of plundering the old world is central to the new wave of alternate history study.

The paintings are a very important piece of the puzzle. A few times we are shown a painting and right in front of it the same scene to show that the paintings represent the movie, and give background detail. Such as the fruit in Bill's house. In the bathroom scene with Mandy is a picture of a similarly posed woman on a sofa. The masked orgy participants were revealed from the paintings on the wall to be members of the European nobility.

One thing we see often is the overplay of the colors red and blue. One researcher claims in the movie that red means danger, while blue is safety. An example of this is on Bill's street walk, before he meets Domino and enters her apartment (red door), he passes a beautiful blue door (which if he supposedly took, would take him away from the danger of the encounter with the woman, which led him to the mansion). I disagree with this interpretation. *The Matrix* movie has the red and blue symbolism as well. There the red is to learn the truth of the matrix, and the blue is to stay in happy sleep land. Thus, every time Bill chooses red over blue, what he is really choosing is to know the truth of his world. Exactly when this comes about (that the truth is what he seeks), is hard to pinpoint. However, there is a moment in the movie where he goes from playing in the world, to wanting to know what the world is. And every time he chooses red, he chooses truth.

Christmas trees and lights are also important in the movie as they are in every scene (except at the Somerton Mansion). The Christmas tree here in a sense represents the fake world of the slaves and their goofy religious and societal ideas, as opposed to the secret world of the elite without any religious games; who know the underlying secrets of reality- where the rainbow (fairy tale version of life) ends.

The Harfords arrive at the mansion of Victor Ziegler for his annual Christmas party. It is important to note that the two parties (the Christmas party and the one at the mansion at the end) are linked. They are not separate. You might say there is only one party that is happening in two images: the first party appears to be a nice upper class Christmas party, the second the satanic ritual orgy. The first party has everything hidden, but we see the eight-pointed star of Babylonian goddess Ishtar, and many pentagram wreaths on the wall to indicate something else is up.

A few quick pieces of this party. Both Alice & Bill mention not knowing a single person at the party (Bill even saying he does not know a soul here... a sly reference to this being a soul-less bunch). When Alice converses with Bill at Ziegler's bash she seems to be testing Bill to see if he recognizes or responds to the environment. She asks him "why do you think Ziegler invites us to these parties?" Bill thinks it is a simple question, but this could also be a statement with emphasis on the word WHY, as if Alice knows why and she is seeing if her husband can figure it out. He however is clueless to what she is hinting at and who she really is.

All of the sudden Bill spots an old friend from medical school, Nick Nightingale, who is playing piano on stage with the band. Notice the band plays no Christmas music. As soon as this happens Alice seems frightened (as if she does in fact know him) and claims to need a bathroom. Instead, she runs quickly to the bar and downs a drink as if in anxiety.

While at the bar Alice meets a man named Sandor Szavost, a Hungarian who drinks her drink (a symbol of wanting to share her fluids, or perhaps an NLP technique). The name Sandor is likely a reference to Anton Sandor LaVey, founder of the Church of Satan. Sandor asks her about Ovid's *Art of Love*. This series of books, written during the times of Ancient Rome, was essentially a "How to Cheat on Your Partner" guide. Just as it seems Alice may fall for his attempt to hypnotize her, she breaks free (does she remember a similar game with him before?) and exits. This scene on the surface makes no sense, it takes up a large amount of screen time, but yet seems to amount to very little from the standpoint of the plot. This is why I feel there must be a scene cut out where we see Sandor and Alice again, likely at the mansion during Bill's voyage. It would explain much more about this scene with a future one that it foreshadowed.

Meanwhile, Bill is discussing with two flirtatious models who tell him that they want to take him to "where the rainbow ends". While the meaning of this enigmatic phrase is never explicitly explained in the movie. This might be the later orgy, it might be simply "upstairs" into the hidden world he soon finds, or it might be referring to something beyond this reality. One of the models introduces her friend as Nuala Windsor, both speak with British accents. Windsor is of course the name of Royal family of Britain. Take note of how overtly seductive the models are with Bill, a distinct parallel to Sandor and his hypnotic attempts to seduce Alice going on simultaneously in the other room. The taller model, mentions to Bill that they had once met in Rockefeller Plaza while she was doing a photoshoot. This reference to the Rockefellers is very significant, as it ties into the rainbow references. The Rockefeller family owned a nightclub at 30 Rockefeller Plaza in New York City called The Rainbow Room. When the model says Bill met her when she had something in her eye, and he was very nice and had a handkerchief could be a code for how they really met. They may have had sex or she gave him a blow job or something, and he is being coy about the whole thing as she is speaking in code.

Their conversation is again interrupted (as interruptions become a recurring event for Bill throughout the film), when one of Ziegler's assistants approaches Bill and asks him if he could help him with something for Mr. Ziegler. Bill enters the master bathroom where he finds Ziegler half naked and getting dressed while trying to revive a fully naked prostitute who has overdosed on drugs. There are no Christmas lights in Ziegler's bathroom. Ziegler then urges Bill to keep everything he just saw a secret. The world "where the rainbow ends" must never be revealed to the outside world. It is also interesting that the nude woman in the painting above Mandy is sprawled out in the same position, as if to allude to the film's thesis of a thin borderline between fantasy or dream, and reality.

You can see the amount of info this movie contains, as I have only touched on the opening 20 minutes or so. The movie keeps this level up right to the end.

*

2001[128]

2001 A Space Odyssey captivated audiences when it came out. People knew they were seeing a masterpiece, but no one knew exactly why, or even what had happened in the film. Thankfully some thirty years later, along came Rob Ager to help sort some of it out, and his work made me go deeper into the film myself to see what could be understood. Kubrick claimed later that the movie's true meaning has been visually encoded to bypass the conscious mind and sink straight into the subconscious, thus was a type of alchemy on film.

> "*I don't like to talk about 2001 too much because it's essentially a non-verbal experience. It attempts to communicate more to the subconscious and to the feelings than it does to the intellect. I think clearly there's a problem with people who are not paying attention with their eyes. They're listening. And they don't get much from listening to this film. Those who won't believe their eyes won't be able to appreciate this film.*" – Stanley Kubrick

The most important character in the movie is not a person, but a giant black stone known as the monolith. Of course, I don't have to remind my readers that in alchemy the great work was designed to reach the Philosopher's Stone, often shown as black in the first stage of the work in Nigredo. What is the monolith exactly? It is claimed that it is the civilizing principle for the apes, and everyone else in the film. But I disagree, for what happens after the rather happy apes come across the monolith? They start killing each other. After the ape killing scene, the movie continues almost

---

[128] mI am not going to go into *the Shining*, except to say that this movie is over the top with symbolism. Its not really a horror movie, or even a ghost movie (though it does have ghosts, it just takes time to figure out who is or is not one). It portrays the history of the United States. In this you can find reference to JFK, the moon landing being faked, the Native Indian genocide, sexual abuse of the characters, start of the Federal Reserve, going off the gold standard and that the fact that every part of the hotel is a type of labyrinth.

two hours longer without any animals, plants, or nature at all. A bone gets tossed into the air, and becomes the spaceship of 2001, and it is as if all of history between those two moments is of no value. So is the monolith an alien implant from space, a metaphor of technology? Many try to show that the monolith creates an evolutionary jump (because it leads to spaceships and planetary travel), yet it could also show a devolution or a sort of imprisonment (as technology takes us away from our natural connection to the earth). At the end of the movie, when Bowman awakens to his True Nature, it is the monolith at the end of his bed staring at him when he makes his great realization.

However, Kubrick's key symbol is for the viewer. Recall specific music appears each time the monolith is drawing in the humans to it. Yet the music appears in a few other places. At the start, intermission and ending, each time over top of a black screen. Ager has wonderfully pointed out that the black screen (more clearly shown at movie theaters) is the monolith turned on its side. Hence at the deepest level the movie screen itself is the monolith, and the monolith is a story of the movie. The wisdom of the monolith in the movie is not for the movie characters, but for the film audience in the theater watching it.[129] I have an additional theory on the meaning of the monolith. That the monolith personifies the Demiurge. The apes lose their connective ability to nature and turn warlike after the appearance of the monolith. The movie ends with Bowman, reaching to the monolith and being reborn. Thus the movie can be the story of the monolith, which is the story of the Demiurge, which is the story of our entrapment in the reincarnation cycle.

What of the ending which has confused everyone? Even Arthur C. Clarke (the book's author) said he did not understand the ending of the film. That is because no one is able to recognize the entire set of scenes which take place in the Renaissance style hotel, is Bowman seeing that he is an actor in a movie, a character in a dream. In the hotel room Bowman is in an alternate universe, but once he gains the true meaning of the monolith, he also gains that knowledge of himself. He is leaving the two-dimensional

---

[129] The monolith appears in the movie over and over again, but not always black. Sometimes it is white, like the screens in the talk rooms, on various computer screens. Sometimes it is red, thus the monolith can represent the three alchemical stages of transformation. Actually there is only one red monolith, when Dave blasts the airlock. Above is a red monolith that says "caution, explosive bolts."

confines of believing what is on the screen, to become part of his own audience, hence seeing himself in the third person in the Renaissance room. The entire film has been a movie within a movie. When the moon pod landed early on, to the left there are three screens. The middle one shows the exact same view we are seeing (why is what we are seeing is being shown as a camera shot to the control base landing area?). We might say that we the audience, are really seeing only one of what may be three movies happening at the same time.

Moreso, the Torus docking station is shaped like the spinning reel of a movie film, and the docking bay might be the projector. The final shot of the Torus docking station has the two wheels of the station rolling towards the camera until they disappear off screen leaving a black emptiness, as if we are entering or exiting the roll of film. As soon as Floyd enters the strange rotating seating area, he comes through odd rotating panels. In the production stills (we don't really see it well in the movie) he seems to enter the scene as if stepping right out of the movie film. And on the main ship, the astronauts are in and run around in, what can be seen as the inside of a movie reel. Meanwhile, when the scientists go to view the monolith, they walk down an isle just like the way they walk down to their seats. Thus, this concept has been presented over and over in the film with the hopes something will break through in our understanding when we come to the ending.

Once in the hotel we notice that the wide-angle camera lens continues as from the ship, similar to Hal's vision, but these will give way in time to more standard camera shots indicating that Hal is no longer watching. When Bowman looks at himself in the bathroom mirror, the close up shows that his helmet is reflecting the bedroom not the bathroom. Another close up of his mask shows a reflection of the film crew in it, while he has a sort of confused look, of ultimate self-awareness as he sees he is a character in a movie. A production still has Bowman half behind a door, half in and out of reality as he leaves the ship and enters the hotel room.

The pod disappears and becomes a dinner table the space suit and muffled breathing become real clothes and real breathing. We see a real toilet in the bathroom, when before there were the cautions about using the special space ones. He eats real food for the first time in the movie. The paintings on the walls symbolize a more natural way of being. He is becoming (even in a hotel room), more natural. The smashed glass is key to Bowman's completed illuminated state. In the original 70mm film, it was commented that at the exact moment the glass shattered, the film noticeably skipped. That meant there was an error in two places at the same time. The mistake of knocking the glass off is a glitch in the matrix, and causes the jump in consciousness- that we have only ever been looking at the monolith all along, and everything happening on the monolith has just been a movie. It seems that when the movie was put onto more recent 35mm format, someone thought the jump was a technical error and cleaned it up for the new production. The smashing of the glass mirrors and the smashing of the skull by the apes, indicate that somehow a code is cracked; like a zen koan, when answered, immediate illumination occurs.

In the final scene, with Bowman in bed looking on at the monolith, the camera pans back behind his head breaking the wall, seeing through the wall, breaking the matrix. The room does not have doors or windows, in a sense it is the monolith that is the only way in or out. Notice that the baby in the final shot slowly turns to look directly at us, as if the reborn Bowman understands the meaning of the monolith. There is almost a feeling that the watcher of the movie should understand this as well.

The problem for us on this search is, this might all be showing the reincarnation trap. If Bowman is claimed to be the baby at the end of the movie, then that means he did not make it out of the matrix, and as such a lot of what I have just mentioned above that Rob Ager presents might be incorrect. So here is another possibility. The long tunnel Bowman went through with all the colored lights, is the famed tunnel of light which we want to avoid, but he didn't. He comes to the hotel room when Ager is correct and he has come to see the truth of his existence, that he has been a character in a movie. But this room is more like a processing, waiting station. He stays there until he is "reincarnated." Perhaps his reaching for the monolith was somehow him "agreeing" to the new life. The next cut is to the baby in the womb, oddly holding its neck. We see the baby looking at the earth, then looking directly at us. Most have thought this is so wonderful, how sweet. But if you see it as this child is just about to be back in the insane hell of the earth realm, this is the last look of "what have I just done?" before being back memory wiped into this matrix.

*

Coda

Just before this book was completed, I came across a clip from the episode "Coda" from *Star Trek Voyageur.* A clip exists on YouTube[130], and it is amazing to see this much information on the subjects presented in this book in a four-minute segment of television time. In it, the Commander Janeway is in a life-death struggle in her physical body, but her mind has gone to the after-death world where she is interacting with someone who looks like her father. This figure is attempting to get her to go with him to the white light. She realizes he is an alien disguised as her father, attempting by any means necessary to get her to go into the light behind him. She makes a couple of key statements in the exchange, "You're more like a vulture, preying on people at the moment of their death when they're at their most vulnerable... What's the real reason you want me in that Matrix? Somehow I don't think it has anything to do with everlasting joy... If you could force me to go, you'd have done it already. You need me to agree, don't you? I have to go voluntarily." The part about us needing to agree is important, and hence the need for a type of "soul contract." We still have sovereignty in the astral realm, just don't agree with these archonic beings to do anything. You can choose.

The alien then shows his true colors and what everything is about when he proclaims. "There'll be another time, and I'll be waiting. Eventually you'll come into my Matrix and you will nourish me for a long, long time."[131]

[130] https://www.youtube.com/watch?v=ghSq2qlwrs0&t=0s
[131] Exchanges from posted script http://www.chakoteya.net/Voyager/311.htm

Appendix 3

Cagots

An odd group over the last 500 years in Southern France and Northern Spain, is one known as Cagots (or Agots in some regions, Capots specifically in the Languedoc). They were another persecuted group, required to live in separate areas (called categories), generally at the edge of any city. They were excluded from all social and political rights. They were only allowed to enter church via a special door (usually very small), of which some still exist in French historic churches of the area. During a church service a rail separated them from the rest of the congregation (similar to the ropes of the Southern US that separated whites and blacks at concerts and other events). They had their own holy water stoop, and should the Eucharist be offered to them, it was given on a very large wooden spoon (so as the priest to not come in contact with them). They were forbidden to drink or eat from the cup or plate of a non-Cagot, and they had to wear special clothes to be identified- which often included wearing a yellow or red goose foot attached to it.[132] They were restricted

[132] As for the goose foot origin for the Cagot badge, the protector of Toulouse, who ruled the Languedoc, was said to be the "goose foot queen." In Norse myth, Bertha (Berchta) means bright or or intelligent. She was goddess of growing, and of the souls of unborn babies. Two of her main items are a goose foot and a golden spindle. Bertha herself was an excellent spinner and spent so much time pushing the treadle that she is often portrayed with a wide flat foot. This portrayal has led to speculation that she was, in fact, the original Mother Goose. As a spinner, on the nights between Christmas and January 6th, she went through every street in every village and town, looking through every window to make sure the spinning was finished and had been done well. For the maidens who had taken care in doing their task, she left a gift of one of her own golden threads or a distaff full of extra-fine flax, but those who had been careless found their wheels broken and their flax spoiled. Thus she is linked to what became the female St. Nicholas of Christmas tradition.

only to the trades of carpenter, butcher and rope maker. They were treated the same as lepers, and for a while many thought they must have been lepers, but this is not the case.

The trouble is, no historian today is really sure who these Cagots were. They did not seem to be a specific ethnic or religious group that can be easily identified. Some wrote at the time that they had blonde hair and blue eyes, others they were dark skinned. One account says they either had no earlobes, or if they did, one ear was shorter than the other. It is more likely though that there were no real distinguishing features to tell them apart, hence the reason they needed to wear the special clothes. The only difference it seems is that they are claimed to have descended from families identified as Cagots. Some say they were descendants of the early Visigoths, others descendants of the eight century Muslim invasion of Spain, while another suggests there were direct descendants of the Cathars. The first documents that mention them are in the 13th – 14th centuries, just after the time of the death of the Cathars, hence the suggestion there must be some sort of link. Another claim of the time suggested them as "beings that fell from the sky and came out of nowhere." This links to an odd account from around 800 AD where the Archbishop of Lyons, Agoband claimed the city was invaded by creatures sailing in aerial ships.[133]

During the French Revolution, the Republic made it clear that the Cagots were no different from any other citizen. The Cagots tended to support the Republic and stormed government offices and burned birth certificates in order to try and conceal their origins. But they were still kept track of by the local population, and whoever they were, the tradition of shunning this group lasted well into the Industrial Revolution. Then, almost by magic, it all just sort of disappeared. To this day no one is sure who a Cagot was, why they were shunned, or what really happened to them. Though in a modern twist, the tale of the Cagot came back to life in 2021, when "anti-vaccination and anti-vaccine passport protesters in France started wearing the red goose's foot symbol that Cagots were forced to wear, and handed out cards explaining the discrimination against the Cagots."[134]

[133] I am sorry, I have misplaced the sources for the final two mentions of beings falling from the sky

[134] https://en.wikipedia.org/wiki/Cagot

Appendix 4

The Apocryphon of James

"*Now when James heard these things, he wiped away the tears in his eyes and very bitter [...] which is [...]. The Lord said to him, "James, behold, I shall reveal to you your redemption. When you are seized, and you undergo these sufferings, a multitude will arm themselves against you that <they> may seize you. And in particular three of them will seize you - they who sit (there) as toll collectors. Not only do they demand toll, but they also take away souls by theft. When you come into their power, one of them who is their guard will say to you, 'Who are you or where are you from?' You are to say to him, 'I am a son, and I am from the Father.' He will say to you, 'What sort of son are you, and to what father do you belong?' You are to say to him, 'I am from the Pre-existent Father, and a son in the Pre-existent One.' When he says to you, [...], you are to say to him [...] in the [...] that I might '[...] of alien things?' You are to say to him, 'They are not entirely alien, but they are from Achamoth, who is the female. And these she produced as she brought down the race from the Pre-existent One.*

"*So then they are not alien, but they are ours. They are indeed ours because she who is mistress of them is from the Pre-existent One. At the same time they are alien because the Pre-existent One did not have intercourse with her, when she produced them.' When he also says to you, 'Where will you go?', you are to say to him, 'To the place from which I have come, there shall I return.' And if you say these things, you will escape their attacks.*" Apocalypse of James, Jesus speaking to James[135]

[135] http://gnosis.org/naghamm/1ja.html

Appendix 5
The Planets

Things can become a bit clearer when the metaphor of the Demiurge as a type of super-AI computer is made. All of this realm is what I call the simulation construct, a type of computer program. It is much more than what we think of as a computer program in our reality, but we have to use that metaphor. All programs come with rules, specific "if this, then that" codes. There can be a variety of possibilities, but they will be limited. Some of the limits are the space available on the computer (which requires limits of options) and processing speed (how quick the AI can make its calculations). Certain events (then that), can only happen with a prior (if this) occurrence. Part of what might be called the value in the first stages of spiritual work is to get to know the "rules of the realm."[136]

An example is Pi, the mathematical constant 3.14159, which is the main code of the computer and relates to the language structure of reality. Phi, the golden ratio 1.618, is the way computer has been designed to grow and interact. The Speed of Light is the barrier. Some have likened it to the operating speed of the Demiurge's computer. The Speed of Light is as fast as the system can compute, not the fastest that movement can occur. As long as you travel at that barrier or below, you are in the simulated matrix. When we see it is the barrier, we get another clue. If one can move faster than the Speed of Light, then we are no longer able to be maintained by the computing speed of the computer matrix, and it might just be forced to "spit us out" to keep from having the whole system crash. That is a metaphor you might want to go over in your head a few times. What will

[136] This is the title of a very interesting series of videos I made with Cambell Purvis of the YouTube channel *Spiral Up*, where we discuss what agreement, we can find about what is a 100% rule of this reality.

happen if you can go faster than the Speed of Light, and what will be the AI computer's response?

*

Planetary Frequencies[137]

The entire planetary realm becomes another "matrix construct," another series of lies that we have to burst through. Both figuratively and literally as it turns out. The Sun and Moon were key elements of the Hermetic art, and people today tend to believe they represent in the tradition gold and silver, or male and female. They can have that connection in early stages of the work. But in the final stage, the Sun and Moon become revealed to be completely different beasts. So what are the Sun and Moon? What are the planets? Are they what NASA tells us they are? I suggest they are frequency projectors.

There is evidence when you look into the ancient writings that there was once two Suns and no Moon in the sky. The main Sun might have been our current Saturn, ring-less at the time. This was known as Ra in the Egyptian pantheon. A great change seems to have happened when this original Sun was "switched off" and our current one "turned on." It is hard to know exactly when this happened, perhaps around 3000BC. I believe it occurred due to a "reset" that happened at that time, producing a new way to lock humans into this realm. This lock was more through a perception-controlling frequency. The world that humans perceive was actually altered at that time. What we experience through the five senses now is not what was experienced before the switch. We are quite literally in a different matrix, only due to the change to the way we perceive based on the frequency coming to us. If one can learn to block that frequency, a new world (what Castaneda called the Separate Reality) appears.

To accomplish the change, the old Sun, Saturn, was changed into something else. Rings were formed, that act similar to the grooves of a record, to hold and project a sound frequency. Saturn became connected with the god Chronos (of time) and associated with Satan. Saturn went from being a positive energy force for the Earth, to becoming a source of an evil mind-controlling frequency.

---

[137] Again this is another section that I cannot prove, but there is enough evidence to claim what I am suggesting here is on the way to being correct.

After this change Ra could no longer be the main Egypt deity, and was merged to become Amun-Ra (the Hidden Ra). Amun-Ra is Saturn. Once Amun-Ra's energy took over the governing elite of Egypt, it was in some way "curtains" for humans. This new Sun became symbolized by the Aten disk, and is what Akhenaten began worship of. He is considered the first Pharaoh of the Illuminati, and perhaps the word Illuminati will make more sense as to what it is pointing towards. A Sun that is not the original Sun, as our reality is not the original reality.

A question comes, what is our Sun's power source? Astronomers will say it is gaseous fire caused by atoms in nuclear fusion. I have earlier shown the connection between the words for Sun and soul, so what if instead of some atomic energy system, that we are being warmed by the sunlight of recently dead souls, who have fused to the furnace of the Sun, to keep it firing, and send energy back to us, so we can die and become food for it? An endless cycle. Some researchers, influenced by the work of Wes Penre, suggest that the Sun also links to a type of astral grid. This grid can be thought of as the limits of the sky, what is being pointed to by the word firmament. This may also be the Van Allen Radiation Belt, which no physical object is able to pass. No the NASA moon landers could not get through the Van Allen Belt. But the grid also seems to be astral as well, so even in the after-death realm it is very challenging to pass through, as was depicted in the 2020 movie *Soul.* This grid was perhaps known in Egypt as the Net of Tehuti."[138]

All the planets had their frequencies re-tuned after the last reset. Originally femininity and masculinity were frequencies mirrored in the sky. Venus was the feminine frequency, while Mars had been the masculine frequency. Each were pure in their origin. During this re-tuning, Mars became a more warlike and controlling frequency, while Venus was not just re-tuned, but possibly shifted. For around this time the Moon suddenly appeared in the sky.

---

[138] The Farsight Institute had a remote viewing experiment the called The Escape. The viewers were looking into whether the earth was a prison, and if so, for how long. Each seemed to indicate a type of grid that surrounds Earth and makes sure no souls can get through it. Though another researcher Wes Penre suggests there are holes in this net, and our job in the after-life is to find the holes in the net and use them to continue our soul journey that had been placed in park by entering here.

"The Maoris called the Moon the 'man-eater', the source of death. In equatorial Africa some tribes said 'the moon looks down over our country and seeks whom she may devour, and we poor black men are very much afraid of her on that account, and we hide ourselves from her sight on that night (the night of invisibility). In Central Asia, the Tartars thought a giant lived in the moon who ate people. The Tupi tribes of Brazil believed that 'all baneful influences, thunder and floods proceed from the Moon. In some shamanic lore, the Moon steals souls, and it is the shaman's task to journey to the Moon and bring them back. The Siberian Inuit tribe conceived death as a loss of the soul, which journeys up to the Moon and then onward to the Sun. Gypsies, many of whom came originally from India as slaves, also claimed their own Romany saviour who carried souls to the Moon."
Wayne Bush

Several myths from over 2000 years ago discuss a time "prior to the Moon's creation."[139] The Moon cannot be described properly. A book[140] came out a decade ago to discuss all of the strange anomalies of this celestial body. Most of the author's questions have never been properly answered by the scientific community. It might be a hollow satellite to act like a base station for monitoring (as seen in *Star Wars* and *Truman Show*). It might be a focusing device for the frequency coming from Saturn, to direct it more strongly to Earth. Gurdjieff claimed humans were "food for the Moon," while some on NDEs claim it is the Moon where they first go when they enter the white light tunnel, a sort of staging center for souls to wait prior to their next incarnation, which can take up to thirty years to occur, though no one can explain why some reincarnate immediately and others take considerable time. Some claim this soul transfer happens during particular Moon stages, full Moons or eclipses. That would explain why there is a natural reaction in our bodies during these Moon periods.

Venus had been the main feminine light in the sky, but part of the Moon's creation was to take the place of Venus in the energy structure. Unlike Mars which shifted masculine energy to something else, the feminine principle of Sophia-Isis-Magdalene was transferred to a new fake satellite called the Moon. No surprise our key slave creation force, money,

---

[139] These include such names as Aristotle, Appolonius or Rhodes and Plutarch. It can be checked in more detail here https://www.lewrockwell.com/2011/12/immanuel-velikovsky/the-earth-without-the-moon/

[140] *Who Built the Moon?* by Christopher Knight.

has as its word root the moon. Now women have been taught to worship the moon, as if it is feminine, but "is really a false feminine," and men are taught to worship the Sun instead of the original Mars. [141]

Lastly to help you take a hard look at what this light in the sky called the Moon is or is not, recall that Frank Sinatra wanted to "Fly me to the Moon." What was flying to the Moon? His hopes, his love, his adventures, or his loosh?

[141] I first heard this idea of the Moon being a copy of Venus from a conversation by Ola Wolny with Tony Sayers. She also mentioned in that interview that according to the old knowledge of her homeland, wolves do not howl at the full moon as a sense of praise, they howl at it in an attempt to scare it away.

Appendix 6

Do We Belong Here?

Another area to examine closely is that humans really do not belong in this realm.[142] Every other creature here is fine with everything they were born with: fir, claws, and instincts. They know where to go and what to do when they get there. They are fully functioning units, and instinctively know what herbs to eat when they fall ill. As long as they have not become "domesticated" by humans, they live free. Really. That does not mean nature is not a cruel world, one simple injury will mean a bird or animal will soon be dead. But until that time, they know how to function. Look at us, if we were sent out in the woods naked, almost everyone would be dead in 48 hours. Even a trained survivalist dropped in the middle of the forest would have a rough day or two until making a shelter, getting a fire going, and making the first few tools.

We are the only creature that needs tools, clothes, shelter or fire just to survive. Animals, birds and fish also do not need lawyers, money, banks and governments. In fact, humans do not live in nature at all. We live in artificial environments, and the bigger the city, the more artificial it all is. We live enclosed, away from nature in homes, office buildings, cars, buses and planes. Oh sometimes we open a window to let some fresh air in, or take a giant step and go out and sit in the sunshine on a fenced in deck (wouldn't want a creature to come by). Humans think they are living.[143] Nature is the great healer, yet humans seem to do everything to hide from

---

[142] All of this was reminded to me in a recent conversation that Dan (*Overwatch* YouTube channel) had with Mark (*Forever Conscious Research* YouTube channel).
[143] Recently deceased Canadian author Brian Fawcett, first made me aware of how humans live now in completely artificial environments, cut off from anything that might be deemed natural living, and that was long before cell phone and Wi-Fi EMF frequencies shooting through our bodies 24 hours a day.

it, save a one hour walk on a very artificial and controlled pathway set out by the local authorities, only to return to the enclosed world of "our homes." Symbolically, our homes, workspaces and whole cities have become a sort of Plato's Cave within Plato's Cave. Just starting to spend more time directly in nature, is a type of exiting these smaller symbolic versions.

There are a lot of things about how we are put together that makes no real sense from the point of being a part of this thing called nature on Earth. For example, I have a grass allergy. What good is an allergy to something that is in my environment 24 hours a day? Have you ever heard of a bear with a grass allergy? No of course not. It would pretty much destroy day to day functioning. We are fragile creatures. We can be color blind, which would make us easy prey if we cannot spot predators, or poisonous plants. Our eyesight goes quickly, our body breaks down after age 40, and on and on. We just do not fit in this realm as a creature originally designed for it. This indicates our original home may be another place, and we were brought here as suggested in the movie *Dark City.* Answering completely who created us, and why, is part of the preparation to exit.

GLOSSARY

Alchemic Stages

The four alchemic stages are: Nigredo (black), Albedo (white), Citrinatius (yellow) and Rubedo (Red). Each was a different stage of inner process, and each had its own symbolism and presentation.

Astral realm

A finer level of reality that one enters either when having an OBE or NDE. Some claim it is a plane of existence between Earth and Heaven.

Cathars

A Christian sect who lived mostly in Southern France and Northern Italy around the 11th - 15th centuries. They are suggested to have developed from previous groups such as the Manicheans and Bogomils, although no one is quite sure where they came from. The Church of Rome initiated the first Crusade against its own people to try and wipe the Cathars out in 1209AD.

Demiurge

A Gnostic term for what they call "the real creator of the material world." This is a false god, and is more like an AI computer that created an artificial realm and trapped human souls in it. Also referred to as Rex Mundane by the Cathars.

Dzogchen Buddhism

An Eastern tradition focused on emptiness, compassion and merging with the Clear Light (Void)

Gnostics

Several groups who follow the tenants of Gnosis (wisdom), which is what one needs to find Truth. One of these groups was responsible for writing the *Nag Hammadi Codex*

Hesychia

Greek Word for "stillness", and also for a group of monks in modern day Turkey who flourished between 1000-1400AD. They have great similarity to modern Dzogchen Buddhism.

Loosh

Term coined by out of body experiencer Robert Monroe, in his book *Far Journeys*. The term came as it was explained to him in an OBE that the alien beings who controlled this realm desired loosh (a type of energy), and they created humans and a world of conflict and suffering as it gave them the best loosh.

Nag Hammadi Codex

A series of books (the first bound and page numbered books in history) in the Coptic Language from a group of Gnostics found near Nag Hammadi Egypt in 1945, and first acknowledged in 1947 - the same year as the Dead Sea Scrolls were announced.

Near Death Experience (NDE)

An experience associated with what seems to be a soon to be death. Generally, NDEs have similar characteristics (but not all) and those who return to a body generally describe it as pleasant and life changing.

Non-player-character (NPC)

In video games, they are the people who populate the game to give it depth, and the one playing the game has no influence on them. NPCs will always follow their script 100% of the time.

Out of Body Experience (OBE)

When someone's awareness enters a non-physical body and can interact either in the physical or astral realms.

Oneness

An experience that can be called non-dual, unity or consciousness. Nothing is seen to be outside of oneself, or anything other than the self.

Plato's Cave

Allegory of a system of exclusionary reality found in the book *The Republic* by Plato

Pleroma

The original home of the Father, the God of Good and his female counterpart Barbelo. This place of Fullness, Absolute and Totality, is the real Home of the divine spark within known as a soul.

Reincarnation-Soul Trap

A term for presenting our world. Non-human beings either created this realm, or control this realm, and bring human souls into an artificial world construct. They do this in order to farm humans for food." Wayne Bush

Void

A place in or beyond the astral realm that can be called "still" or "non-dual". Many describe it as black or dark, but not empty either. This is likely also what is called the "Clear Light" of Dzogchen Buddhism, what is to be the focus of connecting with in life, so as to make it easier to connect with it in death.

White light tunnel

An experience many have during a NDE, seeing a tunnel of white light that is luring them towards it. Generally, it is described as a feeling of the greatest love and joy imaginable, one almost impossible to resist.

ACKNOWLEDGEMENTS

A number of people were very helpful in offering suggestions and giving advice with early copies of the book. I want to single out a few stars who helped with editing and continued suggestions as the book went from idea to finished project: * Verushka Ettlin, Brian Johnston from "Cool Guitar Gear," and my wife, Gro Anita. She also had to deal with a man consumed by 10-hour work days for several months to get this project completed. That gets a star in itself.

BIBLIOGRAPHY

(I highly recommend the sources indicated in bold below)

General Sources

Anagnostou, Angeliki, *Can You Stand The Truth? The Chronicle of Man's Imprisonment: Last Call!*, (2012)

Buhlman, William, *Adventures in the Afterlife*, (2013)

Castaneda, Carlos, *Active Side of Infinity*, (1998)

Castaneda, Carlos, *Eagle's Gift*, (1981)

Good Sky, Dianna, *Warrior Spirit Rising*, (2020)

Fawcett, Brian, *Public Eye: an Investigation into the Disappearance of the World* (1991)

Lash, John Lamb, *Not In His Image*, (2021)

Marshall, Bart, *Becoming Vulnerable to Grace*, (2021)

scott, kenneth, *An Overview of the World System of Bondage*, Gemstone University

Talbot, Michael, *Holographic Universe*, (1991)

http://www.butterfliesfree.com (Stephen Davis website)

htpp://www.trickedbythelight.com (by Wayne Bush)

Various pages on Wikipedia (yes I know, but the site does give the standard viewpoint on any subject)

Forever Conscious Research (YouTube Channel)

Free at Last (YouTube Channel)

www.gnosis.org

Cathar sources

Coppens, Philip, *Servants of the Grail*, (2009)

Douzet, Andre, *The Wanderings of the Grail,* (2006)

Mark, Joshua J. Mark, "World History Encyclopedia" found at htpp://www.worldhistory.org

McDonald, James MA, MSc. "Cathars and Cathar Beliefs in the Languedoc," http://www.cathar.info, Date last modified: 8 February 2017

Palamas, Gregory, *Holy Hesychia: The Stillness that knows God*, ed Robin Amis, (2016)

Pickett, Linda, *The Templar Revelation: Secret Guardians of the True Identity of Christ,* (2007)

Smith, Andrew Phillip, *The Lost Teachings of the Cathars: Their Beliefs and Practices,* (2015)

ABOUT THE AUTHOR

Howdie Mickoski is a researcher and philosopher. He is the author of three previous books: *Falling For Truth*, *Exposing the Expositions* and *The Power of Then*. He speaks on various internet channels under the title *Howdie Mickoski Talks*, and can be found on YouTube (for now), Bitchute, as well as Freevoice.io.

He can also be found via his website:

https://www.egyptian-wisdom-revealed.com/

And through his email:

egypthowdie@outlook.com

Thanks for reading.

Printed in the USA
CPSIA information can be obtained
at www.ICGtesting.com
LVHW041046010424
776064LV00005B/87